The Emergence of the Interior

The Emergence of the Interior considers how the concept and experience of the domestic interior have been formed from the beginning of the nineteenth century. It considers the interior's emergence in relation to the thinking of Walter Benjamin and Sigmund Freud, and, through case studies, in architecture's trajectories toward modernism.

The interior emerged historically as the context for newly articulated desires for privacy and comfort, the consolidation of gendered and familial roles in life, and domestic practices of consumption and self-representation. Charles Rice examines how this emergence related to both the upheavals associated with modernity, and the 'normalizing' influence of the domestic that took hold through the nineteenth century and into the twentieth century. Case studies investigate developments through the English discourse of domestic planning, turn-of-the-century theories of domestic consumption and design reform, and modernist dealings with the interior in the work of Adolf Loos and Le Corbusier.

The book argues that the interior emerged with a sense of 'doubleness', being understood and experienced as both a spatial and an image-based condition. Taking a radical position counter to many previous histories and theories of the interior, domesticity and the home, *The Emergence of the Interior* will be of interest to academics and students of the history and theory of architecture and design, social history, and cultural studies.

Charles Rice is Senior Lecturer in the School of Architecture at the University of Technology, Sydney.

The Emergence of the Interior

Architecture, Modernity, Domesticity

Charles Rice

Routledge
Taylor & Francis Group

LONDON AND NEW YORK

First published 2007
by Routledge
2 Park Square, Milton Park, Abingdon, Oxon OX14 4RN

Simultaneously published in the USA and Canada
by Routledge
270 Madison Ave, New York, NY 10016

Routledge is an imprint of the Taylor & Francis Group, an informa business

Typeset in Univers by Keystroke, 28 High Street, Tettenhall, Wolverhampton
Printed and bound in Great Britain by MPG Books Ltd, Bodmin, Cornwall

British Library Cataloguing in Publication Data
A catalogue record for this book is available from the British Library

Library of Congress Cataloging in Publication Data
Rice, Charles
The emergence of the interior : architecture, modernity, domesticity / Charles Rice.
p. cm.
Includes bibliographical references and index.
1. Interior architecture—History—19th century. 2. Interior architecture—History—
20th century. 3. Architecture, Domestic. 4. Space (Architecture)—Social aspects.
5. Space (Architecture)—Psychological aspects. I. Title.
NA2850.R53 2006
747′.8809—dc22   2006018422

ISBN10 0–415–38467–2 (hbk)
ISBN10 0–415–38468–0 (pbk)
ISBN10 0–203–08657–0 (ebk)

ISBN13 978–0–415–38467–4 (hbk)
ISBN13 978–0–415–38468–1 (pbk)
ISBN13 978–0–203–08657–5 (ebk)

In memory of Paul Hirst

Contents

Illustration credits

The author and publisher gratefully acknowledge the following for permission to reproduce material in this book. Every effort has been made to contact copyright holders for their permission. The publishers would be grateful to hear from any copyright holder who is not acknowledged here and will undertake to rectify any errors or omissions in future editions of the book.

1.1 © York Museums Trust (York Art Gallery), UK/Bridgeman Art Library

1.2 By permission British Library, shelfmark 1261.c.21

2.1, 2.2 By permission Thomas Engelman

4.1 By permission Vera Muthesius

4.2 By permission State Library of South Australia, SLSA B49700

5.1, 5.3 By permission Albertina, Vienna, ALA 2292, 2453

5.5 © F. R. Yerbury/Architectural Association

Acknowledgements

This book began as a PhD dissertation, and I should like to thank Stanislaus Fung at the University of New South Wales and John Macarthur at the University of Queensland for their supervision of that project. Their influence on the development of my work has been decisive. Development of the book manuscript was generously supported by a grant and a period of sabbatical leave in 2005 from the Faculty of the Built Environment at the University of New South Wales. During this period, Morag Shiach welcomed me as a visiting research fellow to the School of English and Drama at Queen Mary College, University of London, and I enjoyed immensely the collegiate environment amongst the faculty and research students there. At the Architectural Association School of Architecture in London, Mark Cousins generously provided a session of teaching and an environment of stimulating discussion which balanced and influenced the writing process. Marina Lathouri and Katharina Borsi were valued colleagues and interlocutors. Colleagues at my new home in the Faculty of Design, Architecture and Building at the University of Technology, Sydney, have made the final stage of the book's completion a very pleasant experience. I am grateful to Tarsha Finney for her valuable and insightful research work, and to Caroline Mallinder and Kate McDevitt at Routledge for their handling of the book's production.

Many people have assisted me with invitations to present my ideas and arguments at various institutions and conferences, and by reading and commenting on my work in draft form. These events and opportunities have proved invaluable in the book's development. I should like to thank Andrew Benjamin, Iain Borden, Vittoria Di Palma, Scott Drake, Adrian Forty, Charlotte Grant, Katja Grillner, Hilde Heynen, Christopher Hight, Jonathan Hill, Anne Janowitz, Marina Lathouri, Stephen Loo, John Macarthur, Brenda Martin, Diana Periton, Jane Rendell, Yves Schoonjans, Bill Taylor and Clair Wills.

Over a number of years, Barbara Penner's friendship and collaboration have been a source of great joy and inspiration for me, and my thinking has benefited immeasurably from her incisive and always constructive critique. Through the generosity of his hospitality, Nigel Talamo has made my visits to London both viable and extremely enjoyable. And I should like to thank Tina Grone for her friendship and support.

Earlier versions of parts of this work have been published in *Architectural Theory Review* (vol. 8, no. 2, 2003), the *Journal of Architecture* (vol. 9, no. 3, 2004) and the anthologies *Negotiating Domesticity: Spatial Constructions of Gender in Modern*

Architecture (eds Hilde Heynen and Gülsüm Baydar, Routledge, 2005) and *Walter Benjamin and History* (ed. Andrew Benjamin, Continuum, 2005). I should like to thank the respective publishers for allowing me to include this work in the present volume in revised form.

Introduction

In 1862, Charles Baudelaire wrote a prose poem entitled 'The Twofold Room'. It begins with a description of 'A room just like a daydream':

> The furniture takes on elongated shapes, prostrate and languorous. Each piece seems to be dreaming, as if living in a state of trance, like vegetable and mineral things. The draperies speak an unvoiced language, like flowers and skies and setting suns.
>
> There's no artistic abortion on the walls. Compared with pure dream or unanalysed impressions, definitive or positive art is a blasphemy. Everything here has its appropriate measure of light and delicious dark, of harmony itself.[1]

The description of this animate, nature-like room changes abruptly halfway through the poem. An intrusion comes with 'a terrible, heavy thump' on the door, at which point Baudelaire remembers:

> Yes, this hovel, this home of everlasting boredom, is indeed my own. Look, there are the fatuous bits of junk, my dusty and chipped furniture; the fireless hearth with not even a glowing ember in the grate all fouled with spit; the dingy windows down which the rain has scrawled runnels in the grime; the manuscripts riddled with cross-outs or left half done; the calendar on which the evil days of reckoning are underlined in pencil.[2]

A context for immaterial, irreal experience, Baudelaire's interior is also the context for his work, for his relation to the productive cycle. It figures at once his removal from the world, and his belonging to it. It is an interior in which time is suspended in reverie,[3] as well as one which registers the reality of the inexorable march of time. These poetic reflections might be compared to thoughts he recorded a year later in

'The Painter of Modern Life': the artist bears witness to modernity as a condition caught between the eternal and the fleeting.[4]

'The Twofold Room' is emblematic of an event which is the subject of this book: the emergence of the domestic interior as both a concept and a material manifestation of the nineteenth century. The poem captures the sense of the emergent interior's doubleness, a sense which, in this instance, involves the reality of the interior's spatiality – Baudelaire's own hovel, a condition marked out in contrast to a bourgeois respectability[5] – as well as its condition as an image, one that can be imagined and dreamed, and inhabited as such.

Doubleness is manifest in a semantic development that marks the emergence of the interior. The *Oxford English Dictionary* records that 'interior' had come into use from the late fifteenth century to mean inside as divided from outside, and to describe the spiritual and inner nature of the soul. From the early eighteenth century, 'interiority' was used to designate inner character and a sense of individual subjectivity, and from the middle of the eighteenth century the interior came to designate the domestic affairs of a state, as well as the sense of territory that belongs to a country or region. It was only from the beginning of the nineteenth century, however, that the interior came to mean 'The inside of a building or room, esp. in reference to the artistic effect; also, a picture or representation of the inside of a building or room. Also, in a theatre, a "set" consisting of the inside of a building or room.' The first use of the word relating to this meaning emphasizes its image-based sense, and comes from an 1829 publication entitled *Companion to Theatres*: 'A few interiors, two or three streets, and about the same number of country views, would last as stock scenery for several seasons.' The entry for 'interior decoration' corroborates the idea of the interior's deliberate fabrication, its staginess, and its distinction from architectural construction: 'The planned co-ordination for artistic effect of colours and furniture, etc., in a room or building.'[6] The first use given is *Household Furniture and Interior Decoration*, the title of Thomas Hope's 1807 publication. A similar pattern of meaning and emergent doubleness is identifiable for the French *intérieur*, which is also taken up in German.[7] Charles Percier and Pierre Fontaine's *Recueil de décorations intérieurs* of 1801, along with Hope's publication, marked the domestic interior as a site of professional struggle between architects and upholsterers. Indeed, the interior emerged as the newly articulated entity at stake in this battle, properly belonging to neither profession.[8]

The interior thus emerged with significance as a physical, three-dimensional space, as well as an image, whether it be a two-dimensional representation such as a painting, a print in a portfolio of decoration, or a flat backdrop that could conjure up an interior as a theatrical scene. This image-based sense also encompasses a reverie or imaginal picture like Baudelaire's, one which could transform an existing spatial interior into something other. Significantly, doubleness involves the interdependence between image and space, with neither sense being primary.

In this way, the interior emerged in a domestic sense as a new topos of subjective interiority,[9] and framed newly articulated and increasingly widespread desires for privacy and comfort, for the consolidation of specific gendered and familial roles in life, for the linking of a consumer culture to the attainment of domestic arrangements that demonstrated acceptable norms, and for practices of self-representation in the context of domestic life. Indeed, the domestic interior as such emerged from the beginning of the nineteenth century. This is not to say that furniture and its arrangement, or indeed domestic habits and mores, did not exist before this time. Rather, the interior conceptualized a particular emerging and developing consciousness of and comportment to the material realities of domesticity, realities which were actively formed in this emergence, and which, as in Baudelaire's reverie, could also become transformed and destabilized through it. The interior as a bourgeois manifestation is key to consider here. In his study of the British, French and Germanic bourgeoisie, Peter Gay has suggested: 'Perhaps the most severe hurdle impeding the enterprise of defining the nineteenth-century bourgeoisie is its troubled attempts at self definition.'[10] So central has the interior's role been in such attempts at self-definition, and in the universalizing of the values associated with those attempts, that the historical circumstances that condition those attempts are often obscured. This book aims to open new ways of thinking about the domestic interior by returning to the concept the sense of its historical emergence.[11]

Architecture

The book focuses particularly on architecture's relation to the domestic interior,[12] taking up the idea that the interior emerged in addition to constructional, ornamental and surface definitions of inside space that were architectural. The interior was articulated through decoration, the literal covering of the inside of an architectural 'shell' with the soft 'stuff' of furnishing. And as an image-based phenomenon, the interior began to be represented in ways visually distinct from conventional architectural representation. Yet this separation also involved an intimate association. The interior impacted in significant ways on the development of particular architectural techniques, and the terms by which architects joined cultural debates.[13] The book considers several key moments of this relationship between the interior and architecture, including the codification of room and corridor planning in England from the middle of the nineteenth century, and how an imagination of the interior enabled a modern sense of comfort to be articulated architecturally; the way in which the material consumption of the interior was a crucial component of the architecturally led reform of design and industry around the turn of the twentieth century, and how it articulated social and national identity; and the question of the interior as image and its relation to space in the work of Adolf Loos and Le Corbusier, where modern architecture's engagement with mass media was articulated through the interior's doubleness. Through these examples, the techniques and concepts that surround the interior's emergence reframe how one might think of architecture's relation to key aspects of its own disciplinarity, and the ways in which this is claimed in wider social and cultural contexts. At the same time, the interior as a specific concept and material manifestation, one that is not reducible to architecture, gains strength in a way that questions thinking that would naturalize and essentialize it.

Modernity

These architecturally based investigations resonate with the emergent interior's implication in several important questions of modernity, including the status of experience, the presence of history, and knowledge about subjectivity. Investigating the role the interior has played in the thinking of Walter Benjamin and Sigmund Freud allows the book to establish what the interior's emergence has meant in relation to these questions. Benjamin's account of the bourgeois interior's 'short historical life' in the nineteenth century is considered in detail, along with what this account meant for the organization of his voluminous history of that epoch, *The Arcades Project*. The interior also played a multiply inflected role in Freud's development of psychoanalysis as a science and therapeutics of the subject. It is examined as the physical site of psychoanalysis' development, the context in which its therapeutics went to work, and an analogy for the structuring of the psyche. These investigations question and move beyond an alignment between the domestic interior and a subject's psychology that tends to naturalize this relationship.[14] They also take into account how the emergence of the interior had a historical and psychological significance that is inseparable from how modern articulations of history and psychology are themselves understood.

Domesticity

The emergence of the interior framed domesticity in its modern form.[15] In turn, this form has tended to frame understandings of domestic life across history.[16] In this way, the interior can seem self-evident, constituting a natural and universal domesticity, as if the movement of historical time bore witness to the progressive evolution of essential aspects of domesticity. This view is often aligned with the notion of home, the site where domesticity is formed and recognized through personal experiences and associations. But the historical formation, variability and contingency of such associations are often obscured in this view.[17] The book investigates the way in which the interior is constitutive of modern domesticity. At the same time, it aims to show how domesticity considered as a stable and timeless aspect of living – a dream of the nineteenth century – is a misconception, albeit a powerful one. Part of this misconception has to do with how the interior's doubleness operates. By and large, histories of the interior, domesticity and the home idealize representations of domestic life, treating them as evidence of a domesticity which is universally recognizable, even if historically distinct. In this way of thinking, the concept of the interior is assumed to stand outside of historical processes. Its spatial sense is dominant, and the image is supposed to provide a transparent window on to the spatial. The doubleness of the interior implies, however, that the image-based and spatial senses of the interior are equally important. As is shown at several points throughout this book, interiors as images have a life independent of supposed spatial referents, and the nature of relations between image-based and spatial interiors is often far from transparent. Indeed, such relations have historically made the interior the site of uncanny qualities precisely through a play between identity and discrepancy at the heart of the interior's doubleness.

In this way, understanding the doubleness of the interior bears most crucially on the status of historical evidence. One cannot simply assume direct access to historical conditions of domesticity through images that would purport to represent transparently those conditions. Automatic associations between historical and contemporary conditions, authorized through a notion like home, and the personal and universal recognition it implies, need to be questioned. As a result, one of the book's preoccupations is with how the emergence of the interior relates domesticity to the past, and conjures up a dreamed idealization that is impossible to realize fully in any present. Thus associations between the domestic and the universal can be seen critically, that is, as an aspect of a nostalgia for lost origins that the emergence of the interior produces.

Here again one approaches the question of the interior's relation to modernity. As already indicated, this is a major consideration for the book, but it is one which counters views of the domestic as that which is opposed to or threatened by the modern.[18] This view is related to an understanding of modernity as a force which renders one homeless, and which disrupts traditional associations with place and community, and hence with an authentic experience of dwelling.[19] Yet counter to this view, which is commonly authorized via a nostalgic reading of Martin Heidegger,[20] the interior does not exist as an answer to this problem of modernity. Rather, it emerges as one of its mechanisms, enacting modern norms of domesticity that are often confused with its timeless and essential features.[21] If this problem were still to be considered within a Heideggerian frame, then the domesticity the interior supports would be at the outset inauthentic; however, the interior emerges to figure such assured notions as authenticity, experience and dwelling problematic.

The book is divided into two parts. The first, entitled 'Orientations', deals with the thinking of Benjamin and Freud in relation to the interior's historical emergence. It also lays out a critique of conventional ways in which the interior has been considered historically. The second part, 'Trajectories', traces architecture's relations to the interior at key moments through the nineteenth and into the twentieth century. These moments are investigated through detailed readings of historically and theoretically significant texts, buildings and images, which act as case studies. Part 1 is not structured as the theory required for Part 2. Rather, each section relates to a different framing of how the emergence of the interior can be considered. Furthermore, the understandings of this emergence developed in each part resonate with one another, building up a complex picture of the interior's historical significance. This complexity, however, should not be aligned with comprehensiveness. The aim has been to identify a number of points where the relationality of the interior's emergence, its linkage to architectural techniques or psychoanalytic practices for example, enables an investigation of the multifaceted and problematic aspects of this emergence. Other examples or case studies could be identified and investigated. The hope is that this book provides something of a framing and a demonstration of possibilities for thinking in new ways about a range of historical and theoretical material on the interior.

Part 1

Orientations

Chapter 1

Irrecoverable inhabitations

Walter Benjamin and histories of the interior

> Ever since the time of Louis Philippe, the bourgeois has shown a tendency to compensate for the absence of any trace of private life in the big city. He tries to do this within the four walls of his apartment. It is as if he made it a point of honour not to allow the traces of his everyday objects and accessories to get lost. Indefatigably, he takes the impression of a host of objects; for his slippers and his watches, his blankets and his umbrellas, he devises coverlets and cases. He has a marked preference for velour and plush, which preserve the imprint of all contact. In the style characteristic of the second empire, the apartment becomes a sort of cockpit. The traces of its inhabitant are moulded into the interior. Here is the origin of the detective story, which inquires into these traces and follows these tracks.[1]

With these lines, Walter Benjamin gives a distilled account of the fabrication and inhabitation of the bourgeois domestic interior. This interior is produced through an infolding, which Benjamin encourages one to consider literally in terms of the interior as a soft and impressionable surface. This surface does not produce a hermetic seal against the external world, but rather is activated through the inhabitant's relation to the city and its world of publicness, business and commerce, and enables a subjectivity and a social identity marked 'bourgeois' to be supported artefactually. The impressionable surface holds on to the artefacts liberated from the world of commodities and interiorized for the securing of a private life; the surface folds to encase the inhabitant and these collected objects. The indefatigable collector understands that such a fabrication of the interior is a continual process, a set of techniques and practices that ensure the ongoing viability of a self. Yet the traces registered on the interior's impressionable surface also position the inhabiting subject in a constricting sense. Such traces imply detection, and the detective inevitably begins an investigation at the discovery of a dead body.[2]

This chapter reads the historical emergence of the interior through the writings of Benjamin, focusing primarily on *The Arcades Project*. It aims to expand upon Benjamin's often gnomic pronouncements, and then focus his thinking in terms of two sets of issues concerning the study of the interior. The first set has to do with the evidence the interior furnishes for historical study. The trace of the inhabitant, caught as it is between securing a private identity, and positioning the subject within frames of detection and governance, suggests that one cannot assume its transparency to something like a stable or true essence of bourgeois private life. Indeed, the supposed stability offered by the interior is a reaction to the alienation and disjunctions of the modernizing city, as well as being complicit with the forms of surveillance and governance produced by and through the city. In this way, the trace has effects both within the historical context of bourgeois domesticity, and in the way one may have access to it as a historical context. As an extension of these issues, a second line of investigation engages with the status of the nineteenth century against an ever-shifting context of the present. Emerging through Benjamin's account of the bourgeois domestic interior is a philosophy of history that reveals critical and illuminating discontinuities in the movement of historical time.

The resources for thinking developed in this reading of Benjamin are used to critique the ways in which historical studies of the interior, privacy and domesticity have been conventionally conceived. These studies have tended to confuse the constricted, mortified inhabitant with its counterpart, the private individual who is supposed to 'live on' through history. Following Benjamin's own historical treatment of the interior, it will be shown that while the effects of the interior's emergence are felt in palpable ways in the present, it is not because of its progressive, stylistic development, or because of the continuity of its inhabiting subject.

The short historical life of the bourgeois domestic interior

'Against the armature of glass and iron, upholstery offers resistance with its textiles.'[3] In this single line, embedded within the voluminous text of Benjamin's *Arcades Project*, arcade and domestic interior come together. This coming together is, however, arranged around a point of resistance. Arcades offer a structural armature and a hardness of material finish that upholstery and textiles resist in their stuffing and covering. Arcades figure the wedded advance of technology and commerce, the emblem of the modernizing city; upholstery and textiles figure the domestic interior as a site of refuge from the city and its new, alienating forms of experience. Yet this resistance heightens their mutual entanglement. Benjamin writes of arcades themselves as kinds of interiors in the city, spaces that reorganize relations between inside and outside: 'The domestic interior moves outside. . . . The street becomes room and the room becomes street.' And: 'Arcades are houses or passages having no outside – like the dream.'[4]

In producing *The Arcades Project* as a fragmentary history of the nineteenth century, a history of discontinuity, Benjamin recognized a productive instability in the emergent concept of the interior, and in its associated concepts such as dwelling and domesticity:

> The difficulty in reflecting on dwelling: on the one hand, there is some-
> thing age-old – perhaps eternal – to be recognized here, the image of that
> abode of the human being in the maternal womb; on the other hand, this
> motif of primal history notwithstanding, we must understand dwelling in
> its most extreme form as a condition of nineteenth-century existence.[5]

Benjamin's difficulty in reflecting on dwelling is the difficulty in capturing the eternal
conception of dwelling as a precise historical condition of the nineteenth century.
While arcades embody technological, commercial and spatial developments of the
nineteenth century – developments which, precisely framed in terms of technological
progress, become radically old from the perspective of the twentieth century –
dwelling appears to stand outside of time, unfolding eternally and naturally within the
interior. Yet one might also think of the resistance offered by the interior's upholstery
and textiles as a necessary response to the emergence of the arcades, and the effects
of the modernizing city that they imply. This is a resistance which does not guarantee
the eternal in dwelling, however much this might have been a desire prevalent in the
nineteenth century. It suggests, rather, the opposite: a specific and contingent formation which defined the interior as the setting for bourgeois domesticity. In this way,
one should think of the bourgeois interior as having a short historical life, or, more
properly, a 'natural' lifespan equal to that of the arcades. The interior is born, matures
and dies out within the span of the nineteenth century. This is the thrust of Benjamin's
thinking in his two exposés (of 1935 and 1939) which offer a synopsis of *The Arcades
Project*.[6] Each contains a section on the interior, giving an account of its emergence
and liquidation within the span of that century. Following the exposé of 1939, the
major aspects of this account will be given.

Interiorization and experience

The quotation at the beginning of this chapter is the key section of the exposé that
describes the interior's historical emergence. For the bourgeoisie, dwelling became
divided from work, and in this division, the conditions for the emergence of the
domestic interior were made possible. In Benjamin's thinking, this division was allied
to a problematization in modernity of the philosophical conception of experience.
Long experience (*Erfahrung*), founded on an appeal and a connection to tradition, and
the accumulation of wisdom over time, comes into conflict with the multitude of
momentary, instantaneous experiences (*Erlebnisse*) that contribute to the dynamic
energy of the modern city. The city alienates long experience; its refuge, and the
context for its amplification, is the domestic interior. Benjamin captured this problematization in his 1936 essay 'Experience and Poverty':

> Everyone knew precisely what experience was: older people had always
> passed it on to younger ones. It was handed down in short form to sons
> and grandsons, with the authority of age, in proverbs; with an often long-
> winded eloquence, as tales, sometimes as stories from foreign lands, at
> the fireside. – Where has it all gone?[7]

The interior's emergence became important in relation to the idea that long
experience might somehow be wrested from objects, that what was carried in the

immateriality of the proverb might, under certain conditions, be provided in a material substitute, that the hearth and its mantelpiece might materially encode the mythical fireside and the situation it provided for the telling of stories. In this way, fabricating and thereby inhabiting an interior was an active, ongoing process, one manifested in Benjamin's account through the figure of the collector. The collector was not one who was simply sealed away in the interior. Rather, this figure negotiated the problematic of experience, realizing that its long and momentary forms were ultimately two sides of the same coin.

The challenge faced by the collector as Benjamin's 'true resident' of the interior was to bestow a 'connoisseur's value', rather than a 'use value', on objects, thereby to '[delight] in evoking . . . a world in which, to be sure, human beings are no better provided with what they need than in the real world, but in which things are freed from the drudgery of being useful'.[8] This drudgery associated with things was consequent upon the rise of commodity exchange through the nineteenth century, a story which has had many tellings. The account of Christoph Asendorf will act as a guide, since it is particularly concerned with elucidating the relation between the object and experience within the rise of commodity exchange.

From the beginning of the nineteenth century, industrial modes of production replaced individual handicraft and workshop modes. The consequent division of labour 'causes the relation between producers and things to lose its basis in repetitive experience, continuity, and an overview of the entire process of production. The new relation that ensues, one already evident in the workshop, is based on partial experience'.[9] Objects once experienced in their totality through the bond between maker and user ('traditionally' the same person) now circulated as abstract entities, stripped of all qualities that were once derived from an embeddedness in time and place (a locality designated by community as *Gemeinschaft*), and a natural necessity of production and use. The experience of the shift in commodity production and circulation reflected the rise in significance of momentary experiences, consequent upon the modernity of industrialization and urbanization. Referring to Robert Musil, Asendorf suggests how these momentary experiences of the metropolitan world (designated by culture as *Gesellschaft*) themselves circulated freely, without requiring a subject to experience them.[10] The man-as-subject was thus also left 'without qualities'.

The fate of objects-become-commodities is that they begin to repossess the categories they seemingly obliterated: they produce a new nature and begin to have their own social relations. As Asendorf suggests: 'Commodities embody the abstract as materiality, as a natural quality of things.'[11] He also recalls Marx:

> the social character of men's labour appears to them as an objective character stamped upon the product of that labour: because the relation of the producers to the sum total of their own labour is presented to them as a social relation, existing not between themselves, but between the products of their labour.[12]

Asendorf's argument suggests that objects as commodities embodied experience as *Erlebnis* in solid, physical form.[13] It is worth arguing, further, that the domestic interior offered the site where the 'social life of things' could be domesticated in a way that was thought to provide compensation for their stripping of qualities away from bourgeois subjects. Objects as commodities could be wrenched from circulation, 'freed from the drudgery of being useful', becoming embedded in the interior to produce a conscious, 'new nature' of domesticity, one that offered an illusion that long experience could be maintained in the interior.

The labour of collecting

Objects become domesticated via the collection. Susan Stewart has located the collection as the final stage of alienation, where the labour of production completed its transmutation into a labour of consumption. She writes:

> What is the proper labour of the consumer? It is a labour of total magic, a fantastic labour which operates through the manipulation of abstraction rather than through concrete or material means. Thus . . . the collection presents a metaphor of 'production' not as 'the earned' but as 'the captured'. . . . The collection says that the world is given; we are inheritors, not producers of value here. We 'luck into' the collection; it might attach itself to particular scenes of acquisition, but the integrity of those scenes is subsumed to the transcendent and ahistorical context of the collection itself.[14]

The interior is the context that allows the collector to capture the commodity, and to become entwined with it. This capturing or domestication takes place through various 'particular scenes of acquisition'. But Stewart also suggests: 'The collection is not constructed by its elements; rather, it comes to exist by means of its principle of organization.'[15] Through this organization, one refers to the collection as finished, the subjectivity constructed through it looking back retrospectively at the narrative of the self built through and into the collection's organization. In Stewart's argument, this narrative replaces a narrative of history; in its classifications, the collection is ahistorical. Yet she qualifies somewhat her earlier statement that the collection is not earned but captured by asserting that the serial manner in which a collection is acquired 'provides a means for defining or classifying the collection and the collector's life history, and it also permits a systematic substitution of purchase for labour. "Earning" the collection simply involves waiting, creating the pauses that articulate the biography of the collector.'[16] While this provides a strong argument for the subject's motivation to collect – collection refashions an alienated self through alienation's final mechanism – Stewart's claim for the ahistorical nature of the collection itself produces a linear concept of its serial acquisition, a history that is the biography of the collector.

Yet the possibility of a collapse in the structural integrity of the collection, or an opening out beyond its supposed structure, reveals the shortcomings in such a linear concept of acquisition. It produces a slippage in the integrity of the collection, and thus in the collector's subjectivity. Recognizing this possibility, Stewart recounts the story of a rare book collector who discovered that there existed another copy of a book he possessed and thought to be unique. The man purchased this other copy from its owner at an extraordinary price and promptly destroyed it.[17] This was not an acquisition per se, but an action that attempted to repair the organizing principle of the collection (uniqueness), and thus retrospectively make sense of an earlier acquisition.

Benjamin's thoughts on the collection become significant at this point, especially since some of them were articulated in terms of his own collecting of books.[18] He was concerned with what he called the 'productive disorder' of the collection, and the ways in which it veers between completeness and openness. He writes of the spectacle of things in dispersion,[19] and draws a relation between the collector as one concerned with bringing things together in an order, and the allegorist who delights in the disorder of things torn out of their context:

> in every collector hides an allegorist, and in every allegorist a collector. As far as the collector is concerned, his collection is never complete; for let him discover just a single piece missing, and everything he's collected remains a patchwork, which is what things are for allegory from the beginning.[20]

For this ambivalent figure of the collector, the spectacle of things in their dispersion produces a particular sense of perception, one Benjamin developed in relation to Henri Bergson's link between perception and time: 'this is the way things are for the great collector. They strike him. How he himself pursues and encounters them, what changes in the ensemble of items are effected by a newly supervening item – all this shows him his affairs in a constant flux'.[21] The link between commodities striking the collector and the tenor of momentary experience is clear. As with Stewart's account, there is also a process of interiorization at work in collecting: 'The true method of making things present is to represent them in our space (not to represent ourselves in their space). . . . We don't displace our being into theirs; they step into our life.'[22] Further to this process of interiorization, Benjamin saw a link between the process of collecting and a certain sort of memory:

> A sort of productive disorder is the canon of the *mémoire involontaire*, as it is the canon of the collector. . . . The *mémoire volontaire*, on the other hand, is a registry providing the object with a classificatory number behind which it disappears. 'So now we've been there'. ('I've had an experience'.) How the scatter of allegorical properties (the patchwork) relates to this creative disorder is a question calling for further study.[23]

Stewart argues for the collection as a classificatory system that erases history and produces an internal, synchronic time.[24] Benjamin's concern is for the collector who is open, at some level, to a productive disorder, one that always lurks at the heart of a classificatory system. Here the concept of the trace becomes crucial, and Benjamin used it to link collection to memory as *mémoire involontaire*. The trace involves not what is manifest at the level of the contents of the collection or their disappearance behind the classificatory system, but rather – to use a decorating metaphor, and one that was important for the psychoanalytical account of the subject – what those contents 'paper over'.

Registering traces

What caught Benjamin's attention more than the objects collected within the interior were the cases made for objects: 'What didn't the nineteenth century invent some sort of casing for! Pocket watches, slippers, egg cups, thermometers, playing cards – and, in lieu of cases, there were jackets, carpets, wrappers and covers.'[25] And here one needs to be reminded of the more insidious sense in which the trace works. In his quasi-autobiographical work 'One-Way Street', Benjamin writes of the fate of the inhabiting subject positioned by traces:

> The bourgeois interior of the 1860s to the 1890s, with its gigantic chests distended with carvings, the sunless corners where palms stand, the balcony embattled behind its balustrade, and the long corridors with their singing gas flames, fittingly house only the corpse. 'On this sofa the aunt cannot but be murdered.' The soulless luxuriance of the furnishings becomes true comfort only in the presence of a dead body. . . . This character of the bourgeois apartment, tremulously awaiting the nameless murderer like a lascivious old lady her gallant, has been penetrated by a number of authors who, as writers of 'detective stories' – and perhaps also because in their works part of the bourgeois pandemonium is exhibited – have been denied the reputation they deserve.[26]

The traces that the inhabitant leaves to construct a bourgeois identity open this newly mortified subject to detection. Beyond the specificity of the detective genre, the trace of individual subjectivity secured in private life emerged along with the trace of bourgeois identity measured in social governance. The trace's indexical quality and separability from its referent (the individual body) became linked with the ability to track illegal and deviant behaviour.[27]

Another way of stating these relations is to suggest that the trace became significant at the moment anonymity became prevalent in the city. In this setting, it is important to consider Benjamin's formulation, via Marcel Proust, of *mémoire involontaire*: 'This concept bears the traces of the situation that engendered it; it is part of the inventory of the individual who is isolated in various ways.'[28] This form of memory is linked to the shocks of momentary experiences that are not registered consciously. As Benjamin suggests: 'Put in Proustian terms, this means that only what has not been experienced explicitly and consciously, what has not happened to the subject as an isolated experience [*Erlebnis*], can become a component of *mémoire involontaire*.'[29]

The collection, when it opens out beyond the ordered system to the patchwork, opens to the province of *mémoire involontaire*. The interior then works not as the space ensuring the coherence of classification, but as the space for the registering of traces, providing the surface against which the qualities of specific objects, which constantly have the potential to open the collection beyond conscious orderliness, might be preserved.[30] It is the unconscious potentiality of *mémoire involontaire* which itself opens to the possibility of long experience. Here again is Benjamin's reading of Proust:

> Proust's work *A la recherche du temps perdu* may be regarded as an
> attempt to produce experience, as Bergson imagines it, in a synthetic way
> under today's social conditions, for there is less and less hope that it will
> come into being in a natural way. . . . Proust tells us that for many years
> he had an indistinct memory of the town of Combray, where he had spent
> part of his childhood. One afternoon, the taste of a kind of pastry called
> a madeleine (which he later mentions often) transported him back to the
> past, whereas before then he had been limited to the promptings of a
> memory which more or less obeyed the call of conscious attention. This
> he calls *mémoire volontaire.*[31]

The madeleine was the object whose trace was registered for the *mémoire involontaire*, that memory which is opened in the bypassing of 'the call of conscious attention', and which links to the possibility of long experience, as far as this is possible 'under today's social conditions'. The collection is an attempt, one always related to a perilous dispersion of objects, to find the madeleine, to (re)encounter this object as a way of opening up its trace in the unconscious. Proust himself comments on objects thus:

> I feel that there is much to be said for the Celtic belief that the souls of
> those whom we have lost are held captive in some inferior being, in an
> animal, in a plant, in some inanimate object, and thus effectively lost until
> the day (which to many never comes) when we happen to pass by the
> tree or to obtain possession of the object which forms their prison. Then
> they start and tremble, they call us by our name, and as soon as we have
> recognized them the spell is broken. Delivered by us, they have overcome
> death and return to share our life.
>
> And so it is with our own life. It is a labour in vain to attempt to recapture
> it: all efforts of our intellect must prove futile. The past is hidden some-
> where outside the realm, beyond the reach of intellect, in some material
> object (in the sensation which that material object will give us) of which
> we have no inkling. And it depends on chance whether or not we come
> upon this object before we ourselves must die.[32]

Benjamin responds to this passage in an extension of his thoughts on experience:

> According to Proust, it is a matter of chance whether an individual
> forms an image of himself, whether he can take hold of his experience.
> But there is nothing inevitable about the dependence on chance in this
> matter. A person's inner concerns are not by nature of an inescapably
> private character. They attain this character only after the likelihood
> decreases that one's external concerns will be assimilated to one's
> experience.[33]

This decrease in likelihood, this atrophying of long experience, gives rise to the private individual as collector. Indeed, it gives rise to the interior and its formation of a bour- geois domesticity. The collection becomes private, or, rather, it demands a container of privacy against the commodification of objects. An early fragment on the collection from the 'First Sketches' of *The Arcades Project* captures this sensibility:

> Happiness of the collector, happiness of the solitary: tête-à-tête with things. Is not this the felicity that suffuses our memories – that in them we are alone with particular things, which range about us in their silence, and that even the people who haunt our thoughts then partake in this steadfast, confederate silence of things. The collector 'stills' his fate. And that means he disappears in the world of memory.[34]

What is interesting here in terms of the collection is the shift from object as the prime focus of thought, to the effect of objects for the inhabitant as collector. In Proustian terms, it is not the madeleine that is itself significant, but the trace it opens up. Memory of the past releases experience from its object-prison, which itself has no significance.

The liquidation of the interior

Yet an overburdening of the bourgeois interior as a space for the registering of traces led to its liquidation. In his 1939 exposé, Benjamin writes: 'The liquidation of the interior took place during the last years of the nineteenth century, in the work of Jugendstil, but it had been coming for a long time.'[35] The idea of the interior as nature was literalized and amplified to the extreme in Jugendstil. This interior confused distinctions between the animate and the inanimate, the living and the dead. The Jugendstil artist/architect began to assume the role of total designer, taking up the tectonic elements of new constructional forms, and naturalizing them with a distinctly animated and vegetal stylistic line. The sense of an interior distinct from the archi-tecture that provided a space for it was lost. The individuality expressed within the interior shifted from being that of the inhabitant, mediated through the collection, and became that of the architect-turned-artist, whose artistic 'vision' constricted the inhabitant.

A specific example of the effect of this constriction will be considered in Chapter 5, along with some paradoxical issues to do with the 'finality' of the interior's liquidation; what is important to consider in the current context is the way in which an appeal to long experience, made through the collection, was based in the maintenance of illusions. In commenting on the German 'battle of the styles' or *Gründerzeit*, which directly preceded Jugendstil, Asendorf suggests: 'the education of a civilized person aims at the creation of a capacity for delusion that is supposed to obscure the irrelevance of culture in a world functioning according to wholly different methods, namely those of the money economy'.[36] He writes of the interior becoming 'the mirror image of the world of commodities that the bourgeois citizen has tried vainly to flee'.[37] The last defence against this inexorable infiltration of the commodity was established through an appeal to art. In the Jugendstil interior, every surface, object and spatial articulation was made to conform to a certain artistic vision. But this vision was completely given up to the commodity via art's capitulation to the market. The interior as a surface for the registering of traces, traces of an inhabitation registered over time, was lost. The Jugendstil interior was completely pre-ordained;

it fixed a frozen, alien image of its inhabitants. The whole idea of the interior as a space of refuge collapsed under the weight of this illusion of an artistic life in the interior.

For Benjamin, the lesson learned from this moment is cast in terms of experience. In 'Experience and Poverty', he presents an argument for the necessity to trade in this desire to leave traces of one's existence in order to embrace *Erlebnis* as a new poverty of experience in the modernity of the twentieth century. For Benjamin, the reworking of interior/exterior relations in the architectural modernism of the 1920s and 1930s provided a material provocation for a change in the under-standing of, and the cultural and psychological possibilities for, inhabitation. The literally transparent glass spaces of modernism, and their possibilities for spatial flow and connection, mitigated the bourgeois idea of the interior as a space of encasing for the inhabitant. Within this 'programmatic' slant on the problem of experience, architectural modernism must win the battle over the bourgeois interior by removing its possibility from the inhabitational game.

Once again, a closer examination of architectural modernism and its relation to the interior will be made in Chapter 5. For now it is useful to recall how Benjamin cast the problematic of experience through asking 'where has it all gone?'[38] In the nineteenth century, long experience was elusive, and the interior was founded in this condition. Securing long experience was the concern of establishing the interior as the domain of private life. The illusions constructed in the interior suggest that this sense of long experience was itself illusory, the 'story' of stories told by the fireside rendered mythical precisely in the substitution of the campfire with the domestic hearth. If the bourgeoisie of the nineteenth century lamented the atrophying of long experience and constructed an interior to support them in their illusions about the possibilities for its sustenance, the continuation of this lament was having dangerous cultural and political consequences in the 1930s. At this time, the nineteenth century already seemed like the archaic past, a past which long experience itself seemed to pre-exist in appearing to be precisely that which had always been transmitted from generation to generation. One discovers here that the temporality of experience is not linear. A key part of Benjamin's account of the interior is that it was written with reference to a particular cultural and political context, a particular 'present'. The bourgeois domestic interior was delineated in its clearest image at the precise moment that the culture of his time could not return to the mode of inhabitation it nurtured. This image flashes in an intense, momentary way, and Benjamin's account of the interior is one that tries, impossibly, to frame its after-image. For Benjamin, the interior is revealed as a dream image upon awakening to present cultural realities which are grasped precisely in their discontinuity from the past.

In this way, Benjamin's account of the emergence of the interior relates in an immediate fashion to *The Arcades Project* as a particular sort of history of the nineteenth century. It is a history of discontinuity, an archaeology of an immediate but largely irrecoverable past. The interior is a key topos within the history, and as such reveals a way of grasping the fragmentary nature of that history. The relations between the interior and the organization of *The Arcades Project* will be considered in more detail later in this chapter. For the moment, it is useful to return to Benjamin's 'difficulty in reflecting on dwelling', a difficulty in reconciling the eternal, mythical, 'long' values of experience with the historically emergent context of the interior. The following section pursues a radical 'application' of Benjamin's thinking to what can be seen as a present difficulty in reflecting on dwelling, one to do with how key histories of the interior, privacy and domesticity have been constructed.

Tracing histories of the interior

The essential history of the interior

As has been shown, the interior was revealed as a condition of illusion precisely in its attempts to capture long experience. One must realize, however, that it was no less real, no less materially inscribed for being illusory, and that it has generated experiences and continuities within its own conditions of existence. Indeed, it was the site of Benjamin's own upbringing, and as such he remained ambivalent about its cultural presence.[39] What might be called these 'real effects' of the bourgeois domestic interior are central to Benjamin's difficulty in reflecting on dwelling. For Benjamin, the eternal conceptions of dwelling are produced out of its specific historical conditions of existence. The problem is that these conditions are themselves taken as eternal. Given this difficulty, Benjamin realizes that history is only graspable as a condition in ruins, a series of discontinuous manifestations whose meanings only carry a force given particular 'present' interpretive conditions. By contrast, historian of the interior Mario Praz sees dwelling as an eternal condition which always finds its materialization in the furnishing of an interior. In witnessing the destruction of houses after the Second World War, their interiors laid open with 'some still furnished corner, dangling above the rubble, surrounded by ruin',[40] Praz muses:

> The houses will rise again, and men will furnish houses as long as there is breath in them. Just as our primitive ancestor built a shapeless chair with hastily-chopped branches, so the last man will save from the rubble a stool or a tree stump on which to rest from his labours; and if his spirit is freed a while from his woes, he will linger another moment and decorate his room.[41]

Praz's book *An Illustrated History of Interior Decoration from Pompeii to Art Nouveau* has been hailed as the first comprehensive history of the interior. What makes it significant is not so much the way in which furnishing is cast as the eternal element of domesticity, but rather how this position has been arrived at through the particular treatment of visual evidence. As the introduction showed, the interior's historical emergence was bound up with its meaning being equally spatial and image based. Yet these spatial and image-based senses do not map directly on to one another. Visual representations of interiors are not simply transparent to spatial referents, even if such spatial referents exist; representations construct interiors on a two-dimensional surface as much as practices of decoration and furnishing construct interiors spatially. This becomes important when considering how a history of the interior might itself be constructed from the evidence supplied in visual representation.

1.1
The Artist in Her Painting Room, York (watercolour on paper) by Mary Ellen Best, c. 1830s. In this instance, the painting emphasizes doubleness as a reflexivity in inhabiting and depicting an interior
Source: © York Museums Trust (York Art Gallery), UK / Bridgeman Art Library

It was from the beginning of the nineteenth century that interior views were painted and drawn as ends in themselves, as a specific genre (Figure 1.1). Echoing the Benjaminian short historical life of the interior, Charlotte Gere suggests:

> The depiction of rooms for their own sake, rather than as a background to a narrative, anecdotal or portrait painting, germinated, reached its fullest flowering and died within the space of one century. It was not unusual for such interiors to form a group, representing different aspects of several rooms. They were intended to be placed in albums rather than to be framed and hung, and remained an almost secret possession. . . . When the interior view went out of fashion in the second half of the nineteenth century, their very existence seems to have been forgotten. They were rendered obsolete by the development of a photographic camera capable of focusing on a great depth of field and thus able to do the job of the interior view-painter much more quickly and no less efficiently. Some of these [photographic] albums survive, giving an invaluable picture of decorating taste in the period 1880–1910, before they too were forgotten, like the albums of paintings they had superseded. Mario Praz's rediscovery of this minor but fascinating art barely thirty years ago (his pioneering *Illustrated History of Interior Decoration* was published in 1964) was a revelation, and the historic no less than aesthetic importance of the subject is now recognized by a group of informed collectors.[42]

In this passage, Gere shifts from discussing the specificity of this representational practice and its private significance to describing how these representations give on to a much broader conception of visual evidence for a history of the interior. Praz's work gleans visual evidence from Pompeii, what one must imagine is the first major moment in Western civilization from which representations of domestic life still survive, to Art Nouveau, which, curiously, aligns with the interior's point of liquidation, according to Benjamin. This chronological sequence is tied to a notion that these representations reveal something like the character of a domestic occupation, and that this character is directly accessible through representation. Praz suggests:

> Perhaps even more than painting or sculpture, perhaps even more than architecture itself, furniture reveals the spirit of the age. And there is nothing like a retrospective exhibition of furnished rooms in a chronological sequence to declare to us, at first glance, the varying personalities of the rooms' occupants.[43]

Praz's book aims to provide the published equivalent of this 'retrospective exhibition', taking what are mostly paintings as windows on to the spirit of various ages. Praz clearly realizes that there is something at stake in the relation between the representational and spatial conditions of the interior, hence there is some understanding of the doubleness of the interior. But he generalizes this nineteenth-century conception as one obtaining across all of history, and in so doing, simplifies the relation between representation and space.

What is the impetus behind this sort of generalizing, essentialist historiography? An answer may be found in another key history of the interior, Peter Thornton's *Authentic Décor: The Domestic Interior 1620–1920*. Thornton takes the cue for his investigation from this quotation from Macaulay's 1848 *History of England*:

> Readers who take an interest in the progress of civilization and of the useful arts will be grateful to the humble topographer who has recorded these facts [about the meanness of the lodgings of those taking the waters at Bath, early in the eighteenth century], and will perhaps wish that historians of far higher pretensions had sometimes spared a few pages from military evolutions and political intrigues, for the purpose of letting us know how the parlours and bedchambers of our ancestors looked.[44]

In these terms, a history of the interior supplements traditional grand historical narratives, whereby one's supposed innate appreciation of domesticity would colour the background of past events. But out of this general desire for historical information on the domestic comes the interior and its decoration as a particular object of historical study. Thornton introduces his history by citing a critic's evaluation of Praz's history. Thornton writes:

> Praz . . . was not at all interested in the history of interior decoration, as Hugh Honour has pointed out. The 'true subject' of this 'conventionally discursive' book, Honour insists, 'is not interior decoration, but the ruminations and memories, the visions and fancies prompted by paintings of interiors.'[45]

According to Thornton, Praz aims to see through representation a psychologized concept of the interior, where visual evidence is read for the character of the inhabitant. Thornton, on the other hand, aims to see the material reality of interiors through representation, where the history of the interior is articulated through a history of interior decoration.[46]

Regardless of their supposed differences, the desire for this sort of visually based history of the interior is one born, in Benjamin's terms, after its nineteenth-century emergence and liquidation. Praz's conclusion of his history with Art Nouveau comes to the heart of what this liquidation means for a conventional history of the interior. He cites Benjamin's exposé at length, but curiously translates the Jugendstil interior's 'liquidation' as its 'consummation',[47] as if the last moment of the interior may indeed be found in Art Nouveau/Jugendstil, but in a way that eternally preserves the interior as the natural and essential context for domesticity.

Struggles over representation

The histories of Praz and Thornton treat all visual representations of domesticity as interiors, despite the specific sense in which the interior emerged as a genre of representation in the nineteenth century. Indeed, the most identifiable and 'popular' images of interiors are said to be those of seventeenth-century Dutch painters such as Gerard Dou, Pieter de Hooch, Nicolaes Maes, Jan Vermeer and Emanuel de Witte. Witold Rybczynski, largely drawing on the work of Praz and Thornton, has identified in these paintings the recognizable qualities of home, crucial to this being a sense of intimacy or what Praz identified as *Stimmung*, 'a characteristic of interiors that has less to do with functionality than with the way that the room conveys the character of its owner'.[48] Home develops from this sense in being demarcated as a private world, and Rybczynski finds Dutch domestic arrangements exemplary in managing this demarcation. He allows a universally dominant idea, or rather a fantasy, of home to claim historical credence through the authority of fine art. In addition, it is a fine art that has broad appeal through its supposed realism and association with the domestic. But as Heidi de Mare has shown, these paintings only gained their 'domestic' appeal in the nineteenth century, the time when 'bourgeois family life became a nucleus around which the [Dutch] nation was formed'. Concepts such as privacy, intimacy, comfort and home were nineteenth-century sentiments that 'were then projected into the past and applied to seventeenth-century paintings, books and houses. Thus was born the wide-ranging, homogenous concept of domesticity'.[49] The popularity of these images was related to the mechanism of their availability. De Mare notes that Dutch paintings were sold abroad, especially in the United States, in the nineteenth century, the newly associated ideas of domesticity being exported along with the physical artefacts which supposedly originated these ideas.[50] Associated with this export was a strain of art-historical analysis which emphasized the social content of the paintings, this perspective still informing those who would read a recognizable domestic meaning and content into the paintings.[51]

In a very different interpretation of these paintings, Martha Hollander relates their visual enticements not to recognizable characteristics of home, but rather to compositional techniques and associated constructions of meaning which were historically and culturally specific. Hollander focuses her investigation on the way space was manipulated in the paintings. Their compartmentalization, drawing on and extending the compartmentalization of rooms and the nesting of vistas, mirrors and other images within rooms, 'makes for a remarkably complex play of meanings'. She locates this development in terms of a 'diagrammatic arrangement of images across a flat surface'[52] that underlies the development of Western image making. As such,

> Dutch artists integrated religious allegories of an earlier era into their secular images of modern life, [and] they adapted a traditional visual formula for their depictions of realistic space. In fact, their interest in perspective co-existed with the diagrammatic structure of earlier pictorial media. The resulting tension between the associative organization of signs and naturalistic perspective is one of the most fascinating and challenging qualities of Dutch art.[53]

For Victor Stoichita, these are examples of meta-paintings, whereby the painted subject offers a comment on the constitution of, and possibilities within, painting itself. The paintings offered a dialogue with the idea of the frame, particularly in the treatment of doors as openings between rooms. This meta-commentary is what defined painting in its modern form, that is, as easel painting.[54]

These interpretations reinforce an understanding of what Hollander calls Dutch art's 'depictions of realistic space', rather than its realistic depictions of space.[55] What was being painted was not, as Rybczynski would have it, 'the material world as he [in this case, Emanuel de Witte] saw it'. Rybczynski's idealism substitutes post-nineteenth-century fascination for historical fact:

> This love of the real world – 'realism' is too weak a word – was evident in many details. We can enjoy the way that the shadow of the windows falls on the partly open door, the red taffeta curtains that color the light in the room, the shiny brass of the chandelier, the rich gilt of the mirror frame and the matte texture of the pewter jug.[56]

Rybczynski is taken in by the actual subject of the paintings, which was the entice-ment to looking itself, an enticement Hollander captures in the title of her book: *An Entrance for the Eyes*. Rybczynski is unable, or unwilling, to be critical about the specificity of such enticements in their historical context, their meanings apart from his pre-ordained and naturalized narrative of home.

What can be considered with seventeenth-century Dutch art is the idea that such paintings, and associated forms such as doll's houses and illusionistic perspective boxes, were made for the Dutch bourgeoisie as furnishings for the houses in which they lived. As visual images, they doubled the domestic space of their reception, setting up a play of relations within this doubled situation, not to mention a play of relations between any one painting and what Stoichita calls 'transposed' paintings within it.[57] Yet this compelling play of doubles does not mean that these paintings belong to the concept of the interior. The interior does not simply emerge from the conceptualization of easel painting, let alone being present in a continuous history of Western image making. Stoichita's argument about meta-painting is compelling in its own terms, that is, as an argument about the emergence of easel painting as such, but it is worth returning to the idea that a genre of the interior view emerged in a specific practice of professional and amateur watercolour painting, and in engravings used to publish interior decoration schemes. As such, this genre emerged outside of fine-art easel painting, and in relation to architecture and techniques of representation proper to architecture.

In these terms, Robin Evans has argued that the interior attained a legibility in representation with difficulty. He notes that the 'room' became a new subject matter for architectural drawing from the mid-eighteenth century. This occurred with the emergence of what he calls the developed surface drawing, one which shows all of the inside elevations of any given room folded out relative to the room's depicted plan (Figure 1.2). Evans notes that this was a more comprehensive

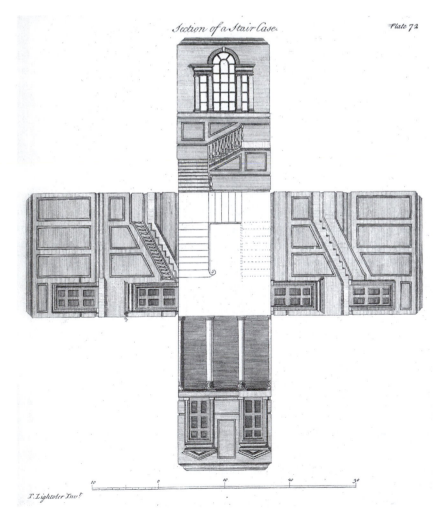

1.2
**Section of
a Staircase
(also known as
developed surface
drawing) by
Thomas Lightoler**
Source: William
Halfpenny, *The
Modern Builder's
Assistant*, London,
1757, plate 72.
By permission
British Library,
shelfmark
1261.c.21

representation of internal decorative schemes than could be achieved through the traditional architectural section drawing, which could only show in detail one inside elevation of any given room at any one time.[58] Developed surface drawings do not partake of the doubled sense of the interior, where the interior as spatial volume is understood consciously, and is accompanied by representational techniques that double this spatial sense. As Evans argues, the developed surface drawing maintains a sense of the decorative treatment of internal walls as flat surfaces, making the space between them void-like. Movable furnishing that might give a sense of spatiality to such decorative treatment was a problem for such a flat representational technique, and tends to sit anchored to the wall, or floats awkwardly in the void between walls.[59]

For Evans, the interior emerged in a spatialized sense in the early nineteenth century when the distribution of furniture became linked to the idea that there were a variety of ways of occupying a room, where previously, differently decorated rooms joined in plan were each to be occupied in one particular way. Humphry Repton was the major figure in this shift: 'It was the call for variety *within* the social landscape of the room that broke the hallowed ring of peripheral furnishing.'[60] Such a shift in distribution, both for furniture and for a room's occupants, began to outstrip the ability of the developed surface drawing to represent this condition adequately.[61] What emerged as a response to the inadequacy of the developed surface technique were representations that showed that 'the *furniture* occupies the room and then figures inhabit the furniture'.[62] These emerging representations were, in a historically specific sense, interiors (Figure 1.3).

1.3
**Drawing Room
by Thomas Hope**
Source: Thomas
Hope, *Household
Furniture and
Interior Decoration*,
London, 1807,
plate 6

In a domestic context, representational techniques emerge, develop, transform and are abandoned together with spatial practices that emerge, develop, transform and are abandoned. At a particular moment, specific representational and spatial practices claim, and can be claimed as, the interior. This claim is not to do with the interior 'as it is', let alone 'as it has always been'. Rather, the very concept of the interior, and specific changes in the practices of inhabitation, are produced as much in representation as they are in spatial practices. This is why representation and spatial conditions need to be considered as doubling each other, rather than representation bearing objective and transparent witness to developments, more often than not cast as continuities, in spatial practices. What one might actually learn from someone like Praz is about particular representational practices and their construction of meanings at particular moments in time, rather than about continuities of life in the interior.[63]

'The private individual makes his entry into history'

If representational and spatial practices are variable in this way, stability might be conceived through the inhabitant as a figure of continuity, and the idea that domesticity is formed around this figure. With the emergence of the interior, Benjamin claims that 'The private individual makes his entry into history.'[64] But here again returns the 'difficulty in reflecting on dwelling'. This nineteenth-century emergence of the figure of the private individual is ripe for uptake within an eternal conception of dwelling.

Volume 4 of *A History of Private Life* is the major historical work on the rise of privacy and domesticity through the nineteenth century.[65] It takes up the idea that the traces of inhabitation constitute, and can be found in, the interior, and further, that taken together, such traces provide a broad historical account of the experience of private life in the nineteenth century. Certain moments from *A History of Private Life* can be pinpointed to show how the evidence of the interior is treated in this way.

Michelle Perrot and Roger-Henri Guerrand broaden the idea of the trace beyond bourgeois practices of decoration in describing the first impulses towards decoration by the French working class of the nineteenth century: 'Moving meant changing wallpaper', the low price of wallpaper in that context having a significant impact.[66] They also cite the wide use and availability of lace curtains: 'they even turn up in the wretched shanties of the Cité Jeanne d'Arc photographed by Atget at the turn of the century'.[67] And they suggest that it was in a choosing and arranging of objects more so than the physical nature of space that marked off a private, individualized interior. Perrot and Guerrand note with respect to elderly people who were confined to hospice care, and who hoarded old household objects and utensils, that 'The only value these things have for them is that they are not part of the house-issued clothing and furnishings. These things belong to them, and taken together they symbolize a kind of home.'[68] For Perrot and Guerrand, the first movement of decoration is in demarcating a personalized domestic interior from an existing inside space, where this interior is made, and perceived as such historically, through the idea of decoration as trace of the inhabiting subject.[69]

In turning their focus specifically to bourgeois practices, Perrot and Guerrand go on to suggest that the significance for the Parisian bourgeoisie of decoration as 'trimming' or covering was in its symbolic protection from the violence and danger of the streets of Paris, and as a way of banishing the look of poverty:

> People became obsessed with the desire that no wall or floor be left bare; bare floors became a mark of poverty. The leading Bourgeois magazine, *L'Illustration*, described the new conception of space in its February 15, 1851 issue: 'We gathered in a small saloon, which was tightly sealed by door curtains, silk pads, and double drapes. . . . A good carpet lies underfoot . . . a profusion of fabrics graces the windows, covers the mantle piece and hides the woodwork. Dry wood and cold marble are concealed beneath velvet and plush.'[70]

Yet even as these motivations to decorate stem from a desire to establish the interior as a stable, personalized space, further on in volume 4 of *A History of Private Life*, Alain Corbin identifies the development of certain neuroses within this interior condition. He likens the 'bourgeoisie's obsession with drapery, slipcovers, casings and upholstery' with the 'perverse effects of modesty' seen in the increasing sumptuousness and complexity of fastenings in lingerie, and the subsequent negotiations and rituals of dressing and undressing. Corbin suggests: 'The desire to preserve, the concern to leave a trace of one's existence, the fear of castration, and the omnipresent reminder of the menace of desire joined in a neurotic encounter.'[71]

This account of the claiming of a space through the leaving of traces sets up a charged and ambivalent relation between an inhabitant's objects and an inhabitant's subjectivity. A mark of this ambivalence is that the other side of the menace of private space – or perhaps it is that the menace of private space is the other side of this dominant tendency – is the desire for a private space in which to define and cultivate one's individuality. *A History of Private Life* does much to emphasize the interior as a setting for crucial aspects of private life in the nineteenth century, with activities such as the keeping of a diary, reading, whether in private or as a family (partaking of both secular and religious texts), the cultivation of gendered domestic duties, and the habits of grooming.[72]

Even from these brief expositions, one can see how arguments about domestic privacy are drawn from the minutiae of daily life. In the introduction to volume 4 of *A History of Private Life*, Michelle Perrot gives an account of the diverse range of historical documents used for the history, including theoretical treatises on the family; police, court and criminal records which give evidence of legal intervention into private matters; private archives which may have been preserved, and which hold personal letters, diaries, etc.; and the novel, which takes the family and private matters as its subject. Perrot suggests that the difficulty with reading these sources comes from the fact that they are 'overabundant yet wanting, garrulous but silent, frank yet reticent',[73] leaving the researchers 'with the difficulty of understanding anything more than the external and public face of private life, with the impossibility of passing through the looking glass';[74] however, Perrot betrays this difficulty by seeing the necessity 'to attempt a synthesis without the needed analyses; we have been forced to cobble together a narrative from fragmentary findings'.[75] Perrot is suggesting that privacy is too individual and heterogeneous a field to construct a grand historical narrative, yet this is what *A History of Private Life* tries to do. What is important to note about this is that the project of volume 4 drives the entire *History of Private Life* project. In his foreword to volume 1, *From Pagan Rome to Byzantium*, Georges Duby writes:

> We had decided that our research should cover all of Western history and that it should emphasize the *longue durée*. To a period of more than two millennia and to all of Europe, with its diversity of regional ways and customs, we would therefore be applying a concept – that of personal life – that had come into common use in certain parts of Europe only quite recently, in the nineteenth century. How should we go about writing the prehistory of such a concept?[76]

Duby recognizes the historical formation of a concept of private life that is linked to the emergence of the interior, and that is organizing a project to uncover what he terms the prehistory of private life. Yet the 'prehistorical' basis of the first three volumes of *A History of Private Life* prior to the 'event' of privacy in the nineteenth century is denied by Duby a few lines later, when he falls back on a notion of the a priori division between public and private in history: 'We started from the obvious fact that at all times and in all places a clear, commonsensical distinction has been made between the public – that which is open to the community and subject to the authority of its magistrates – and the private.'[77]

The tension between the *longue durée* and the 'event' in French historiography has been explored by Emmanuel Le Roy Ladurie, who suggests, in his investigation of two approaches to a particular historical example in the context of social history, that a 'passing event has produced a lasting mentality – a short-term phenomenon has produced a long-term structure'.[78] Ladurie's explanation of the 'event–structure' relation accounts for the way in which the production of a mentality from an event can be mistaken for the existence of the mentality as a function of long-term factors. This is the problem inherent in Duby's invocation of the *longue durée*. Even as he acknowledges the role of an event, his view as a historian is broadly retrospective in terms of the mentality of private life. His idea of a prehistory for the concept of privacy is one which seems inevitably to have led to its nineteenth-century manifestation.

Traditional history/effective history

What is common in the histories of the interior, privacy and domesticity that have been considered so far is that they attest to a post-nineteenth-century way of seeing. This way of seeing authorizes a general historical retrospection which is itself not appreciated within a historical context. This situation approaches what Michel Foucault terms traditional history:

> We believe in the dull constancy of instinctual life and imagine that it continues to exert its force indiscriminately in the present as it did in the past. But a knowledge of history easily disintegrates this unity, depicts its wavering course, locates its moments of strength and weakness, and defines its oscillating reign.[79]

Foucault's effective history, designated above as arising from a 'knowledge of history', is a history of discontinuity, for the sake of breaking tendencies for recognition and 'rediscovery of ourselves'[80] in the construction of history. In Foucault's terms, the emergence of the interior, in its doubleness, can be cast as an event in the schema of effective history, an event that, when perceived, enables a 'reversal of a relationship of forces'.[81] Benjamin's adoption of the interior's emergence into his historical account of the nineteenth century is a perception of this as such an event. It is one topos of the nineteenth century that enables a particular sort of reversal, a waking up from the dream of recognition and 'rediscovery of ourselves' in the image of history as the record of progress. For Benjamin himself, the entire *Arcades Project* amounted to a critique of the historicism which had governed German historiography within modernity.[82]

The traditional history of *A History of Private Life*, Praz, Rybczynski and Thornton does not subject its conceptual and organizational structures to historical analysis. Each of these histories, in their desire for comprehensiveness, seeks to establish a domain of study wherein one can recognize the continually present themes of privacy and domesticity in relation to the stable categories of the interior and its inhabiting subject. These categories provide reference points against which representation, treated as transparent visual evidence, can be verified as to changes in decorative style, and in understanding how the practices of inhabitation can be perceived as timeless but also progressive. These histories of the interior are 'living' histories in which 'we' might rediscover ourselves.

In the manner of effective history, however, Benjamin's work shows a method of gathering and presenting evidence in order to investigate these stabilities as myths. The interior is inextricable from a temporal complexity that means that evidentiary traces become significant through the 'mortification' of objects and inhabitants alike. Benjamin's larger historical project seeks to preserve the fragmentary and occluded nature of this sort of evidence as a radical critique of narratives of historical progress. Embedded within Benjamin's fragmentary history of the nineteenth century, the interior takes on the role of estranging us from, rather than connecting us to, bourgeois domesticity. In allowing for this, Benjamin is able to provide an account of the historical emergence of the interior that seeks to understand precisely the effects of its historical emergence, effects which reverberate through the way in which its history has traditionally been written. The following section returns to Benjamin's project to analyse the position of the interior within this anti-essentialist thinking.

Benjamin's interior history

For Benjamin, the liquidation of the interior presaged a cultural necessity to overcome the sort of thinking that would essentialize the experience of dwelling in the interior, that would make it something timeless and essential to identity. In 'Experience and Poverty', Benjamin remarks:

> If you enter a bourgeois room of the 1880s, for all the cosiness it radiates, the strongest impression you receive may well be, 'You've got no

business here'. And in fact you have no business in that room, for there is no spot on which the owner has not left his mark – the ornaments on the mantelpiece, the antimacassars on the armchairs, the transparencies in the windows, the screen in front of the fire. A neat phrase by Brecht helps us out here: 'Erase the traces!' is the refrain in the first poem of his *Lesebuch für Städtebewohner* [*Reader for City-Dwellers*]. . . . This has now been achieved by Scheerbart, with his glass, and the Bauhaus, with its steel. They have created rooms in which it is hard to leave traces. 'It follows from the foregoing', Scheerbart declared a good twenty years ago, 'that we can surely talk about a "culture of glass." The new glass-milieu will transform humanity utterly. And now it remains only to be wished that the new glass-culture will not encounter too many enemies.'[83]

Benjamin writes of the need to overcome experience (*Erfahrung*), and the connections to tradition that it implies, by overcoming the way in which the interior resists the revolutionary aspects of an architecture of glass. This overcoming was a political necessity, a necessity in not re-establishing a connection to tradition and timeless values from the rubble of its destruction, but instead in accepting destruction, and the poverty of experience which it produced, as a way of moving beyond a culture organized upon such an appeal to tradition.

Beyond his particular construal of this situation in relation to the political realities of his time, Benjamin opens the possibility for thinking critically about the interior's relation to history in revealing this problematic relation between the eternal and the historically specific. Rather than the interior being the exclusive object of its own history, where the tendency towards the timeless and the eternal is amplified, the specific conditions of the interior's historical emergence provide a way of structuring a thinking that recognizes the critical value of the discontinuous and the fragmentary. The interior thus emerges as a particular way of construing crucial questions of modernity.

The interior of thought

Convolute I from *The Arcades Project*, entitled 'The Interior, the Trace', is organized through an interior structuring which carries the force of Benjamin's thinking on historical time.[84] Initially, the convolutes of *The Arcades Project* can be considered the polar opposites of the exposés. Where the exposés are pithy, the convolutes seem to be directionless meanderings; the line of thought travelling between the commentaries and quotations that they contain is often obscure. At one level this has to do with the fact that the convolutes were the notes to a historical narrative on the nineteenth century that was never finished, a narrative for which the exposés offer a synopsis. Yet much of Benjamin's thinking has been explored through the convolute material. This material has often been treated in a way that casts his thinking in terms of what *The Arcades Project* could or should have been in complete form.[85]

Rolf Tiedemann presents the incompletion of *The Arcades Project* thus: 'The fragments of the *Passagen-Werk* [*Arcades Project*] can be compared to the materials used in building a house, the outline of which has just been marked in the ground or whose foundations are just being dug.' He describes the exposés as:

> outlines of the plan[.] . . . The five or six sections of each exposé should have corresponded to the same number of chapters in the book, or, to continue the analogy, to the five or six floors of the projected house. Next to the foundations we find neatly piled excerpts, which would have been used to construct the walls; Benjamin's own thoughts would have provided the mortar to hold the building together.[86]

The metaphor is architectural, one of structural coherence from which an image of completion can be projected. Yet in incomplete form, Tiedemann remarks upon the oppressive weight of the excerpts. As editor of the original German edition of *The Arcades Project*, he mentions the temptation to publish only Benjamin's comments. But the necessity of including the excerpts, which are largely quotations from nineteenth-century sources and which make up the bulk of the convolute material, comes with the possibility of seeing *The Arcades Project* as a complete edifice, one which the reader should construct through their own reading of it. Graeme Gilloch has a more ambivalent account of *The Arcades Project* as an incomplete edifice:

> the 'Arcades Project' may be seen as a disorderly construction site comprising a vast pile of building blocks interspersed with a few scattered sets of opaque, repeatedly redrawn blueprints for assembling them. . . . It is the place where construction and ruination interpenetrate and become indistinguishable from one another.[87]

Howard Eiland and Kevin McLaughlin, the editors and translators of the English version, invoke a more structurally complex metaphor in describing its ordering. *The Arcades Project* is 'the blueprint of an unimaginably massive and labyrinthine architecture – a dream city, in effect'.[88] They comment that this might describe the project as research rather than the finished writing-up or application of research. But they also note that the convolute material was itself subject to revisions, itself being treated as a manuscript. Eiland and McLaughlin ask: 'Why revise for a notebook?' They describe the combining of quoted fragments and Benjamin's own commentaries as a deliberate montaging. Such a

> transcendence of the traditional book form would go together, in this case, with the blasting apart of pragmatic historicism – grounded, as this always is, on the premise of a continuous and homogeneous temporality. Citation and commentary might then be perceived as intersecting at a thousand different angles, setting up vibrations across the epochs of recent history, so as to effect 'the cracking open of natural teleology'.[89]

For Benjamin, this transcendence had much to do with the material he was researching: 'The particular difficulty of doing historical research on the period following the close of the eighteenth century will be displayed. With the rise of mass-circulation press, the sources become innumerable.'[90]

Susan Buck-Morss also confronts the reality of the compositional form of
The Arcades Project, writing of 'this nonexistent text'.[91] Yet for Buck-Morss, such a
non-existent text can still be described as having an overall philosophical conception,
bringing together an earlier, theological stage in Benjamin's intellectual development,
and a second Marxist phase. She describes this conception as 'a dialectics of
seeing'.[92] To aid in making manifest an overall sense of order in the project, Buck-
Morss develops several organizational diagrams or displays that aim to give different
forms of overview for the project. She explains that there is no narrative continuity
in the project, but there is a conceptual coherence. Her own analysis of the project
aims to show its 'coherent and persistent philosophical design'.[93]

Metaphors and diagrams of structure drive these analyses. Yet it is
important to return again to one of Benjamin's key aphorisms on the relationship
between the interior and the city, the public and the private: 'Against the armature
of glass and iron, upholstery offers resistance with its textiles.' Against the stability
of an architectural ordering, a form of surfacing and filling which privileges a complex,
non-hierarchical weave (emphasized through a shuttling, a back-and-forth motion),
resists, offering a different possibility for thought, yet one which is entangled
with the structuring provided by architecture. In contrast to the act of building, and
following up Benjamin's own thinking on the formation of the interior, the act of
upholstering denotes the preparing of an interior to receive objects, where the soft,
upholstered materials of that space receive the impression of those objects.
Benjamin's own commentary can be thought of as the moulding of this soft surface
around the collected quotations, the taking of their impression, their being enfolded
softly rather than fixed rigidly with mortar, and, as such, allowing their positioning to
be provisional in both time and space. This supple sense of the upholstered surface
links to the idiosyncratic subjectivity of the collector, who is open to the dispersion
of things and their innumerable number, rather than the idealizing subjectivity of
the master builder, who wants to control their organization. After all, as Benjamin
notes in the exposé of 1939, architecture's attempt to control the interior through
Jugendstil's totalizing art led to the literal downfall of the artist/architect; Ibsen's
master-builder Solness plunged from the height of his tower.[94]

One is brought closer to the interior's opening up of a specific sort of
ordering. Gilloch captures a sense of the collector in describing *The Arcades Project*
as 'an agglomeration or plethora of interconnected, related enterprises, begun at
various times, dropped, taken up with renewed zeal, transformed, and eventually
abandoned in favour of something else'.[95] Pierre Missac writes of an 'internal composition' in some of Benjamin's writings, and which might be seen to result from
such an approach to things: 'what seems to result is a deepening of the composition,
an interiorization of the dialectic (in the object dealt with, not in the writing subject),
which also indicates an advance in Benjamin's thinking and a concealing of his
intentions'.[96] Missac also calls to mind a fragment from Benjamin's *One-Way Street*
entitled 'Interior Decoration':

> The tractatus is an Arabic form. Its exterior is undifferentiated and unob-
> trusive, like the façades of Arabian buildings, whose articulation begins
> only in the courtyard. So, too, the articulated structure of the tractatus is

invisible from the outside, revealing itself only from within. If it is formed by chapters, they have not verbal headings but numbers. The surface of its deliberations is not enlivened with pictures, but covered with unbroken, proliferating arabesques. In the ornamental density of this presentation, the distinction between thematic and excursive expositions is abolished.[97]

Taking the interior as a mode of organization for Benjamin's thinking resists claims for structural coherence, even ambivalent ones, that derive from architectural metaphors of structure and blueprints. What Benjamin recognizes at the level of the organization of his thinking are the interior's conditions of historical emergence. The antagonism between architecture and the interior is where Benjamin begins his 'convoluted' account of the interior. The bourgeois domestic interior may have a short historical life, but it is never simply finished. Following the trajectory of his thinking through the convolute material gives a sense of the efficacy of incompletion when thinking about the interior.

The convolutions of the interior

To the extent that there is a beginning to Convolute I, 'The Interior, the Trace', it is one where furniture, which is movable, begins to take on aspects of architecture's immovability. Architecture and furniture enter into battle: 'You see beds and armoires bristling with battlements.'[98] Architecture itself becomes interiorized. The interior becomes bigger than architecture, enfolding it in a kind of dream space where scale shifts. Considering furniture as the movable – as opposed to architecture as the immovable – allows Benjamin a more immediate access to the dreamworld of the nineteenth century: 'The importance of movable property, as compared with immovable property. Here our task is slightly easier. Easier to blaze a way to the heart of things abolished or superseded, in order to decipher the contours of the banal as picture puzzle.'[99]

Benjamin next moves to the idea of the interior 'furnished in dreams',[100] as an explanation of the stylistic mixing and differentiation in bourgeois interiors, where the faraway and exotic are brought together in an instantaneous and total effect. More comments and quotations are devoted to the qualities of exotic, dreamlike interiors, until the idea of furniture as fortification surfaces again, this time with a more pointed comment about spatial arrangements of furniture that mark out a defensible space in the interior. Benjamin quotes architectural critic Adolf Behne on the diagonal placement of carpets and furniture:

> the deeper explanation for all this is, again, the unconscious retention of a posture of struggle and defense. . . . Just as the knight, suspecting an attack, positions himself crosswise to guard both left and right, so the peace-loving burgher, several centuries later, orders his art objects in such a way that each one, if only by standing out from all the rest, has a wall and moat surrounding it.[101]

This defensive posture in the interior leads on to the idea that interiors provide 'the costumes of moods', the interior itself 'a stimulus to intoxication and dream'.[102] Benjamin then recalls his second experiment with hashish.

Comments and quotations on the purity of an interior vision, masquerade, the interior features of the city, the emergence of genre painting, and the *fumeuse* as an extinct piece of furniture culminate in a citation from Theodor Adorno on the relation between environment and the inwardness of thought in Kierkegaard. This passage leads Benjamin to more considered notes that can be seen to underpin the exposés' comments on the interior, these comments having to do with 'the difficulty in reflecting on dwelling'.[103] At this point the theme of the trace emerges more strongly: 'Plush – the material in which traces are left especially easily.'[104] He includes material on how particular people are positioned within interiors, and then an idea, in a kind of interiorization of the city, of a 'Multiplication of traces through the modern administrative apparatus'.[105]

While this might be a radically reduced iteration through Convolute I, it shows as much how Benjamin's thinking moves in the interior as it does the interior's emergent historical contours. The interior offers a space of immersion for his thinking, and, in turn, the trajectories of his thinking can be traced out, in the sense of a detection of his thinking. To postulate that such traces belong to a pre-ordained and rigid structure of thinking is to impose a system of thought – indeed, systematic thought – over an idiosyncratic gathering together of fragments, a gathering together which performs an interiorization of these fragments. The way in which this organization is taken up in *The Arcades Project* doubles the interior. There is no attempt here, as there is with volume 4 of *A History of Private Life*, to produce a seamless narrative from fragmentary evidence, and thereby to attempt to produce a transparency between historical representation and the historically inscribed material of the interior. Rather, the convolute registers as a plane of immanence, a surface gathering but also being formed and deformed through the impressions made by the collected quotations. As Gilles Deleuze and Félix Guattari suggest: 'the plane of immanence is ceaselessly being woven, like a gigantic shuttle'.[106]

Mortification and the interior as image

But the question still remained for Benjamin: how is the force of these fragmentary, interiorized impressions to be divined? How is the illuminating potential of historical material on the interior – indeed, the very idea of the historical emergence of the interior – to be presented without an appeal to a narrative history? These questions might be approached by thinking through the relation between the convolutes and the exposés in *The Arcades Project*. The exposés can be seen as a way of exteriorizing thinking, of letting it be imaged within a world of intellectual formalities; yet the counterpart to this exteriorization is the deepening interiorization at work, one which, as Missac suggests, conceals intentions. The trajectory of Benjamin's thinking arcs between these conditions. Akin to an electrical charge, this arc illuminates a dialectical image, an image which allows the fragments wrested from their temporal and associational embeddedness to deliver a force of argument to a present context of reception. Here is Benjamin on the dialectical image:

> What distinguishes images from the 'essences' of phenomenology is their historical index. . . . These images are to be thought of entirely

apart from the categories of the 'human sciences', from so-called habitus, from style, and the like. For the historical index of the images not only says that they belong to a particular time; it says, above all, that they attain legibility only at a particular time. And indeed, this acceding 'to legibility' constitutes a specific critical point in the movement at their interior.[107]

The dialectical image carries the trace of the nineteenth century as archaic past into Benjamin's temporal present. Being seized in the present, the image mortifies the past. This involves the same sense as the interior's mortification of its inhabitant. Mortification both destroys and redeems particular past moments in order that a kind of originary value be returned to them. As Michael Jennings suggests: 'Only this sort of ongoing purgative labour which "mortifies" the past can reveal those few images that might have a positive effect in the present.'[108] These images are a link to the *mémoire involontaire*, the illumination of a forgotten past.[109] Yet the material kernel that delivers this past in a present of reception is the interior, itself the context for the possible link to the *mémoire involontaire* via objects wrested from the world of commodities. The interior is revealed as the ultimate commodity form via this illumination. It gives itself up to the *mémoire involontaire* as a kind of final act, one combining both redemption and destruction.

The dialectical image carries a force that produces an awakening to the problems of the present. Specifically for the interior as a cultural form, this awakening had to do with its newly illuminated impossibility as a space of retreat and immersion. In the crystallization of a concept of modern dwelling as rootless, open and on the move, the bourgeois domestic interior is delivered of its regressive resistance, being delivered instead into a different kind of resistance, one of revolutionary thinking, where the radical potential for dwelling of a glass architecture is illuminated.[110] The force of Benjamin's interiorized thinking breaks the interior apart. This breaking apart, only possible through an immersion within the interior, renders the eternal sense of dwelling radically historical. But this radical historicity renders the broken fragments archaic. An image of the interior – the interior as image – arises with most clarity at the moment of its historical passing. The intention concealed within the bourgeois interior was the critical exposition of its own historical demise.

This exploration of Benjamin's thinking through the interior has given a complex and critical sense to the interior's historical emergence. The interior organizes a thinking that seeks to divine the source of its affect and criticality in the present. In turn, this thinking seeks to preserve the fragmentary nature of the historical conditions of the interior's emergence, one which recognizes its impossibility in the present. Such thinking has enabled a critique of conventional accounts of the history of the interior, privacy and domesticity. The major effect of this traditional, essentialized historical work is to render timeless a sense of the interior's inhabitation, allowing a progressive and unproblematic reading of the domestic. A further corrective is needed to this traditional historical thinking, one that focuses on what it might mean to inhabit the interior infused with both a sense of the new and the archaic. Chapter 2 investigates a particularly modern, psychoanalytical account of the subject that was theorized in an intimate relationship with the bourgeois domestic interior.

Chapter 2

Lost objects

Sigmund Freud's psychoanalytical interior

Chapter 1 considered how the subjectivity of the collector as 'true resident' of the interior developed along with the collection as a particular construal of a world of things. This chapter examines relationships between subjectivity and the interior in a more specific way. Three framings of Freudian psychoanalysis will be considered: first, a consideration of psychoanalysis as a technology of subjectification, with the interior as a key part of its mechanism; second, an examination of Sigmund Freud's Viennese consulting rooms as the domestic scene of his psychoanalytic practice; and third, speculations about the role of the interior in the formulation of a psychoanalytic theorization of subjectivity.

A domestic technology

The rise of the social, the family, and the deployment of sexuality

In his foreword to Jacques Donzelot's study *The Policing of Families*, Gilles Deleuze writes: '"Having a room of one's own" is a desire, but also a control.'[1] With the historical emergence of the interior, desire and control appear as two sides of the same coin: desiring an interior means submitting to its mechanisms of control. In the late nineteenth century, desire was theorized psychoanalytically in relation to the controlling mechanism of the domestic interior. In this way, psychoanalysis can be seen to have developed as a technology of subjectification. For Nikolas Rose:

> Technologies of subjectification, then, are the machinations, the being-assembled-together with particular intellectual and practical instruments, components, entities, and devices that produce certain ways of being-human, territorialize, stratify, fix, organize, and render durable particular relations that humans may truthfully establish with themselves.[2]

The interior can be considered as a practical instrument or machine working as part of the technology of subjectification that psychoanalysis enacted. Within this technology, the interior territorialized particular relations to the self which were accorded the status of truth. In other words, an explicit relation between the interior and interiority was enacted within this technology. Both were assembled together. As Rose suggests: 'all the effects of psychological interiority, together with a whole range of other capacities and relations, are constituted through the linkage of humans into other objects and practices, multiplicities and forces'.[3]

The first step in considering the interior's role as part of a technology of subjectification is to understand the historical emergence of 'the social', the field that makes the workings of this technology both possible and analysable. Like the interior, the social needs to be considered as a historically formed category, and not a natural ground against which the workings of society can be understood. The social is itself an apparatus for governance and the production of knowledge. Deleuze describes the social as having its origins in the late eighteenth century, and emerging in relation to other domains such as the economic, the judicial, the medical and the educational. These sectors are not reducible to the social, nor vice versa. Rather, the social 'is able to react on them and effect a new distribution of their functions'.[4] For Deleuze, this new distribution hybridized the public and private, and the family became the milieu on which the social acted. This was not a pre-existing form of the family that began to be seen with more clarity, or a form that was put in crisis through social changes. Rather, the family was constructed in a particular form through the workings of the social. Part of this construction had to do with the means by which the social went to work on the family. Roles, responsibilities, significances and shortcomings were all produced for and within the family, to the extent that in their identification, monitoring and correction, the assembled mechanisms of the social were deployed.

This way of conceiving of and studying the social stands in contrast to what Donzelot calls the history of mentalities, the kind that *A History of Private Life* records. Against this general historical approach, Donzelot posits the family 'not as a point of departure, as a manifest reality, but as a moving resultant, an uncertain form whose intelligibility can only come from studying the system of relations it maintains with the sociopolitical level'.[5] Psychoanalysis, rather than being a way of explaining the mentality of private life, is seen as a particular line of force that contributes to the tracing out of the social. For Donzelot, the power of psychoanalysis within the family is 'regulatory and noncoercive'.[6] And as Michel Foucault has shown, this form of power arises from psychoanalysis' 'deployment of sexuality' within the family.[7] This deployment was not simply focused on the family as defined by the conjugal couple and their children. Rather, it worked through spatial articulations. Foucault writes of spaces haunted by sexuality,[8] spatial conditions created to produce, regulate, separate and link multiple sexualities:

> The separation of grownups and children, the polarity established between the parents' bedroom and that of the children (it became routine in the course of the [nineteenth] century when working-class housing construction was undertaken), the relative segregation of boys and girls, the strict instructions as to the care of nursing infants (maternal breast-feeding, hygiene), the attention focused on infantile sexuality, the supposed dangers of masturbation, the importance attached to puberty,

the methods of surveillance suggested to parents, the exhortations, secrets and fears, the presence – both valued and feared – of servants: all this made the family, even when brought down to its smallest dimensions, a complicated network, saturated with multiple, fragmentary and mobile sexualities. To reduce them to the conjugal relationship, and then to project the latter, in the form of a forbidden desire, onto the children, cannot account for the apparatus which, in relation to these sexualities, was less a principle of inhibition than an inciting and multiplying mechanism.[9]

Psychoanalysis is not simply reducible to the 'family drama', but must be considered in relation to a spatialization of its power and effects. In turn, it is useful to consider how this spatialization brought into discourse the particular subjectivities at stake in the domestic interior.

The domesticity of psychoanalysis

The spatialization of sexuality gained its discursive form in psychoanalysis in several ways. Initially, the symbolism of the domestic in Freud's theory of dream interpretation is important to consider. A crucial aspect of this theory had to do with breaking up the manifest appearance of a dream, and reassembling the constituent parts into a narrative of interpretation.[10] Often this manifest appearance was associated with the domestic interior. In his writings on dreams, Freud produced a litany of interpretations of their domesticity. In developing these, he drew on and critiqued earlier theorists of dreams who associated parts of a house, especially its interior, with parts of the body. The advance Freud made from these earlier theorists was in suggesting that associations were made in dreams between unconscious impulses and domestic scenes, and further, that sexual imagery was hidden behind these supposedly innocent scenes.[11] In one particular example, Freud highlighted the association of a derogatory German term for women, *Frauenzimmer* (literally, 'women's room'),[12] with the dream symbolism of rooms:

> Rooms in dreams are usually women ('*Frauenzimmer*'); if the various ways in and out of them are represented, this interpretation is scarcely open to doubt. In this connection interest in whether the room is open or locked is easily intelligible. . . . A dream of going into a suite of rooms is a brothel or a harem dream. But, as Sachs has shown by some neat examples, it can also be used (by antithesis) to represent marriage.[13]

This sexualized consideration of the interior as dream symbol is augmented in the later theorization of the psyche by what might be called an organizational consideration. In his introductory lectures on psychoanalysis from the beginning of the twentieth century, Freud used a suite of rooms to explain the structure of the unconscious:

> an individual process belongs to begin with to the system of the unconscious and can then, in certain circumstances, pass over into the system of the conscious.

> The crudest idea of these systems is the most convenient for us – a spatial one. Let us therefore compare the system of the unconscious to a large entrance hall, in which the mental impulses jostle one another like separate individuals. Adjoining this entrance hall is a separate, narrower, room – a kind of drawing-room – in which consciousness, too, resides. But on the threshold between these two rooms a watchman performs his function: he examines the different mental impulses, acts as a censor, and will not admit them into the drawing-room if they displease him. . . . The impulses in the entrance hall of the unconscious are out of sight of the conscious, which is in the other room; to begin with they must remain unconscious. If they have already pushed their way forward to the threshold and have been turned back by the watchman, then they are inadmissible to consciousness; we speak of them as *repressed*. But even the impulses which the watchman has allowed to cross the threshold are not on that account necessarily conscious as well; they can only become so if they succeed in catching the eye of consciousness. We are therefore justified in calling this second room the system of the preconscious.[14]

What is striking about this spatial analogy is the way in which it doubles the domestic situation experienced by Freud's clientele, a situation which, in many cases, had driven them towards the therapeutics of psychoanalysis: impulses held on the threshold of rooms, jostling between individuals, acts of guardianship that permit or deny access, the important eye needing to be caught. There is a sense that regulated behaviour in the bourgeois domestic interior offered a powerful explanatory tool in Freud's understanding of the structure and workings of the psyche, and also that this sort of domesticity was the context wherein psychoanalysis went to work.

Dora, or the psychoanalysis of domesticity

Freud's account of one of his most important case histories, that of Dora, is a narration of the norms and deviations within the bourgeois domestic realm. As he remarks in the preface to its publication under the title 'Fragment of an Analysis of a Case of Hysteria', Freud perceived a great deal of difficulty in making the intimate details of a young woman's sexuality public. Yet – and here Foucault's account of psycho-analysis' releasing of sex into discourse echoes loudly – he felt he must do so for the good of science, not apologizing for the 'frankness' with which he is to describe these intimate details. Dora's illness is a case study of the regulating role of the family in bourgeois life, and of the complications which arise – and the point at which the therapeutics of psychoanalysis intervene – when the normal state of familial and interpersonal relations goes awry. Freud writes:

> It follows from the nature of the facts which form the material of psycho-analysis that we are obliged to pay as much attention in our case histories to the purely human and social circumstances of our patients as to the somatic data and the symptoms of the disorder. Above all, our interest will be directed toward their family circumstances – and not only, as will be seen later, for the purpose of enquiring into their heredity.[15]

The case study will be recounted in detail to shed light on the importance to Freud of 'family circumstances'. It was Dora's father who brought the 18-year-old to see Freud. This action of parental authority was intended to restore order to familial relations, yet it was the action that allowed the instabilities in these relations to be released into discourse. Dora's father had wanted Freud to '"talk" Dora out' of her belief that he was having an affair with Frau K., a close family friend.[16] The affair had started when Frau K. began to nurse Dora's unwell father, a role which Dora had herself fulfilled, and which her mother did not. Dora also became close to the young Frau K., who acted as a kind of mother figure in place of the lack of attention paid her by her own mother. Herr K. was also interested in Dora, and had propositioned her on an occasion when the families were on holiday together. Dora reacted with disgust at this advance, and a brief while after it had taken place, she informed her parents of it. Herr K. denied that he had made an advance, and made allegations to Dora's parents about the young woman's lack of innocence in sexual matters. When Dora tried to persuade her father to break ties with the K.s, ostensibly as a result of this event, she suffered an attack which brought to a head a series of depressive symptoms and negative feelings towards her father, whom she had previously adored. It was at this point that Dora was taken to Freud.

Dora recounted to Freud how she felt she had been 'handed over' to Herr K. so that her father's relationship could continue with Frau K. Yet rather than acceding to this account, Freud interpreted it as a situation where Dora was actually complicit with the staging of her father's relationship because of her love for Herr K. Freud interpreted her hysterical symptoms and actions, including her relation to a governess who she was convinced was in love with her father, and whom she had had dismissed, as indications of a repressed love. It was Dora's identification with the governess that was, according to Freud, the reason for her repudiation of Herr K.'s advance; in the manner of the advance, she felt she was being treated like Herr K. had once treated one of his own servants. Dora had waited two weeks to let her parents know about the incident so, Freud says, that Herr K. could renew his advance, but that two weeks was effectively the period in which she 'gave her notice', much as a servant would. Furthermore, Freud suggested that the maintenance of the affair between Dora's father and Frau K. was actually for Dora's convenience. One of Dora's dreams that Freud analyses in detail suggests her desire to depart from her family and Herr K., a vengeance Freud detects as also aimed at himself due to Dora's premature departure from analysis, giving, in her mind at least, two weeks' notice.

Freud's narration and interpretation of the case is about the reorganization of a familial order through Dora's assent to Herr K. Had his proposition been received by Dora, this would have opened the way for his divorce from his wife, also ostensibly opening the way for Frau K. and Dora's father's relationship to have a legitimacy at the expense of Dora's mother, towards whom no one seems to have been able to be more than tolerant.[17] At the point Freud offered Dora this interpretation, she ceased her analysis. He concludes the case history by recounting that many years after her treatment Dora married a man Freud initially mistakes as a suitor who had appeared in the second of two dreams, whose analysis forms a large part of the case study. The study is neatly tied up by Freud at this supposed restoration of familial values:

> Just as her first dream represented her turning away from the man she
> loved [Herr K.] to her father – that is to say, her flight from life into disease
> – so the second dream announced that she was about to tear herself free
> from her father and had been reclaimed once more by the realities of life.[18]

Yet in the concluding passages to his account of the case, Freud acknowledges two
blindspots in his analysis which explain why he considered it to be an incomplete
one. The first has to do with his failure to realize Dora's love for Frau K., a failure that
casts doubt not only on Freud's solution to the treatment being proposed in a
restoration of familial order, but upon the very normalizing tendency of this order, its
reliance on a model of heterosexual love supported through the analytical apparatus
of the Oedipus complex.[19] The second has to do with Dora's transference with Freud,
where he initially assumes the role of Herr K., and then that of Dora's father. Freud
relates Dora's termination of the therapy to his failure to detect this transference and
manage its effects. Yet Lisa Appignanesi and John Forrester argue that Freud also
played the role of two women during this transference: Frau K. and a governess
figure. They suggest that Freud was '*unconsciously* very much at ease with playing
the part of a woman'.[20] But consciously, of course, Freud was wary of the contamination that such an identification with the feminine could threaten for the science of
psychoanalysis. The pseudonym Dora was one Freud drew from his own sister's
nursemaid. He gave a servant's name to the patient whose treatment, and its lack
of 'success', was infused with the figure of a servant.[21] Peter Stallybrass and Allon
White suggest that the servant figure was written out of case studies that served to
crystallize the Oedipus complex as structured around the mother and the father. They
argue that Freud conceived of what they call the 'family romance' biologically, that it
was 'ontologically prior' for Freud, not subject to change or contamination that the
historical circumstances of class and labour might bring.[22]

But this potential threat of the feminine and the servile points to the very
domesticity in which the Freudian discourse of psychoanalysis was produced. Dora,
whose real name was Ida Bauer, was born in 1882 at Berggasse 32 in Vienna. From
1891 Freud and his family lived at Berggasse 19, and it was in Freud's consulting
rooms at this address that Ida Bauer underwent her analysis.[23] Turning to consider
the interior environment of Freud's consulting rooms provides a way of framing some
particular questions to do with his analytic practice.

Freud's consulting rooms

An interior collected

The most striking aspect of Freud's consulting rooms was the way in which they
amplified Benjamin's notion of the interior as refuge of the collector. From 1908,
Freud's rooms were contiguous with the Freud family apartment at Berggasse 19.
Domestic spaces by circumstance, these rooms were made into interiors through
the arrangement of Freud's vast collection of antique sculpture and imagery. The collection was housed in vitrines and arrayed on every available flat surface. Photographs
of the rooms taken by Edmund Engelman in 1938, just prior to their dissolution and

Freud's flight to England, have captured this interiorized scene of his analytical practice. As Diana Fuss has noted in her detailed reading of the consulting rooms:

> Engelman's photographs dramatically capture what half a century of Freud commentary has overlooked: the location of the analytic scene within the four walls of a crypt. When patients arrived at Freud's office, they entered an overdetermined space of loss and absence, grief and memory, elegy and mourning. In short, they entered the exteriorized theatre of Freud's own emotional history, where every object newly found memorialized a love object lost.[24]

This exteriorized theatre was the spatialization of Freud's own psychological interiority. Patients undergoing analysis were caught up in this interior which set the scene for the exteriorization of their own psychological interiority. The interior was thus not simply a passive context for analysis. It actively participated in analyses, and became implicated in the discourse of psychoanalysis produced through Freud's practice. Fuss herself has analysed how patients having their first consultation with Freud would be interviewed in the study, the scene of Freud's writing. They were seated in front of a table adjacent to Freud's writing desk (Figure 2.1), a position at the very centre of the study and its collected objects. A small mirror positioned in the plane of the window adjacent to Freud's desk would reflect the patient, effectively severing his/her head and making a bust of the patient. In assuming his position at his desk, Freud's own head would come between the patient and the mirror. In analysing the optics of this situation, Fuss remarks: 'Freud's clinical assumption of the function of the mirror, and the substitution of other for self that it enacts, sets in motion the transferential dynamics that will structure all future doctor–patient encounters.'[25]

2.1
Freud's study, showing part of his antique collection arranged on his writing desk, 1938
Photograph by Edmund Engelman. By permission Thomas Engelman

2.2
**Freud's
consulting room,
showing the
couch and
Freud's adjacent
armchair, 1938**
Photograph by
Edmund Engelman.
By permission
Thomas Engelman.

Subsequent sessions between Freud and his patients would take place in the consulting room proper. This was joined to the study through double doors which were always kept open. The patient would lie on the couch positioned against a wall, with Freud seated in an armchair next to the head-end of the couch (Figure 2.2). Freud would look out into the room as the reclining patient looked along the line of the couch towards another vitrine of objects positioned against the adjacent wall. From a spatiality of seeing, where the patient was the centre of a gaze directed at him by Freud and his objects, and where the patient also became a kind of object, Fuss argues that the analysis proceeded in the consulting room through a spatiality of listening, where Freud's ear became the sense organ most acutely attuned to the analytical situation. Fuss describes Freud's spatial positioning as producing a 'passive listening technique'[26] that corresponded to the practice of free association that Freud encouraged in his patients.

The process of free association took place within an interiorized world of antiquities. Yet Freud himself remarked on the role of the space of analysis in a way that denied the overburdened atmosphere of his own consulting rooms:

At least once in the course of every analysis, a moment comes when the patient obstinately maintains that just now positively nothing whatsoever comes to mind. His free associations come to a stop and the usual incentives for putting them in motion again fail in their effect. If the analyst insists, the patient is at last induced to admit that he is thinking of the view from the consulting room window, of the wall-paper that he sees before him, or of the gas-lamp hanging from the ceiling. Then one knows at once that he has gone off into the transference and that he is engaged upon what are still unconscious thoughts relating to the physician; and one sees the stoppage of the associations disappear, as soon as he has been given this explanation.[27]

When it is brought to the patient's attention that he/she is associating with the interior without really knowing it, transference as an unconscious process is set in train. Considering Freud's interior as the 'exteriorized theatre of Freud's own emotional history', transference takes on a spatial dimension, and more than mere wallpaper and gas lamps are at stake. The collection, and its relation to antiquity and archaeology, becomes constitutive of the scene of transference. That Freud does not remark upon – or may actively have dissembled – the particularity of what one of his own patients would have seen looking around his consulting rooms relates to an ambivalence about what the collection's contents and formation reveal about his psychoanalytical method.

Psychoanalysis and the archaeological metaphor

Numerous analogies have been made between psychoanalysis and archaeology, but Freud himself seems not to have made the connection between his psychoanalytical method and his own collection of antiquities.[28] Yet there is a potential to do this, given what the photographs reveal about Freud's consulting rooms, and given issues surrounding the archaeological metaphor in psychoanalysis. By pursuing this relationship, important questions are raised concerning the representation of the interior.

Kenneth Reinhard has given the most productively critical account of the archaeological metaphor. He argues that psychoanalysis is not simply a therapeutic process of 'plumbing the subject's unconscious "depths" and bringing repressed material to the conscious "surface"',[29] as might an archaeological dig, the recovered objects of which would become collector's items. Rather, the archaeological metaphor relates to a lost cause, the inability to recover hidden meanings. As Reinhard suggests:

> Freud's antiquarian things are less metaphors of the psychoanalytic process or symptoms of his acquisitive personality than they are manifestations of what Lacan calls the Freudian 'Thing'. . . . [T]he Thing, for Lacan, is the traumatic materiality that both gives rise to and is sublimely in excess of the symbolic categories of exchange, attribute, and positionality which determine the symbolic structure of the object.[30]

For Reinhard, a concept of construction is at work in the collection which produces a particular sense of meaning. In a way that resonates with Benjamin's sense of temporality, meaning is not simply recovered, but is rather the result of a complex temporal transcoding. In analysing an early use of the metaphor of archaeology in Freud's writing on hysteria, Reinhard argues that the scattered remains uncovered

> must be 'filled out' and 'translated' before they become meaningful. Moreover, the monuments that are unearthed are not so much *of* the past as *to* the past, built by lost civilizations to 'commemorate' their own passing. That is, the monument that was originally intended to immortalize its historical moment in stone disintegrates into relics or fossils which mutely record the inexorable passage of time. . . . [I]f the relics of antiquity speak to the analytic reader, they always speak of something other than the moment they were intended to represent, and always in the foreign and stony tongue of untimely epitaphs.[31]

In Reinhard's argument, this sense of the 'untimely epitaph' relates to symptomatic elements in cases of hysteria which remain 'exterior to the processes of symbolic conversion'.[32] These 'stigmata' are elements which cannot be subsumed within the archaeological metaphor. They are both prior to and in excess of psychoanalysis' treatment, but they are those things which mark the hysteric, and thus instantiate treatment. 'Neither simply foreign to hysteria nor fully within it, the stigmata are, in Lacan's expression, "extimate" – intimately exterior – to both the theory and the phenomenology of the symptom.'[33] This sense of the 'extimate' pervades the interiorized scene of Freud's consulting rooms, his own antiquities revealed 'objectively' within an environment that attempts to domesticate them, to collect them into an interiorized world, a world of the interior. Yet their 'significance' precisely resists this domestication, and a symbolic reading that this domestication would entail. They are ex-centric to the analytical scene while at the same time constituting that scene:

> Thus, the non-specular 'fascination' of Freud's antiquities is a function of neither what they look like (their imaginary similitudes) nor what they represent (their symbolic interpretations), but their constitution as signifier-things in a collection. Like signifiers, that is, they promise a legibility which they deny; like things, they opaquely, mutely point only to themselves.[34]

In Reinhard's reading, the significance of the collection is in its deliberate construction, and what the constructive process reveals about Freudian psychoanalytic method. A late reworking of the metaphor in Freud's writings on psychoanalytic technique emphasizes the usefulness of an extreme type of construction of the elements of a patient's psychological history as a point of intervention in an analysis. This is not a reconstruction of the truth that had pre-existed in past time, but rather one that offers a fictional lure that might catch the 'truth' of the subject precisely through its constructed nature, its 'falsehood'.[35] This truth has the status of the Thing, 'an originary trauma, in which something disavowed is nevertheless preserved as a denied fragment of the real'.[36] This trauma cannot be represented in the construction in the same way that it is not simply unearthed through the 'digging down' of analysis. The construction, like the delusions of the psychotic patient, is fabricated around the Thing 'as what Freud calls a "fragment" or "kernel" of truth'.[37]

It is useful to recall at this point Benjamin's account of the collection discussed in Chapter 1. In that discussion, the collection was considered as an attempt to reconstruct the alienated individual within the interior through wresting objects from their circulation as commodities. This action can be explained as an attempt to win something back for experience as *Erfahrung*. Yet the collection could never simply re-member the subject, as the collection itself veered between completeness and complete openness. The interior instantiated as 'container of privacy' subjectified the collection, giving rise to this instability. In this psychoanalytic context, collecting can thus be cast as the drive to seek out the Proustian madeleine that might allow the collector to 'take hold' of their experience, an experience that was not simply the subject's 'conscious' personal history, but one that was registered below the level of consciousness as the 'shock' or trauma that left its mark on the subject. The collection might, in its failure to find that object forever lost, take on this consequence of becoming the subject's personal history, and as such, act as a kind of compensation for the subject alienated from themselves. Yet this compensation is a false one, the collapsing of the 'extimate' memory trace (designated by memory as *Gedächtnis*) into the remembrance (*Erinnerung*), which Benjamin recognized, through Freud and Theodor Reik, as destructive.[38] For Reinhard, the Thing lurks in the collection as proliferation, 'the object' being irrecoverable. Ultimately, the subject becomes possessed by the collection;[39] the interior which encases the collection encases the subject also. The traces registered by objects in the interior become more intimately related to the traumatic memory-traces of the subject, though in a way that denies their easy compatibility.

A doubled scene

Ultimately, in Freud's consulting rooms, there is more than one subject at stake. For Reinhard, 'the "cause" or *la chose* of the subject as well as of the subject's delusion . . . hangs between analyst and analysand, the kernel of a *délire à deux* in excess of the dialectic of negation and affirmation which sets the tempo for interpretation's *pas de deux*'.[40] Thus the status of the collection, and the interior's housing of it, is not reducible to Freud's own biography as a collector, just as the collector's biography cannot, in any true sense, be formed from the manifest content of their collection. Freud's consulting rooms constitute the interiorized scene of his analytical technique, the scene of a relation between subjects mediated by objects that, however material, are forever beyond possession. From this point, one can return to Fuss's argument about the spatiality of the analytical scene in the consulting room proper:

> Transferential force emanates from Freud's possessions; these over-invested forms operate, for the patient, as shadowy substitutes for the analyst who must not be seen. Whether or not Freud's patients actually related to their physician's objects in this way is perhaps less interesting than the revelation of Freud's own deeply cathected relation to his things [.][41]

In this passage, Fuss proposes a clear interpretation of the role of Freud's collection within the analytical scene, and then appears to break off this interpretation, returning instead to one centred on Freud himself. Yet there is room to pursue this relation of objects beyond Freud as an individual collector, given that such a consideration comes up against the problem of the archaeological metaphor.

A productive step would be to consider the very materiality of the photographs of Freud's rooms, that is, to consider them outside a frame of representation. The analytic 'scene between two' is no more than a collection of photographs that double a scene which is itself forever lost.[42] Reinhard mentions how Lacan recalled seeing the 'remains [débris]' of Freud's collection in the house Freud occupied for a short period in London before his death.[43] As was noted earlier, Engelman's photographs were taken as a record of the rooms in Vienna shortly before Freud's departure, and the rooms in London, also a part of the house the Freud family shared, are said to have been arranged much as they had been in Vienna.[44] Yet the idea of a separate study and consulting room, and, along with it, the complex optics and acoustics of the analytical scene which Fuss so carefully reconstructs and analyses, was not retained. In London, the study and consulting room were combined together, the couch being situated opposite Freud's desk, and without the same intermediary presence of objects from Freud's collection.[45]

What is at stake here is not a lost fidelity between photographs, objects and their spatial arrangements. The preceding analysis of the archaeological metaphor has displaced such a consideration. Rather, these photographs, and the way they relate to Freud's practice and the theorizations that arose from and directed this practice, raise crucial questions concerning how photography is understood as evidencing the interior.[46] In her interpretation, Fuss explores the scene of analysis in terms of 'the porous boundary between the two-dimensional space of photography, and the three-dimensional space of architecture'.[47] This boundary, however, is more like a yawning gap, one produced through a locational (rather than purely spatial) excentricity between images and space. In this sense, there is a much more compelling and unsettling relation between photography and space emerging at the heart of Fuss's argument when she remarks on a 'highly unusual mode of museum exhibition'[48] that exists now at Freud's apartment in Vienna. Engelman's photographs hang on the walls of the largely empty, though still cramped, consulting rooms. This collection of photographs has returned to this space to offer an image of the absent interior, or, put the other way, Freud's interior has returned to this inside architectural space as a collection of photographs. Rather than a porous boundary between representation and space, there is an uncanny doubling, a sense of discrepancy, a gap which produces the most palpable of doubled interiors.[49] The photographs do not mediate this discrepancy; rather, their material presence in the interior produces it. They show precisely the absence of the things they picture, but also the uncanny, anamorphic reappearance of the interior. Reinhard's description of Freud's collection of antiquities is apt to repeat here as an account of these photographs' uncanny reoccupation of the site of their genesis:

> Thus, the non-specular 'fascination' of Freud's antiquities [read: Engelman's photographs] is a function of neither what they look like (their imaginary

> similitudes) nor what they represent (their symbolic interpretations), but
> their constitution as signifier-things in a collection. Like signifiers, that is,
> they promise a legibility which they deny; like things, they opaquely, mutely
> point only to themselves.[50]

This description emphasizes the thing-like, and the Thing-like, nature of the photographs, their manifestation as flat objects hung on walls, walls they themselves
have interiorized, but which in no clear way do they represent.

These arguments concerning Freud's consulting rooms begin to reach
beyond the particularity of their historical circumstance, raising broader issues concerning representation and the constitutive role the interior has in theorizations of
psychoanalysis. It is worth reframing the account of psychoanalysis once more to
deal with these issues. This will occur through a consideration of the uncanny and
the double in psychoanalytic theory.

The doubled interior of psychoanalytic theory

Representing the uncanny

In his writing about the uncanny, architectural theorist Anthony Vidler has pointed
to the sense of a modern unhomely, a phantom, unsettling double that arises out of
the cosiness and protection offered by the domestic interior.[51] He has traced the
emergence of this uncanny in an aesthetic of the sublime that is experienced in
relation to the interior, 'a domesticated version of absolute terror',[52] projected in the
fairy tales of E. T. A. Hoffmann and the writings of Edgar Allan Poe:

> Its favourite motif was precisely the contrast between a secure and
> homely interior and the fearful invasion of an alien presence; on a psy-
> chological level, its play was one of doubling, where the other is, strangely
> enough, experienced as a replica of the self, all the more fearsome
> because apparently the same.[53]

Vidler argues that the development of the uncanny as a sensibility of the nineteenth
century also arose with the alienating and anxiety-inducing forms of experience in
the burgeoning metropolis, captured in the sense of an estrangement from sure
foundations that was coupled with a sense of the march of progress. The conditions
of modern estrangement involve for Vidler the interactions between subjects and
spaces, but he sees that these interactions are only analysable at the level of their
representation. He suggests:

> As a concept, then, the uncanny has, not unnaturally, found its metaphor-
> ical home in architecture: first in the house, haunted or not, that pretends
> to afford the utmost security while opening itself to the secret intrusion
> of terror, and then in the city, where what was once walled and intimate,
> the confirmation of community . . . has been rendered strange by the
> spatial incursions of modernity. In both cases, of course, the 'uncanny' is
> not a property of the space itself nor can it be provoked by any particular
> spatial conformation; it is, in its aesthetic dimension, a representation of

a mental state of projection that precisely elides the boundaries of the real and the unreal in order to provoke a disturbing ambiguity, a slippage between waking and dreaming.

In this sense, it is perhaps difficult to speak of an 'architectural' uncanny, in the same terms as a literary or psychological uncanny; certainly no one building, no special effects of design can be guaranteed to provoke an uncanny feeling. But in each moment of the history of the representation of the uncanny, and at certain moments in its psychological analysis, the buildings and spaces that have acted as the sites for uncanny experiences have been invested with recognizable characteristics.[54]

In discussing the uncanny, Vidler assumes that all effects of possible slippage or leakage between the representational and the spatial occur solely within representation. The spatial is curiously absent in a commitment to analysing its representation.[55] Vidler sees that buildings and space are '*emblematic* of the uncanny, as the cultural signs of estrangement for particular periods'.[56] His caveat that 'there is no such thing as an uncanny architecture, but simply architecture that, from time to time and for different purposes, is invested with uncanny qualities'[57] seems to be made in defence of a possible charge that he is suggesting it is possible to *build* an 'objectively' uncanny architecture, or that any subject should be able to experience the uncanny in relation to certain spaces specified as such. When he writes of 'real space' rather than its representation, Vidler refers to states of 'real homelessness' and the effects of social estrangement as opposed to an unhomeliness represented in architecture. While sound on its own terms, this argument remains locked within representation when specifying the workings of the uncanny. Vidler is unable to argue convincingly that the uncanny can arise spatially.[58] Yet it is precisely in a double relation between image and space where the interior has significance for understanding the uncanny, and vice versa.

It seems that if the uncanny is to be located as affect, rather than simply represented as such, it is in the moment where the subject is not sure of the distinction between a representation and a spatial condition. In the case of Freud's consulting rooms in Vienna, this would occur when the photographic capture of the interior uncannily revisits the site of this capture. In a similar way, an act such as reading a story (perhaps by Poe or Hoffmann) about a domestic uncanny while seated in a cosy domestic interior might create an uncanny effect through the unsettling homology between the represented interior, and the interior in which a subject engages with this representation. As Ernst Bloch has suggested vis-à-vis the detective novel:

Something is uncanny – that is how it begins. But at the same time, one must search for that remoter 'something', which is already close at hand. [. . .] Who indeed is not moved by such a thing more than superficially and fleetingly? The setting in which detective stories are enjoyed the most is just too cosy. In a comfortable chair, under the nocturnal floor lamp with tea, rum, and tobacco, personally secure and peacefully immersed in dangerous things, which are shallow.[59]

In Bloch's description, it is not simply that the story represents an uncanny situation. The uncanny feeling manifests itself in the slippage between the situation represented, and the situation in which this representation is encountered. A domestic horror story or detective novel is affecting because it makes one sense this uncanny in one's own home as an immediate spatial affect. A crucial part of the conceptualization of the uncanny for Freud occurred in relation to its experience as an affect of a doubled interior. A confusion between a two-dimensional reflection and the three-dimensionality of space provided the spur to Freud's theorization of the uncanny, and, at the same time, his articulation of the psyche in terms of the double.

The interior uncanny, or the double and the psyche

In a footnote to his essay on the uncanny, Freud mentions several anecdotes, two from Ernst Mach and one of his own, that describe coming across one's double. Freud's anecdote describes how, while on a train trip, the washroom door between his compartment and the one next to his swung open, and another traveller appeared to be entering into Freud's cabin from the washroom. Thinking that this person had simply exited the washroom in the wrong direction, into Freud's cabin instead of his own on the other side, Freud jumped up to set the man straight, only to realize that he was looking at his own reflection in the mirror on the open washroom door:[60]

> I can still recollect that I thoroughly disliked his [Freud's reflection's] appearance. Instead, therefore, of being *frightened* by our 'doubles', both Mach and I simply failed to recognize them as such. Is it not possible, though, that our dislike of them was a vestigial trace of the archaic reaction which feels the 'double' to be something uncanny?[61]

In this anecdote, a mirror image posed a threatening image to Freud as he was seated in his cabin. But when he recognized the nature of this image, that it was a mirror reflection of himself seated in his own space, rather than another entering through space towards him, the image became non-threatening. Freud felt an uncanny effect when he was confused over the relation between the image and the space from which he perceived the image, or, more precisely, when he read the reflected image as spatial extension.[62]

This situation is reminiscent of Lacan's description of the mirror stage as the situation where the child identifies with an image of its body presented in a mirror. Triggered by the double in the mirror, this identification produces an ego always alienated from itself. Elizabeth Grosz has called this an image of an 'imaginary anatomy' which 'reflects social and familial beliefs about the body more than it does the body's organic nature'.[63] She also emphasizes the way in which the mirror image 'also duplicates the environment, placing real and virtual space in contiguous relations'. And she emphasizes in Lacan 'the crucial role the body-image plays in the subject's capacity to locate itself and its objects in space'.[64] In Grosz's argument, space is not a pre-existing container into which a body projects itself. Rather, it is formed around the reflection of an imaginary anatomy. In his train cabin, Freud was only able to locate himself spatially when he recognized his own imaginary anatomy. As Grosz argues: 'The representation of space is thus a correlate of one's ability to locate oneself as the point of origin or reference of space: the space represented is a complement of the kind of subject who occupies it.'[65] This argument provides another way of describing the doubled interior. The space of the interior, and a subject's ability to locate themselves as the 'point of reference' of this space, comes about through the recognition of an image that is by no means a transparent representation of a space. In Grosz's sense, representation refers to the subject's ability to master their space. It is a question of the spatial locatability of the subject. Lacan himself writes:

> The mirror stage is a drama whose internal thrust is precipitated from insufficiency to anticipation – and which manufactures for the subject, caught up in the lure of spatial identification, the succession of phantasies that extends from a fragmented body-image to a form of its totality which I shall call orthopaedic – and, lastly, the assumption of the armour of an alienating identity, which will mark with its rigid structure the subject's entire mental development.[66]

A kind of orthopaedic locatability within space, or, in other words, the inhabitation of the interior, is explained in this way through the concept of identification, a concept more attuned to spatial affect than empathy, and one at the core of Freud's theory of the psyche as it forms a key part of his discussion of the uncanny. Early in the uncanny essay, Freud writes that the experience of the double was not always uncanny or frightful. It becomes so through processes that constitute a fully differentiated psychic apparatus. More specifically, Freud describes the shift in the double (manifest through reflections, guardian spirits) from a relation of narcissism with the subject, and as such existing as a denial of death, to becoming a harbinger of death. It is in the production of a self-regarding capacity within the psyche, what Freud developed into the concept of the ego ideal, that the double becomes the figure of a kind of self-critical 'conscience'.[67] The formation of the ego ideal results from processes of identification. Identification is described by Freud as ambivalent: wanting to be someone in the sense of having someone as one's ideal also involves taking that person's place.[68] Identification can thus involve annihilation of the object of identification through its introjection into the ego. The object is renounced or lost, and as a substitute for this loss, it is set up inside the ego, hence becoming the object of identification.[69] Thus, in certain instances, such as 'melancholia' or depression, Freud notes the division of the ego into two parts, 'one of which rages against the second. This second piece [the ego ideal] is the one which has been altered by introjection and which contains the lost object.'[70]

Here it is useful to return to another crucial interior moment in the development of Freud's theory of the psyche: the analogy with a suite of rooms introduced earlier in this chapter. In analysing this analogy, Kaja Silverman has extended a Freudian theorization of identification towards a theory of desirous looking. She writes: 'The basic drive in the human subject is the urge to see once more what has been seen before. . . . It is because it is primarily at the level of vision that we apprehend what was in what is that the passion of every subject's signifier is conducive of the appearance of certain creatures and things.'[71] Silverman calls this appearance of the world with a particular affectivity an image, an entailment of perceiving subject and world perceived. It releases latent, anterior visual experience, the sort of unconscious impulses that jostle in the 'entrance hall' of the unconscious, impulses which 'seem, indeed, to be the site of a certain desire – of a desire for what might be called "affiliation"'.[72] The transfer of energy involved in the production of an image, a production involving constant displacements and shifts of investment, acts as a kind of definition of subjectivity, which, for Silverman, 'is a constellation of visual memories which is struggling to achieve a perceptual form'.[73]

The classic case of affectivity and affiliation can be recalled to explain these theoretical formulations: Proust's madeleine. In thinking about his childhood in Combray, Proust was concerned with how memories are revived. His experience of tasting tea in which a madeleine had been dipped produced a cascade of visual memories, arising, as Proust writes, like stage sets that augmented spatially and topographically his initial, voluntary recollections of his childhood.[74] Even though the spur to this revival was not itself a visual experience – the simple sight of madeleines had previously produced no effect – the result of this affiliation manifested in visual terms. Silverman's account of affiliation, of unconscious impulses catching the eye of consciousness, can be compared with Proust's account of his experience:

> Undoubtedly what is thus palpitating in the depths of my being must be the image, the visual memory which, being linked to that taste, is trying to follow it into my conscious mind. [. . .] Will it ultimately reach the clear surface of my consciousness, this memory, this old dead moment which the magnetism of an identical moment has travelled so far to importune, to disturb, to raise out of the very depths of my being?[75]

Proust initially struggled to account for his strange sensation, felt bodily, on tasting the tea and madeleine, and he ruminated over the gap he experienced between the sensation and its source. His conscious attempts to seek the source were only leading to the dissipation of the sensation: 'Seek? More than that: create. [The mind] is face to face with something which does not yet exist, which it alone can make actual, which it alone can bring into the light of day.'[76] This struggle to recognize the source of affect is, in Silverman's terms, a creative act, the production of 'certain creatures and things':

> And suddenly the memory revealed itself. The taste was that of the little piece of madeleine which on Sunday mornings at Combray (because on those mornings I did not go out before mass), when I went to say good morning to her in her bedroom, my aunt Léonie used to give me, dipping it first in her own cup of tea or tisane.[77]

Compare this moment to Freud's recognition of the presence in his train carriage as his reflection, a presence initially felt bodily, uncannily. In drawing from this experience, the interior provides Freud with the analogy by which these affiliations can be understood in terms of the organization of the psyche. Referring back to Benjamin's reading of Proust discussed in Chapter 1, it is possible to see the way in which this organization is also that of the *mémoire involontaire*. While for Benjamin, the interior was the figure within which the problematic of experience in modernity could be grasped, a conceptualization of the subjectivity formed from this problematic of experience can be added to this understanding. It is a subjectivity emerging from processes of the psyche understood in terms of identifications, affiliations of unconscious impulses. Recognition of the type Freud and Proust wrote about re-members the subject, though for Lacan, the interiorized scene of the mirror stage produces the alienation that constitutes identification as a continual process. Thus re-membering can only be articulated, and can only carry its subjectifying force, to the extent that an uncanny gap, a gap between sensation and its source, or a slippage between image and space, is felt palpably as the uncanny. This gap allows the very movement of subjective impulses to be sensed and theorized. In this, the interior takes on a role internal to the theoretical formulations of psychoanalysis, which are formulations of modern subjectivity.

Coda: from orientations to trajectories

The three framings of psychoanalysis' relation to the interior presented in this chapter figure this relation as a kind of enmeshing. Particular aspects and understandings of psychoanalysis become unthinkable outside of the interior, and vice versa. Yet the interior is not essential to psychoanalytic thinking. Rather, this enmeshing is historical and, as such, circumstantial. In other words, it relies on the particular availability and construal of evidence within a psychoanalytical frame, and the linkages and conjectures that may be formed in this construal. At the same time, this enmeshing raises questions to do with what might constitute the evidence of the interior. Together with the reading of Benjamin performed in Chapter 1, these thoughts provide orientations to the historical emergence of the interior. As such, they echo in Part 2 of this book, which is concerned with the emergent interior's linkage with particular contexts of architectural thinking and practice.

Part 2

Trajectories

Chapter 3

Imagining the interior

Plan and comfort

Around the middle of the nineteenth century in England, a particular conjunction occurred between the emerging architectural technique of asymmetrical planning, and the strengthening domestic desire for comfort. Several treatises on domestic architecture positioned the plan as the centrepiece of domestic design and construction. Yet a measurement for the efficacy of the planning techniques the treatises codified could only be found through the imagination of a comfortable interior from the organizational conditions that the plan inscribed. Interiors needed to be imagined by the architect and client alike, as if both were the 'future inhabitants' of the plan.

This chapter examines this condition by analysing two key treatises on domestic planning, Robert Kerr's *The Gentleman's House* (1864), and J. J. Stevenson's *House Architecture* (1880). In their differing ways, these treatises show that comfort gained meaning and significance in relation to the planimetric apparatuses deployed for imagining interiors: Kerr's apparatus valorizes comfort in relation to the separation of functions and inhabitants from each other; Stevenson suggests comfort is to be found in an organization that promotes the commingling of inhabitants. The plan allowed these architects to think through the interior, realizing a linkage between possibilities that could be imagined, and the technicalities of design and building. Kerr was well aware of the 'battle' between architects and upholsterers in the nineteenth century, writing: 'the architect must not venture to reckon without in the first place his client, and in the second place his client's upholsterer'.[1] Imagining the interior as part of a process of planning enabled the architect to have a freer understanding of the qualities of a domestic arrangement being projected, outside of the presence of a competing profession. Crucially, this imagining fed back into the ongoing planning process, and offered a particular vantage on how the competing elements of a plan should be arranged, thereby consolidating a claim for architects' expertise in matters domestic.

As with the chapters of Part 1 of this book, the interior is being treated here in a way that emphasizes conditions surrounding its historical emergence. In its imagination, there are elements of temporal disjunction that resonate with Walter Benjamin's account of the interior's emergence. Imagination itself, while not being deployed here within a Freudian conceptual apparatus, is bound up with the interior's conditions of historical emergence in a way that indicates how the interior could make further linkages with apparatuses for regulating the domestic subject, most notably, the one constructed by psychoanalysis.

Considering the interior in this manner also affects the way in which the history of English domestic planning has been conventionally understood. A key text on the discourse of planning, Jill Franklin's *The Gentleman's Country House and its Plan*,[2] combines a general historical survey of the literature with an account of the social aspects of domesticity. Franklin writes of 'a whole range of customs and conventions [lying] enshrined in the country house plan',[3] and she tracks social and architectural changes through the nineteenth century. In addition to engaging in a close reading of architectural plans, she turns to nineteenth-century periodical and book publications on domestic architecture, Kerr's treatise key among them. In a way similar to volume 4 of *A History of Private Life*, Franklin also turns to letters, diaries, memoirs and novels, reading them as historical sources in order to embellish her account of the social life of the country house.

Robin Evans has situated nineteenth-century English developments in relation to a consideration of domesticity from the Renaissance to modernism. In his article 'Figures, Doors and Passages', and in a way similar to Franklin, Evans looks beyond plans for evidence of modes of inhabitation, and he pays particular attention to visual representations of domesticity: 'Take the portrayal of human figures and take house plans from a given time and place: look at them together as evidence of a way of life, and the coupling between everyday conduct and architectural organi-zation may become more lucid.'[4] Across this period of time, Evans is able to signal shifts in both planning and representational techniques. He argues that nineteenth-century English domestic planning, and most notably Kerr's treatise, consolidated a technique of 'room and corridor planning', with its resultant division of served and servant spaces defined in terms of movement and access. From his reading of pictorial representations from this time, Evans argues that forms of inter-personal relation and forms of identity were displaced on to objects and furnishings that assumed a greater presence in the space pictured, while the body became removed from the possibility of direct contact with other bodies.

In terms of the historical projects on the interior and domesticity critiqued in Chapter 1, Franklin's account belongs within the frame of general, or 'mythic', history. She marshals a range of historical sources to strengthen her reading of the social and architectural cultures surrounding the country house plan. Evans, on the other hand, looks for the ways in which inhabitation escapes usual understandings, and instead, how it is constructed in particular ways through representation. Franklin would want to see her approach to the plan drawing as critical: 'Architectural plans can be analyzed in two ways: architectural historians have often concentrated on their aesthetic qualities, seeing them as a series of patterns on paper; the users of a building are more likely to be concerned with its convenience or inconvenience.'[5] Evans, however, would want convenience and inconvenience to be understood not as abstract values existing outside of their emergence and formation in relation to the specific techniques and practices of planning, themselves emergent in the nineteenth century.[6] Yet ultimately both of these historical projects are bound to a method of reading both plans and visual representations as evidence of actual inhabitations. In analysing the relation between plans and imagined interiors, this chapter moves away from this sort of project, and its interest in furnishing evidence of 'ways of living in times past'. Instead, the particular efficacy that doubleness gives to the interior's historical linkage with the discourse on domestic planning will be investigated. The reading of Kerr's and Stevenson's treatises focuses on the way in which imaginative possibilities for the male figures of the architect and the client/inhabitant are encoded by the text, and articulated through particular ways of reading plans. Through analysing these treatises, the interior and its imagination are shown to be crucial to the way in which techniques of planning became conceptualized.[7]

The imaginative inhabitation of the plan

In *The Gentleman's House*, Kerr gives a particular account of the utility of the plan:

> No room ought to pass muster on the plan until the designer has in imagination occupied it and proved it comfortable. It is not too much if he plots upon the drawing every important article of furniture which the room has to receive, and so establishes its capacities and qualities beyond all hazard. A little of this fastidiousness on paper will save much discomfort in the building.[8] (Figure 3.1)

The plan is useful to Kerr for its possibilities of what will be termed 'imaginative inhabitation', a type of mental picturing of a future interior possible within the inside space of the house being planned.[9] This picturing is not an externalized representation – Kerr includes no pictures of interiors in his publication – but the internal imagining undertaken when constructing and reading a plan.[10] The unpicturable condition of the interior suspends the relation between pictorial representation and inhabitation, a relation which Evans and Franklin rely on in their use of pictorial evidence. Instead, imagination becomes, for Kerr, the test of his technique of planning.

The vivacity of imagining

In order to frame Kerr's position on imaginative inhabitation, Elaine Scarry's work on imaginal picturing will be drawn upon. In her discussion of Marcel Proust's remembrance of his childhood bedroom at Combray, Scarry asks the question: 'How, then, does a writer get us to imagine a solid surface: a wall, for example, or the four walls that will make up a room?'[11] In answering this, she suggests that Proust's description of the image of a magic lantern playing across the walls of his bedroom serves to solidify them. The importance of this solidification is in the creation of a space of inhabitation for the literary characters: 'It is impossible to create imaginary persons if one has not created a space for them.'[12] Doubling the characters' space of inhabitation is a space for the projection of the reader into the text:

> Even more important than the provision of an inhabitable space for imaginary persons is the creation for the reader of a fiction's *vertical floor* that, by promising to stop our inward fall, permits us to enter capaciously

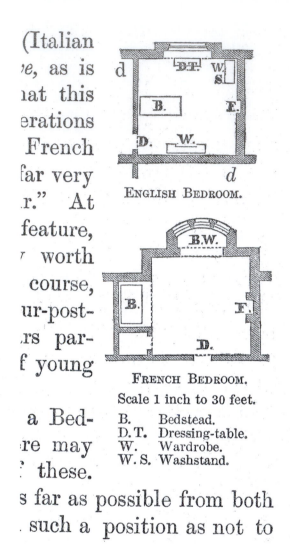

(Italian
e, as is
ıat this
erations
French
far very
r." At
feature,
worth
course,
ur-post-
rs par-
f young

a Bed-
re may
these.

s far as possible from both
such a position as not to

ENGLISH BEDROOM.

FRENCH BEDROOM.
Scale 1 inch to 30 feet.
B.   Bedstead.
D. T.   Dressing-table.
W.   Wardrobe.
W. S. Washstand.

3.1
Bedroom furniture plotted on to plans of rooms
Source: Robert Kerr, *The Gentleman's House*, 3rd revised edn, London: John Murray, 1871 [1864], p. 133

into the projective space without fear and therefore with the lifting of inhibitions on vivacity.[13]

While they might initially seem to be applicable only to a certain sort of literary production – one, however, intimately tied to the domestic interior – Scarry's arguments actually serve to highlight the instructional quality of literary texts, the ways in which they position the reader relative to the characters and situations the reader is instructed to imagine.[14] Taking these ideas into a reading of treatises on planning underpins the sense of spatial imagining they encode with a sense of how they operate as treatises to be read, rather than as documents that evidence a process of planning and building that would take place in reality.[15] Indeed, these treatises have a stake in putting off constructions that might actualize conditions they ask their readers to imagine.

A crucial point in Scarry's argument is her suggestion that 'Our freely practiced imaginative acts bear less resemblance to our freely practiced perceptual acts than do our constrained imaginative acts occurring under authorial direction.'[16] Scarry is relating directed imagining to perception in order to suggest that in the verbal rather than the visual arts, imagined objects acquire the vivacity of perceptual objects.[17] An imagined object is the creation of the subject in the absence of a competing perceptual stimulus. Thus it can attain the value of what Scarry calls vivacity. She defines three phenomena which aid in the sort of distinctions she is making: first, immediate sensory content, which refers to perceptual acts; second, delayed sensory content, or what she calls 'instructions for the production of actual sensory content',[18] which refers to something like a musical score, which itself has no sensory content, but provides the directions for the production of music as actual sensory content. The third phenomenon Scarry defines is mimetic content, which has no given sensory content. This refers to the fact that one can see content in one's imagination, though this content is not given externally. Prose which makes one imagine an interior is an example of this.

The last two phenomena, delayed sensory content and mimetic content, provide a useful structure for understanding the reading of plans in conjunction with textual commentary. There is an interaction between these two phenomena under what Scarry calls instruction; however, the quality of instruction is slightly different between delayed sensory content and mimetic content. The architectural plan can initially be categorized as providing delayed sensory content. If one were to follow the plan and build the building, one would produce an actual sensory environment – a piece of architecture. But in Kerr's treatise, there is a presentation of plans joined by a commentary Kerr gives, not only about certain technical aspects of the house as a building, but about how to imagine and test a possible sensory environment that could be made within the building after its actual construction, but which can be imagined without the building having been built. In this way, the plan also provides mimetic content in terms of the imagining of inhabitation. It could be argued that Kerr excluded pictures of the interiors he discusses in *The Gentleman's House* in order not to confuse the act of imagining with the act of perceiving. But as Scarry makes clear, this separation of imagining and perceiving means that imaging can be directed in a way that more strongly resembles perception.

These theoretical renderings of imagination help draw out the significance of imaginative inhabitation as it plays out across two distinct moments in the construction of the plan and its discourse, moments that are demonstrable in Kerr's treatise. The first of these is the shift from a consideration of domestic architecture within the frame of general accounts of architectural style towards an understanding of the plan in its fitness to a domestic programme; the second moment has to do with how the plan form enables the imagination of comfort when the scale of domestic arrangements is considered in relation to the needs of an individual client.

The domestic plan: from style to fitness

Kerr's treatise begins with a history of the domestic plan, categorized in terms of architectural style.[19] The purpose of this history is to assess the fitness of two broadly defined plan types to an English sensibility of domestic comfort: one variously described as classical, Palladian and Italian, the other as Elizabethan, Gothic and medieval. Kerr makes general distinctions between these two broad plan types on the basis of a reading of climate in terms of geographic region, which then in turn comes to stand for national characteristics: the medieval plan, which, according to Kerr, favours privacy and seclusion, developed in northern climates, and is therefore more suited to England; and the classical plan, which favours publicity and openness, developed in southern climates, and is therefore more suited to Italy.[20] This argument marks Kerr's preference for the Gothic in terms of English conditions; however, beyond this simple polarity between classical and Gothic, Kerr does make several remarks on the question of the suitability of plan types to a contemporary English domestic situation, one that responds to the prevailing debates about historical revivals and national styles.[21] Kerr writes that neither plan type carries the authority of a national or climatic authenticity. To think of authenticity in an archaeological vein – the revival of exact medieval or antique plan conditions – does nothing to answer to the practical needs of contemporary domesticity: 'That either style will supersede the other becomes then a question of competition under such modification, indeed under such mutual influence and aid, that it involves all that is required for such harmonious co-operation.'[22] The competition itself between plan types becomes the contemporary English inheritance.

Kerr argues further that considerations of the plan are not to be subsumed under considerations of the ways in which architectural styles, once again falling into the general categories of the classical and the Gothic, were argued over at the level of suitability to functional or representational requirements: 'it is enough to remark that in both cases [i.e. the classical and the Gothic] the development of opinion was gradual but well defined, and that the only inquiry pertaining to our present investigation is one which can be readily met, – namely, how far the two principles respectively produced any change in the subject of *Plan*.'[23] Kerr proposes that the revival of the antique had little or no effect on domestic arrangements, and the revival of the Gothic had a great effect:

> For the old English model, with all its crudities, was English, and not even obsolete; and such a thing as the Pompeian house, with all its refinement, foreign and antiquated; – the one specially calculated to meet practical requirements of English comfort and convenience, and the other the growth of altogether different circumstances.[24]

This further explanation of Kerr's preference for the Gothic plan turns on the issue of asymmetry, and the way in which it is supposed to lead to comfort and convenience. In a comparison of two contemporaneous plans of 'small dimensions' (Figure 3.2), Kerr links the irregularity of plan disposition to an idea of convenience in inhabitation:

> The Ground-plan of Llwyn House [1860] is, for so small an example, particularly expressive of classical principle. The central lines of vista and approach throughout, and the perfect symmetry of division, are admirably contrived.

3.2

Plans of Llwyn House, Oswestry, 1860, and Old Connaught, Wicklow, 1859

Source: Robert Kerr, *The Gentleman's House*, 3rd revised edn, London: John Murray, 1871 [1864], plate 16

LLWYN HOUSE, OSWESTRY.
By M. Blake, 1860.

From the Building News.

GROUND FLOOR.

OLD CONNAUGHT, WICKLOW.
By Mess.rs Lanyon & Lynn, 1859.

From the Builder.

GROUND FLOOR.

Scale 1 inch to 30 Feet.

Plate 16.
Llwyn House &
Old Connaught.

Contrast this with the Ground-plan of Old Connaught [1859] on the same Plate, and the Mediaeval features of the latter will readily be perceived. The Porch, with its uncentral position; the Hall, with its Screen and Bay-window; its communication, at the Dais end (so to speak) with the Family-rooms, and at the Entry-end, with the offices; the privacy of the Staircase; and the characteristic irregularity, although perfect convenience, of the thoroughfare lines, are especially interesting and ingenious. At the same time the absence of affectation in this plan is worthy of great praise.[25]

In discussing the plan of Llwyn House, Kerr's language is couched in terms of abstract principles of composition. The greater space he devotes to Old Connaught allows him to develop the specificity of each room in the arrangement, along with a greater sense of imaginative moving-through of the 'characteristically irregular' plan.[26] This difference in ways of looking at classical versus Gothic plans becomes a significant issue in another of Kerr's comparative analyses. In comparing two royal palaces sharing Prince Albert as their client (Figures 3.3 and 3.4), Kerr argues that similar needs in accommodation can give rise to different planimetric interpretations:

> The Royal Marine Palace of Osborne [1848] . . . is a serviceable illustration again of Classic plan largely modified to accord with the habits of the present day in England. The Royal Castle of Balmoral [1855], also, . . . is an equally serviceable specimen of Mediaeval plan modified in like manner. What constitutes these plans more particularly eligible for such a contrast as the present is the fact that the supervision of the late accomplished Prince Consort is understood to have minutely and intelligently governed both during the process of their design. We do not require to assume that any intention existed on the part of either the architect or the client, in whichever case, to produce a specimen of style in plan; but so much the better for our purpose. Two Palaces, for the self-same occupation, and in circumstances by no means dissimilar, are designed under the self-same control, but by different architects, each in his own style unconsciously; and the result is the interesting contrast in question. The architect of Osborne produces an Italian Villa; the architect of Balmoral an Elizabethan Manor-house. Neither of them pretends to be punctilious;

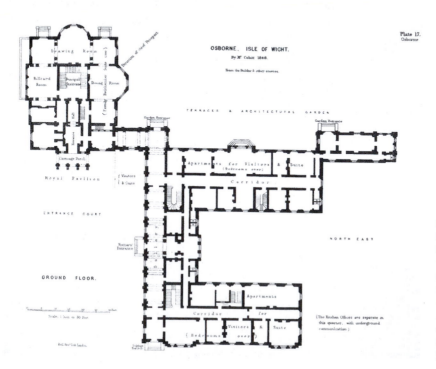

3.3
Plan of Osborne, Isle of Wight, 1848
Source: Robert Kerr, *The Gentleman's House*, 3rd revised edn, London: John Murray, 1871 [1864], plate 17

3.4

**Plan of
Balmoral Castle,
Aberdeenshire,
1855**

Source: Robert
Kerr, *The
Gentleman's
House*, 3rd revised
edn, London:
John Murray, 1871
[1864], plate 18

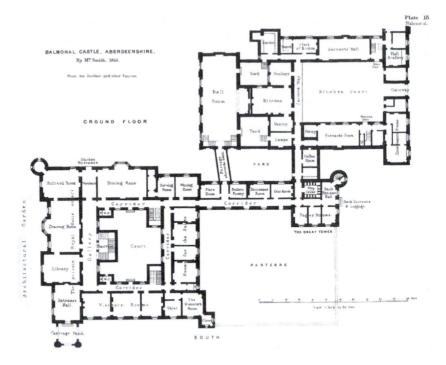

on the contrary, both are anxious to attain perfect domestic convenience
of a modern rural kind, independently of anything like mannerism of
arrangement . . . and yet the two present, throughout their entire scheme,
a striking dissimilarity of style.[27]

Kerr makes further distinctions between the symmetry and regularity in partitioning
of Osborne, and a convenience of disposition which eschews 'all needless or fictitious
correspondence'[28] of Balmoral. This sort of distinction once again emphasizes the
different ways of looking at these plans. Yet another sort of question becomes prominent here. The above comparison suggests that Kerr had a conception of style as a
kind of unconscious disposition of an architect which would not unduly compromise
any programme, given the strength of the client's input.[29] But in his conclusion to
the comparative analysis of plans, a sense of equivocation about how to judge the
competition of styles emerges:

That all Classic motive is based on regularity, and all Gothic on irregularity,
is still a first principle; but that the Classic manner may pervade a plan in
spite of irregularity in detail, and the Gothic manner similarly in spite of
symmetry, is the final lesson this contrast is meant to convey . . . both
are essentially and persistently grounded on every-day modern arrangements; to live in the one would be precisely the same as to live in the
other . . . and yet this is our argument, – that the one exhibits throughout
an all-pervading balance which need not be constrained, and the other an
all-pervading freedom which need not be unruly, as two distinct styles of

> Plan between which there seems to be thus far really no difference of
> value.[30]

This equivocation says much about the professional stakes influencing Kerr's treatise:
that he was available as an architect to produce plans in either broadly defined
manner.[31] The larger problem of this equivocation is that it represents the point at
which Kerr's historical analysis (and the history of nationalism and style in architecture)
meets the outlining of Kerr's own practice as an architect. At this point, Kerr's notion
of an imaginative inhabitation of the plan emerges as one useful in picking up on what
the Gothic plan has bequeathed to Kerr's contemporary situation: 'all-pervading
freedom' as opposed to abstract compositional balance.[32] It is the freedom of the
Gothic plan, visible in the attribute of asymmetry, that can allow for a certain
imaginative freedom of architect and client. This freedom is discussed in more detail
in Kerr's comments on the scale of domestic arrangements, and the quality of
domestic comfort. In these discussions Kerr argues his preference for the Gothic on
'imaginative' terms.

Comfort, scale and imaginative freedom

After the comparative analysis of Gothic and classical plans, Kerr lists ten primary
principles that must be considered in domestic planning. Among these principles are
issues of aspect and prospect, salubrity, the overbearing considerations of style which
compromise these values, and these last few principles:

> 8. Generally speaking, architects have to learn this golden rule – 'take care
> of the inside, and the outside ought to take care of itself'. – 9. Architects
> must especially consent to provide for the furniture. – 10. Nor must other
> minutiae be neglected; nothing is too small to be seen when it is too late
> to mend.[33]

In these last principles, Kerr privileges the architect's attention to the interior
possibilities of a dwelling, and he defines the gentleman's house in terms of its
'accommodation':

> No question of mere magnitude is involved; no degree of embellishment;
> no local or personal peculiarity; but there is indicated an entire class of
> dwellings, in which it will be found, notwithstanding infinite variety of
> scale, that the elements of accommodation and arrangement are always
> the same; being based, in fact, upon what is in a certain sense unvarying
> throughout the British Islands, namely, the domestic habits of refined
> persons.[34]

Kerr neatly avoids the question of style, and instead displaces the issue of plan
suitability on to English domestic habits. He argues for this in terms of a series of
room-types, with the gentleman-client being left to 'discern for himself' (or imagine)
the scale of his requirements:

> Let us instance the chapter on the *Drawing-room*, or that on the *Kitchen*;
> this treats of *all classes of such rooms together*: the reader being left to

discern for himself (as he easily may do, it is hoped) the precise bearings of the argument on any particular scale of Drawing-room or Kitchen which may be in his mind, – the *principles* being in all cases the same. But let us go farther, and take the chapter on the *Boudoir*, or the *Billiard-room*, or that on the *Still-room* or the *Steward's room*; the reader has here to discern, not only what such a room ought to be, but to what scale of building the possession of such a room pertains.[35]

The possession of a conveniently planned array of rooms at the correct scale for one's needs acts as a definition of domestic comfort, which comes under the provision of what 'a room ought to be':

What we call in England a comfortable house is a thing so intimately identified with English customs as to make us apt to say that in no other country but our own is this element of comfort understood. . . . The peculiarities of our climate, the domesticated habits of almost all classes, our family reserve, and our large share of the means and appliances of easy living, all combine to make what is called a comfortable home perhaps the most cherished possession of an Englishman.[36]

For Kerr, comfort includes the idea of environmental controls for individual rooms,[37] but he is keen to make the principle of comfort primarily a subjective one:

Comfort includes the idea that every room in the house, according to its purpose, shall be for that purpose satisfactorily contrived, so as to be free from perversities of its own, – so planned, in short, considered by itself, as to be in every respect a comfortable room of its kind.[38]

This notion of comfort becomes a kind of circular argument: that comfort is what appears to be comfortable. Comfort is the subjective state of experiencing a 'satisfactorily contrived' interior as much as it might be a material attribute of the interior itself. For Kerr, the imagination of comfort takes precedence at the level of the plan. One has to sense being comfortable by an imaginative inhabitation of the plan, by imagining the correct scale for one's needs, in light of a recognition of what English comfort means in relation to the history of plan types.

The interaction of plan and textual commentary in Kerr initially comes under the provision of what Scarry calls delayed perceptual content. Considered in terms of the history of plan types and the comparative analysis of the classical and Gothic, the plan provides the structure for imaginatively recognizing the salience of certain plan forms in terms of such factors as climate and national sensibility, that is, in terms of the plan's organization of a future building; however, considering scale and comfort, where imaginative inhabitation is given a more prominent account, Kerr's text slides further to the side of providing for mimetic content, whereby the subject is given the 'room' to imagine inhabitation largely free from the material constraints that the plan organizes. This imagining feeds back into the planning process, but is not determined by the plan's future outcome as a built structure. A doubled condition arises here: the plan exists as a coding of a proposed material reality on the one hand, and on the other, a device by which to inhabit this condition immaterially, in advance of the way in which a built architecture would frame inhabitation.[39]

At this point it is useful to refer this reading of Kerr back to the frame of argument employed by Franklin and Evans to gauge how it is beginning to move beyond this frame. At one level, the reading of Kerr has opened an element of the undefined in his writing. There has not been an attempt to read the treatise for evidence of modes of inhabitation. Rather, it has been read for the way in which the inhabitation of an interior is managed in relation to the plan through an apparatus of imagining. Finding 'evidence of inhabitation' cannot yet be proposed as a way of dealing with this material, as imaginative inhabitation is precisely concerned with putting off this question of evidencing an interior in representational or material form. Imaginative inhabitation is concerned with the inhabitant's sense of a future possibility of an interior that can feed back to an adjustment of the particular variables of the planning process. For Kerr, these processes are informed by a history of plan types. Thus – and here it is useful to recall Benjamin's thoughts on the interior – time does not operate in a strictly linear or progressive sense with regard to imaginative inhabitation.

But this complexity of time in the processes of planning reveals the mechanism by which plan suitability is to be judged. Imaginative inhabitation forecloses on the future possibility of inhabiting the materially complete house by promoting comfort as the measure of proof for successful inhabitation, and therefore a successful plan. Comfort is proposed as fully imaginable, and thus, following Scarry's alignment of imagining under instruction with perceptual acts, as fully perceivable at the level of plan arrangement. The delayed sensory content that the plan encodes is forgone for the more immediate and 'real' sense of imagining mimetic content. The tension that is revealed here is mirrored within the formation of the concept of comfort itself, which gains sense in a double register: at one level able to be imagined as a continuous condition of repose, but at another level, needing to be constantly renegotiated through inhabitation.

The double register of comfort

As the means to imagine comfort, Kerr advocates considering each room of the house as isolated from the others. This is particularly evident in his discussion of the principle of privacy. For Kerr, privacy relates to the separation from the family of the servants' location, activities, and movement through the house.[40] Kerr underscores his argument about this separation by suggesting that it is of mutual benefit to both 'communities': 'Whatever their mutual regard and confidence as dwellers under the same roof, each class is entitled to shut its door upon the other and be alone.'[41] As the subject of planning, comfort is made possible by juggling the individual demands of spaces, and the relations between them. As the subject of a client's desire formed through an imaginative inhabitation of the plan, comfort is found at the end of a corridor behind a closed door. Thus comfort arises for Kerr in a double register: as a relational condition, the way in which the family and the servants need privacy from each other under the same roof, and as a fixed state, when a door can be closed and an interior inhabited in total privacy.

The double register of comfort plays out between architect and client, and between the technique of planning and the act of imagining. The way in which comfort has been discussed in the existing literature suggests this double register, but also an impending friction when the plan gives way to a subjective projection into a realized spatial condition. This idea of friction will be discussed in terms of Stevenson's *House Architecture*, where a description of the spatial attributes of certain types of rooms predominates over a focus on plan conditions. But as a more immediate task, it is necessary to flesh out the idea of the double register of comfort.

In his investigation of the emergence of a modern sensibility of comfort, John Crowley has noted a crucial shift in the term's meaning. Comfort became significant in the eighteenth century as an attribute of the body and its physical environment, supplanting an earlier sense of comfort meaning moral and spiritual support.[42] This emergence of the body gave rise to the double register of comfort: while the notion of comfort as support remained consistent, the shift from spiritual to physical support suggests both a physical relation, for example between a person and a chair, and a fixed state of being comfortable while seated. Further, Crowley suggests that through the eighteenth century, comfort became taught and learned and thus was used as a criticism of the existing material culture of life, and as a way of articulating and evaluating improvements to the qualities of life. He argues that this sense developed in writings on political economy, where material comfort legitimized new consumption patterns. Material comfort gained force through the eighteenth century as a human right, where it could be incorporated into developing humanitarian ideologies, until 'at the end of the eighteenth century, physical comfort could be asserted as a right of the unprivileged and a humanitarian responsibility of the propertied'.[43]

In Crowley's argument, there is a shift on the one hand from an immaterial sense of comfort – comfort as emotional support – to its material sense. On the other hand, however, as the sensibility of comfort develops into a progressive idea related directly to material culture, Kerr shows that its necessity to be imagined also gains strength. But no longer is the imagination of comfort to do with the comfort of one's soul. Rather, it has to do with the way in which a particular material condition can be imagined. Imaginative inhabitation as occurring in advance of – and as the desire for – the acquisition of a comfortable material condition creates an expectation that will itself be tested and revised with bodily inhabitation.

Adrian Forty provides another angle on the concept of comfort that is pertinent to extending this idea of its double register, and the way in which the plan encodes particular possibilities for imagining comfort. In the context of a discussion of the concept of function, Forty traces a derivation of comfort from the architectural discussion surrounding the 'fit' between people and buildings. Forty discusses the French term *convenance* as an expression denoting this idea of fit. He cites J.-F. Blondel's explanation of this term: 'For the spirit of *convenance* to reign in a plan, each room must [be] placed according to its use and to the nature of the building, and must have a form and a proportion relative to its purpose.'[44] Blondel wrote these words in 1752, and Forty traces the translation of the idea into English through

J. C. Loudon's *Encyclopaedia of Cottage, Farm and Villa Architecture* in 1833. Loudon translated *convenance* as 'fitness for the end in view'.[45] After this translation, Forty sees *convenance* becoming 'an increasingly undynamic concept that gradually collapsed into "comfort"'.[46] But Kerr saw a crucial role for the imagining of comfort in relation to the scale and disposition of a house. It was the very technique of imagining comfort that was a crucial test for the 'fitness' of the plan.

A third account of comfort takes it as a conceptual and material device for the disciplining of the family in the nineteenth century, in this way bringing together its physical parameters, and the way in which architecture and social relations manage those parameters for a particular cultural sensibility of comfort. In 'The Idea of Comfort',[47] Tomás Maldonado argues that it arose as a compensation for the rapidity of urban and industrial development and expansion into the nineteenth century, a compensation that was achieved for the nuclear family, but in relation to larger structures of governance and control. Maldonado deals with comfort within a set of terms that includes privacy and hygiene; privacy is an ideal, and the opportunity for domestic comfort is planned in order to maintain the stability of the family as a nuclear unit within this ideal: 'But at the same time, the dream (for it is a dream) of bourgeois privacy is based on a close regulation of material things.'[48] This regulation, which is also one of the body and the person, is given relationally by comfort and hygiene, but as a 'dreamed' condition. Maldonado explicitly considers the relational and reposeful registers of comfort across gender lines in the context of mid-nineteenth-century English ideas of comfort. In terms of female domestic duties, comfort can be understood as the alleviation of domestic toil. In relation to the male's position in the household, comfort, especially in relation to comfortable furniture, can be considered as a state of repose.[49] Maldonado notes, however, that towards the late nineteenth century, there was an equalization of these differentiated considerations of comfort in spaces such as the parlour, which break a strict gender division in the household and give comfort the signification of a shared domestic experience.

In this literature on comfort, the term, in its double register, resolves in three ways: for Crowley, there is a shift in the eighteenth century from an emotional sense to a physical sense; for Forty, there is a shift between a planimetric and a subjective sense from France to England between the eighteenth and the nineteenth centuries; and for Maldonado, there is a material and spatial regulation of the family cast in the sense of a gendered relation to the double register of comfort. Each of these investigations brings to light the shifting sense of comfort, suggesting that Kerr's invocation of comfort cannot be related to any 'natural' or stable meaning, and further, that in the ways in which comfort is constructed as a domestic value, the material and the immaterial go hand in hand.

This literature does, however, contextualize Kerr's invocation of the term, and this allows an insight into how the term is useful to him, and how it plays out more widely in the English discourse of domestic planning. At one level, the double register of comfort mirrors in Kerr the relation between the imagining of comfort as an ideal condition, and the ongoing imaginative work that produces the plan as an apparatus for the imagination of this ideal. For this relation to be productive, the material resolution of the plan as a built condition must be put off, and the attainment of comfort treated as an imaginary condition at the level of the plan's perceived suitability. Kerr forecloses on a physical possibility for the measuring of comfort, but in *House Architecture*,[50] J. J. Stevenson begins to investigate what this physicality could mean for the imaginative inhabitation of the interior. In doing so, he moves away from the planimetric consideration of comfort towards a spatialized sense, where inhabitation is presented to the reader of his treatise as a 'pictured' condition.

The friction of domestic space

Franklin suggests that Stevenson's *House Architecture* went back over ground Kerr established sixteen years previously, but with more information on environmental matters such as ventilation, heating and drainage, which Kerr had not included.[51] But the importance of Stevenson's difference from Kerr lies elsewhere. Kerr's concept of comfort was as a fixed state for his gentleman-client, his role as architect being a juggling of the plan requirements to achieve this end, that is, a sorting out of comfort relationally, so that this reposeful condition could be imagined. Stevenson sought to present comfort as a relational quality for the inhabitants themselves, a quality that was couched in a language which described the types of frictions and interrelations brought about by revising ideal plan conditions in a lived domestic situation. Mark Girouard captures this sense of the difference between Stevenson and Kerr by suggesting that Stevenson had the feeling that 'houses should be designed to be enjoyable as well as convenient'.[52] Girouard also notes that, along with a loosening of the compartmentalization and social divisions inscribed in Kerr's planning, there is also a way in which Stevenson's publication is appealing to a different architect/client grouping, those of the 'upper-middle class' rather than the country-based aristocracy. Consequent upon this shift is a moderation in the scale of domestic dwellings, leading to the sort of 'moderately' sized late-nineteenth-century work of British architects that became internationally known.[53]

Inhabiting the already inhabited

In a way similar to Kerr's, Stevenson's history of the domestic plan in England is a history of forms of inhabitation which privilege privacy as a value.[54] More specifically, Stevenson's history is one of the changes in the concept and inhabitation of the space of 'the hall'. Stevenson argues that in the Middle Ages, the hall was the space of the house itself, and the hearth in its centre was the focus of domestic sociality. Complexity in planning emerged from subdivisions and annexations of this space, corridors and galleries becoming the means of communication between rooms, but also major architectural features themselves.[55] Here there are two major departures from the model laid down by Kerr. The first is on the question of Kerr's advocacy of a strict separation between servants and family, the second is Stevenson's account of the spatiality of the hall which critiques the strict separation of thoroughfare and destination, and allows for something of the confusion of the meeting of bodies to be counted as the precondition for a comfortable form of domestic inhabitation.[56]

In his account of the 'Servant's Offices', Stevenson directly admonishes Kerr for insisting on a strict separation between servants and family because a closer interaction between them would enable more familiarity and equity, therefore more loyalty and pride in work from servants. And he adds: 'should the mistress not have the run of her own house?'[57] But Stevenson believed the private lives of both family and servants should be respected.[58] It is not through an actual openness that what Kerr called each community should know of what the other does, but through a kind of picturing. Stevenson remarks: 'Household work is not a thing to be ashamed of or hidden out of sight; it has been a favourite subject with many painters, but a sense of fitness will keep it to its proper place.'[59] Here Stevenson is using a trope of picturing inhabitation which can usefully be compared to Kerr's sense of imagining inhabitation. Stevenson asks the reader to treat a particular domestic scene as the subject of representation, and one sees this scene not as a freely imagined one, but as the imagination of the way one would perceive a picture, in this case, a framed genre painting. This situation can be referred back to Scarry's categories of imagining to understand the difference between Kerr and Stevenson on this point. Kerr's sense of imagining was explained as the production of mimetic content, where no direct perceptual stimulus of what is to be imagined is given to the subject who imagines. Imagination can then have a vivacity normally associated with sensory perceptions. Stevenson's imaginative act, however, entails the imagination of a perceptual act, that is, the imagining of looking at a representation of an interior scene, or even at a further remove, the imagining of someone in the act of painting an interior scene. This appears to be a hybrid of the verbal and the visual arts: the mimetic content imagined is actually the creation of direct visual content which would be the object of visual perception.[60] This hybrid encourages imagining as looking, bound as looking is by the close attention to material details, rather than the freer act of imagining proper, that is, the production of mimetic content, where the compensation for not directly perceiving the world is an ability to stretch it, and literally make it up, wherein lies imagining's vivacity.[61]

In Stevenson's text, the reader is instructed to imagine a series of interior genre pictures. The instruction interprets the picture at the same moment that it sets it before the reader's imagination. This is demonstrated in Stevenson's account of a typical drawing-room, a word-picture he presents in order to argue against what Kerr argued for, that is, the separation of function into discrete rooms:

> Except on rare occasions, the [drawing-]room remains unused, in dignified and dismal desolation, all the more cheerless that it is kept in perfect order – the furniture all swathed in brown holland, everything in its proper place, the books on the round table in the centre of the room (without which, no lady's drawing-room is considered to be complete), radiated at equal distances around its circumference. It serves its purpose, in producing that consciousness of being as good as our neighbours, in which consists so much of the happiness of life.[62]

Stevenson follows this description of the drawing-room by advocating the idea of the general-purpose medieval hall, and after having discussed the planning of domestic dwellings in full, he again returns to the idea of the hall, both as a form of communication between rooms, and as a space of inhabitation by the family. He advocates it as a kind of multi-purpose space, able to reduce the size, and even the necessity of, separate and specific sitting rooms.[63] The hall returns, for Stevenson, as the medieval space of the dwelling itself.[64] The strength of this idea comes from the way it is presented as an already inhabited picture to the imagination. Stevenson discusses an anonymous plan of a large-scale dwelling to indicate his thinking:

> Another bedroom and dressing-room is provided on this [ground] floor near the entrance, where ladies arriving as guests for the evening might disrobe, or for older people for whom climbing the stairs is a burden. Probably one good sized room, which might be used for other purposes, might be more generally useful.
>
> One of the great difficulties of designing a house is to adapt it to the scale of living of the family; arrangements which are excellent in a small house being out of place in a grander one. And it frequently happens that people adapt their new house to a scale of living, which, when they get into it, they find they have outgrown; or, on the other hand, that they burden themselves with a house too large for them, which it is a toil to live in.
>
> It is always safe, in a country house especially, to have one great room; in this case we may dispense with great size in the others. This room should, I think, be made like the Hall of an old English house, which may be used for a dinner, or a dance, or sports, and even when the family is alone is not unpleasant as a sitting-room.[65]

The picture of the hall which the reader is instructed to imagine is inhabited by people other than the reader, and it takes on the functions normally assigned to separate rooms as part of its ever-changing inhabitation. The reader imagines looking at a series of pictures, rather than being present in the space of the hall as one would seemingly be in Kerr's notion of imaginative inhabitation. Stevenson's distaste for the picture of the drawing-room comes out of this notion of inhabitation: the drawing-room makes a bad picture because it is uninhabited, and further than that, because it presents itself as uninhabitable. The projection into an already inhabited milieu thus has to do with the identification of the imagining subject with those already inhabiting this milieu.

But for both Stevenson and Kerr, the relation between imaginary and physical inhabitation is managed by a particular temporality. Comfort can be achieved at the level of the imaginary inhabitation of the plan, or of a picture of space, in the extent to which this imaginary act feeds back into the ongoing planning process. Yet the fulfilment of comfort is also left open as the future possibility of physical inhabitation, a possibility beyond the techniques of architects.[66]

The future possibility of inhabitation is the province of the inhabitant as consumer. In its conceptual separability from architecture, the interior increasingly came to be seen as a series of consumable objects, and this meant that it began to travel in a geographical space of exchange. More specifically, a particular manifestation of the interior that became prominent in England around the turn of the twentieth century, having developed within the frame of asymmetrical planning, became the means by which a progressivist sense of design governed by architecture travelled to Germany – or so the story goes. The next chapter shows that consumption treated within a geographical space of exchange opens on to other trajectories of the travelling of modernity. Moreover, the sense of the interior's exchange shows how progressivist thinking in architecture attempted to control the interior's material realization. No longer a question of the imagination of a condition of inhabitation beyond the provision of an architectural frame, the interior became architectural, or, rather, architecture became interiorized in the extent to which the interior was the staging ground for modern practices of consumption which were debated and directed through architectural discourse. The very modernity of architecture was claimed in terms of how it might make coherent a reorganization of design and manufacturing at the level of emerging national unities, particularly that demarcated by Germany. Yet an Australian example will be examined, one which offers a critique of the exclusivity of this Anglo/German axis of exchange.

Coda: gender and geography

In invoking geography in this way, it needs to be noted that this discussion of domestic planning has had a particular geographical bias. As a consequence, it has also had a gender bias. As is manifestly clear, the English discourse of domestic planning was controlled by male architects, and addressed to male clients. This might be compared to the situation in America, where discussions of domestic planning took place in the context of domestic advice literature, the most prominent of which was written by women for women. In the work of Catharine Beecher, for example, domestic planning was a practical technique of domesticity that sat alongside other practical techniques such as cleaning and household economics. That a reader – the female domestic subject – might be interested equally in areas of domesticity that in England were split between domestic advice literature and more properly architectural literature points to the importance of considering the issues of architecture's relation to the domestic within a geographical frame. While, perhaps paradoxically, extensive work on the American discourse of planning and domestic advice is beyond the scope of this book for reasons of geography – the focus is on the history of modernism as it has been dominated by the Anglo/German axis – this focus still points to the crucial role geography plays in thinking about historical relations between architecture and the interior. The next chapter will thus be framed by this geographical concern.

Chapter 4

Consuming the interior
Geography and identity

Chapter 3 analysed the way in which architecture staked a particular claim for the domestic with the codification of asymmetrical planning. The interior as an imagined condition was crucial to the articulation of this claim. It aided an architectural discourse that was oriented along new lines inscribed by domestic comfort and the management of domestic relations, without simply being reducible to it. This chapter considers how the interior became the staging ground around the turn of the twentieth century for a reconsideration of nineteenth-century architectural values, particularly around the question of style. The interior performed this role at a crucial moment, the moment, in Walter Benjamin's terms, of its liquidation. In examining this context, the English interior is investigated as it travels, as both an image-based condition and a set of material artefacts, to the different geographical contexts of Germany and Australia.

The German context is considered through architect Hermann Muthesius's role as both the first thorough historian of English domestic architecture at the turn of the twentieth century, and as a theorist and policy maker for the reinvigoration of the German manufacturing sector's production of domestic consumer goods. Muthesius's text *Style-architecture and Building-art: Transformations of Architecture in the Nineteenth Century and its Present Condition* of 1901/03 is the centrepiece of this examination. The situation of wealthy Scots-Australian pastoralist Robert Barr Smith and his wife Joanna forms a counterpoint to the German context of debate. The Barr Smiths imported entire interiors from the London firm of Morris & Co. for their houses in Adelaide, South Australia. They managed an identity as subjects moving within the geographical space between Britain and Australia, taking up the English interior in a way that critically reframes what it made possible in Germany.

This structuring constitutes a geohistorical analysis of the interior at the turn of the twentieth century. Peter Taylor has used this concept to elucidate an idea of multiple modernities that are at play when one considers the geographical interconnectedness of nations, societies and cultures. This geohistorical understanding refuses an abstract definition of modernity, as well as the use of examples or contexts that would merely be illustrative of modernity as an abstraction. It also allows a critique of diffusionist geography, whereby the impetus of progress is said to be passed from an imperial and cultural centre to new centres of progress – for example, in the historical story emphasized by Nikolaus Pevsner, where the baton of progress in design is seen to be passed between England and Germany around the turn of the twentieth century – and eventually to peripheries which come under the sway of centres of power.[1] In discussing architecture's relation to the interior at the turn of the twentieth century in geohistorical terms, this chapter emphasizes the different geographical possibilities that gave a multifaceted sense to modernity at this time.

While the examples of Muthesius and the Barr Smiths are the figures for this geohistorical account, each belongs to a different order of historical example. Muthesius is a central figure both in the history of English domestic architecture and in the efforts to reform design and manufacturing in Germany through the German Werkbund. The Barr Smiths have no such historical significance. Through their consumption practices, they have become exceptional though marginal figures in the history of Morris & Co., and of the English Arts and Crafts movement more generally.[2] The aim of juxtaposing these two examples is not to raise the status of the Barr Smiths to one that is 'generally' important when considering consumption and the interior, or the history of English Arts and Crafts domesticity. Rather, this juxtaposition attempts to use their very marginal, exceptional position as a point of leverage against received ideas about how the English interior has been taken up outside of England. The specific geographical contexts in which these figures were embedded, and across which they travelled, provided diverse opportunities for the consumption of the interior, both as image and as material reality.

Individual interior/national interior

Photographic similarities

An 1896 photograph shows Hermann Muthesius and his wife Anna,[3] seated in the heart of English Arts and Crafts domesticity in Hammersmith, London (Figure 4.1). This was the beginning of Muthesius's attachment to the German embassy, a position he held until 1904. The photograph immediately inscribes gendered roles in a scene which can be understood in terms of the double register of comfort discussed in Chapter 3. Anna pours the tea, offering comfort in a relational setting, and Hermann drinks it in a state of comfortable repose. There is also a particular relation to objects enacted in this scene. It is not J. J. Stevenson's gloomy drawing room, where objects forsake a functional role and attempt only to stand for a neighbourly competitiveness in taste and wealth.[4] The teaset is in the process of being used, the comfort of the chairs is being tested. The small table, in its weight and size, is employed for the specific function of taking tea, and a small burner next to Anna keeps the kettle hot. The photograph is picturing use, a use of space and a use of objects. In terms of the history of photography, this marks a particular shift away from the use of studio interiors for the taking of family portraits. The technical factors of shortening exposure time and the increasing portability of camera equipment from the 1880s onward meant that one's actual home could be the setting for a portrait.[5] Yet this is not so

4.1
**Hermann and
Anna Muthesius
at The Priory,
Hammersmith,
1896**
By permission Vera
Muthesius

much a portrait as an interior in the image-based sense of the concept. It is a depiction of the Muthesiuses' domestic milieu, their comfortableness as husband and wife.

There is a remarkably similar photograph of Robert and Joanna Barr Smith taking tea in their home Auchendarroch in the Adelaide Hills of South Australia, circa 1897 (Figure 4.2). In their interior, they are surrounded by furnishings and decorations from Morris & Co. In the 1880s and 1890s, the Barr Smiths decorated two of their Adelaide mansions, Torrens Park and Auchendarroch, with the most expensive Morris & Co. furnishings. During this time, they were reputed to be the largest international customers of Morris & Co.,[6] and until 1929, three generations of the Barr Smith family decorated seven houses in Adelaide with their furnishings.[7] Robert Barr Smith managed trading, pastoral and mining interests in South Australia, and the family moved back and forward between Scotland, London and Adelaide.[8] Their application of Morris & Co. furnishings to the interiors of Torrens Park and Auchendarroch was total, employing the full range of products in schemes coordinated by Morris & Co. designers. The products were purchased in person directly from Morris & Co. in London by the Barr Smiths, then shipped to Adelaide with written instructions provided by Morris & Co. designers as to their correct installation. The installation was coordinated by architects in Adelaide, but Robert Barr Smith was himself very involved with the ongoing renovations of the two houses through detailed correspondence with his Adelaide architects while he was overseas.[9] Each interior imported by the Barr Smiths was literally transmissible. The image of the desired English 'at ease, at home' fantasy captured in the photograph of the Barr Smiths was, at the level of the interior, divisible into a series of artefacts and components that could be bought, transported and reassembled at the periphery of empire.

Despite the visual similarities between these two photographs, each captures the creation and inhabitation of an English interior as the result of vastly different geographical possibilities for consumption. These enticing similarities must first be ignored in order to investigate these different possibilities. One will then be in a better position to explain what these similarities mean.

Clothing and cleanliness

Via Muthesius, English Arts and Crafts domestic architecture received its first major critical analysis. Muthesius's three-volume study *Das englische Haus* was published in Germany in 1904–5, immediately after his return there from England.[10] The study was informed by his experience of living in London, and his personal acquaintance with many of the English architects studied in the book.[11] But it is Muthesius's slightly earlier polemic *Style-architecture and Building-art* which gives an account of the English domestic interior framed by the relation between England and Germany.[12] The polemic presents a particular image of the English interior to a German bourgeois audience in the context of a call for this audience to emulate the English experience and develop an interior, and an attendant sense of inhabitation, capable of reflecting the culture of the German people. This audience was one which had to imagine the spatial condition of the English interior, and 'revise' this condition in a German context.

By situating such 'personal' practices of inhabitation in relation to an architectural and cultural discourse operating in an international context,[13] one of the central themes of the treatment of the interior in a context of travelling around the turn of the twentieth century is raised: the relation between fashion and style conceived at the level of the individual subject, and the influence of this conception on debates in architecture and design.

In his discussion of the ways in which the engineering and industrial advances of the nineteenth century could offer a new way for architecture to manage a contemporary symbolic content at the turn of the twentieth century, Muthesius used an analogy with dress, and echoed the importance of the *look* of cleanliness:

> They [the new industrial structures and products] must embody an expressive modern form; they must mirror the sensibility of our time just as the richly acanthus-laden cannon barrel did the seventeenth century or the carved and gilded sedan chair the eighteenth century. . . . Nevertheless it would be dangerous to assume that merely satisfying purpose is itself sufficient. Today's simple clothing is also not without its unnecessary elements. Our elegantly dressed gentleman still wears a top hat, patent leather shoes, and silk lapels – elements that might almost be compared with certain polished and nickel-plated parts of a machine. In both cases they seem to have been brought into being by a specific requirement for cleanliness – a demand not only to hinder undesired accumulation of dirt but also to demonstrate symbolically that it is not present, that everything is neat and in the best of order. Our starched white linens also follow the same example.[14]

Muthesius saw a 'coincidence here of certain sanitary and aesthetic concerns. . . . These reforms [evident in contemporary English domestic architecture] follow the same tendency as our clothing, the closer dwelling that envelops us'.[15] Yet it was not an abstract notion of cleanliness per se that was symbolized architecturally. Rather, it was that domestic subjects could manage and symbolize their own cleanliness, and live within this symbolization as a kind of attitude and orientation to contemporary conditions and expectations. Here Muthesius is slipping between architectural concerns of ornament, and what might be called concerns of a subject's identity as they are formed in relation to the interior. One could embody cleanliness and feel comfortable in making this embodiment clear in an individual disposition, initially developed in relation to the comfort felt within the private, domestic sphere, and then implicated with the way one conducted oneself in public. In this sense, Mark Wigley has argued for dress as architecture, and architecture as dress, their implication in debates in the early twentieth century involving more than just a metaphorical relation.[16]

Individual and national subjectivity

Yet in pursuing Muthesius's characterization of the English interior further, there is a crucial link visible between a subject's identity formed in the interior – and described by Muthesius in terms of clothing – and the way in which that identity was articulated with a reform of design and industry at the level of German national culture. The relation between clothing and the English interior positions the interior as a kind of linking space between the private sphere of the individual and the possibility of the individual participating in a larger, collective sense of identity formation. As Muthesius writes:

> Art begins, like so much else, at home. Only he who takes an artistic interest in his four walls, who is himself naturally inclined to shape his personal surroundings, will give form to his taste and bring that sensitivity for art from his rooms into the street and the larger environment.[17]

The surety with which Muthesius could argue for the role of the interior in a larger cultural programme only emerged after the interior became separated from pre-existing architectural determinations, and folded into a call for a building-art. In *Style-architecture and Building-art*, Muthesius came to certain conclusions about the recent history of architecture, and on that basis made a diagnosis about its condition at the turn of the twentieth century.[18] 'Style-architecture' represented the nineteenth-century condition of architecture and the legacy of its effects at the turn of the twentieth century. 'Building-art' is Muthesius's coinage for describing the desirable possibilities latent in the turn-of-the-century condition. There is a clear series of values and the seeds of a reforming programme inherent in the opposing of these labels: style-architecture was what building-art must overcome if architecture was to give direction once again to artistic and cultural life. And what was to be expended here was precisely 'architecture'.

Muthesius's text favours an individualized, realist and nationally based building-art, historically found in the Gothic, as the basis for a renewal of German culture. The English house provided Muthesius with an immediate example of such a position.[19] The progressive proponents of England's domestic building-art were opposed to and eschewed the monumental, style-driven, idealistic and universalist conception of architecture that had, with the late-nineteenth-century battle of the styles, so debased the idea of consolidating a national culture. As if to show the absurdity of maintaining the coupling of style-architecture, Muthesius gives a caricature of the 'style-architect', an absurd sort of subject designing in a medieval manner, in order to make the distinction between style-architecture and contemporary needs more apparent:

> He [the style-architect] then takes care to achieve purely superficial, often arbitrary groupings, which again have nothing to do with the essence of

the thing. He introduces little towers, little gables, and oriels where they appear to him to be desired for the painterly grouping, and he lays out the stairs, if possible, in such a way that their ascending windows make a good image from the street . . . [H]e makes primarily a style-architecture, rather than primarily solving the task in a straightforward [*sachlich*] manner. He creates a hallucination of abstract beauty under which the user can twist and turn as he will.[20]

Muthesius connects style-architecture with exterior conditions, where the 'image from the street' exists in ignorance of whatever might occur within. The twisting and turning of the user, to the extent that this twisting and turning epitomized Muthesius's characterization of the ills of present culture, was an issue of the interior.[21]

Yet the issue of the interior was not one for architecture to solve, even if it had served to highlight, by its exterior 'fashioning', the crucial nature of the interior as the site of a transformation at the turn of the twentieth century: 'it follows that it was not from architecture but from the arts and crafts, and not from architects but from artists of a quite different type . . . that leadership came for that fundamental shift in our artistic situation'. He continues: 'Yet since the arts and crafts in the final analysis are only directed to the design of interiors, they work hand in hand with architecture, even if one understands architecture, as is customary today, under the narrow notion of erecting buildings.'[22]

Muthesius writes of the 'arts and crafts' in the general sense of being techniques allied with architecture, but he also refers explicitly to the English Arts and Crafts movement, and William Morris's leadership.[23] Muthesius suggests that Continental movements, such as Jugendstil and Art Nouveau, are the descendants of the English Arts and Crafts, yet they differ from the Arts and Crafts in seeking new forms, 'thus once again basically the old miseries of style and ornament'.[24] The English Arts and Crafts movement, which is given a slightly mythical air in Muthesius's writing, sought for an individualization of design, so that one would attend to the particularity of each situation for which a designed response would be called, and one could also see the possibility of using this approach to attend to the shaping of one's own immediate, personal surroundings. This represented a twofold shift of approach to the role of design in culture. The most immediate was a shift towards what Muthesius described as the objective conditions of each situation in the absence of a determining or pre-emptive style. The other was the shift away from design being a situation calling for a specialist. The implication was that anyone could, and indeed everyone should be able to, shape their own interior. This aspect marked the movement to a kind of ethics of conduct born of and reflected in one's relation to the interior, and reflected most strongly the romantic socialism of Morris, which itself did not make the transition to Germany.

As a part of the polemic embedded in *Style-architecture and Building-art*, Muthesius's conceptualization of the English domestic interior is made in explicitly 'subjective' terms. In its various forms, the arts and crafts was for Muthesius 'an emotional art, it may provide support for and perhaps altogether capture our present emotional life'.[25] This was a precarious task because the arts and crafts swung between either pole within which it presented its possibilities. The 'soft, flowing' or 'whiplash' line of the Continental versions perhaps was more malleable and capable of more indeterminate forms of expression. Indeed, this line had an anthropomorphizing tendency in that, as Muthesius suggests, 'one seeks to clarify certain static images more forcibly than before with the vigorous assistance of human "empathy." The chair becomes something straddle-legged and crouching, the table leg an elastic line like the weight-bearing human foot.'[26] Colour was also in unison with form: 'both strive to embody the same emotional constituents of feeling'.[27]

All of these tendencies appeared fruitful to Muthesius in showing possibilities of siting the work of cultural renewal in the interior, and with the individual subject. But they inevitably fell across the shift that marked the difference between the two editions of *Style-architecture and Building-art*: the initial possibility of the artistic (Jugendstil) dwelling, and the subsequent perception of its failings. In terms of the possibilities for the interior, what would survive the 'pendular sweep of emotional values', values highlighted by Walter Benjamin,[28] would be the 'necessary and constant demands of material, purpose and construction'.[29] Muthesius's purpose in expounding the values of the English interior above those of the Continental movements rests, ultimately, on a constellation of 'objective' values which needed to be promoted to the German bourgeoisie above the more fickle emotional values that were having a momentary appeal at the turn of the twentieth century. Yet these values were still promoted in terms of the subjective affect of the interior felt through inhabitation:

> Here, amid the architectural extravagance that the architects promoted, one found all that one desired and for which one thirsted: adaptation to needs and local conditions, unpretentiousness and honesty of feeling; utmost coziness and comfort in the layout of rooms, colour, an uncommonly attractive and painterly (but also reasonable) design, and an economy in building construction. The new English domestic building-art that developed on this basis has now produced valuable results[.] . . . It has created the only sure foundation for a new artistic culture: the artistic house[.] . . . In contrast, our new Continental movement will have to wander in journals and exhibitions until we Germans will finally have an artistic house.[30]

The sort of inhabitation that Muthesius was promoting for the German bourgeoisie was an imaginative one, the stimuli for which would be found in exhibiting the interior publicly.[31] But the impetus for this thinking can be related to Muthesius's own inhabitation of an English interior in London. At one level, Muthesius's description above is a direct doubling of the photograph of him and his wife at home in Hammersmith, the photograph demonstrating an exemplary instance of a couple shaping their own four walls. Yet there is also a large-scale shift evidenced here. In comparing photograph and description, a private and individualized domesticity is placed next to the beginnings of a reform programme for the German nation as a whole. The affectivity that the photograph gave to the Muthesiuses' remembrances of their life lived in London was borne out in a domesticity conceived at the scale of the German nation. An individualized practice of inhabitation comes to organize a nation's inhabitation.

While the Muthesiuses have their direct remembrances of their time spent in London, journals and exhibitions would be the only means for Germans to experience the Continental translation of this English building-art. One might cast an eye over journals and exhibitions, and imagine an interior environment in relation to photographs, texts and discrete objects. But in these cases, interiors would be framed and displayed firmly in the realm of the public, of publication. In this way, they would fight in the same space as the style-architecture that Muthesius deplored, and a 'fashionable' sensibility would make them prey to simplistic translations in the context of commercial exploitation. This problem can be examined further in relation to how Muthesius used his position as a central member in the German Werkbund to theorize and promote the shift from an inhabiting subject considered individually, to one considered nationally.

Objectivity and imitation

Key in Muthesius's promotion of the English interior are the notions of 'objectivity' and 'straightforwardness' in design. The German adjective *sachlich*, variously trans-lated as reasonable, matter-of-fact, simple and straightforward, the noun *Sachlichkeit*, or objectivity, and the resultant artistic occurrence, *sachliche Kunst*, or realist art, are all employed by Muthesius to capture what he championed as the objectivity visible in certain unstylized contemporary products of culture.[32] *Sachlichkeit* was crucial in the context of the wider cultural debate in Germany at the time about fashion and style, which were opposed terms in a similar way to style-architecture and building-art. But there is some confusion of terminology here. Muthesius's characterization of style-architecture is akin to fashion, whereby ornament, and ornamental schemas that could be identified with particular historical styles in architecture, are treated as affixed decoration in the name of an individuality that does not participate culturally. Building-art refers to style in the sense of Muthesius's hope for a 'new style', a 'style of our age', that was not a recycling of the historical styles – this would be a descent into fashion – but a grasping of the way in which a unity of style connects with cultural coherence and strength. Frederic Schwartz sums up this argument: '*Sachlichkeit* is not the aesthetic payoff of functional form . . . it is, rather, the avoidance of form as Fashion, and thus a certain *semantic neutralization* of the surfaces of the everyday object and environment';[33] however, in a slightly different take, Wigley sees fashion as a structural determinant that cannot simply be avoided in an appeal to a unity of style. He argues that 'Style is seen to be that moment within fashion that transcends fashion and yet cannot be produced outside of fashion. To produce it, fashion has to be "disciplined" by reducing decoration.'[34]

This complicated difference between fashion and style is also that between the exteriorized and superficial fashioning of architecture and domestic objects, and the sense of a building-art based in an interior. These are differences which involve not only the objects of cultural production, but also subjects' relation to these objects, and the way this relation manifests a subject's identity within culture. As Francesco Dal Co argues:

> The 'creation of the German style' had to entail a convergence of the most active forces of production and commerce and the most important

formations of intellectuals and artists, a synthesis of economic exigencies and cultural aspirations, since, according to a tendency typical of the German people, and here expressed by Hermann Muthesius, 'that which the individual cannot obtain can be obtained by a well-ordered association, a unified general will.' A common aspiration is therefore not enough: the concept of *style* demands a corresponding concept of *organization* – of social organization, political will, economic expansion.[35]

This concept of organization corresponds to the organization of the German Werkbund itself, in whose theoretical debates and policies is found a formulation of how the German bourgeoisie would be encouraged to shape their own four walls with a particular national cultural benefit. The Werkbund emphasized inhabitants as the producers of design through the arrangement of interiors. But in terms of Muthesius's reliance on an English image of the interior, this sort of situation of inhabitation was not straightforward, as Mitchell Schwarzer suggests: 'For writers advocating the English model, cross-cultural imitation was envisioned as the redis-covery of a progressive tradition of Central European national design.'[36] Schwarzer takes imitation in two senses, negatively as the cheap, mass reproduction of inferior-quality goods, and positively, 'as the means to unite contemporary design with tradition conceived as progress'.[37] It was this second sense for which the Werkbund was aiming in its theories and policies for the reform of design and industry, theories and policies which articulated the relation between how an object was to be produced and how it was to be consumed, and which were aimed explicitly against imitation as inferior production and fashionized consumption. The difficulty with a positive sense of imitation, however, is also suggested by Schwarzer:

> How were Central Europeans to reconcile their admiration for English individuality with their own preference for social order? England, unlike France or the other previous centres of classical authority, did not really exemplify universal design principles. Although Central Europeans looked to England for guidance, the further they penetrated into the English state of mind, the more they were frustrated to derive from it an importable formula for their own national design.[38]

The difficulty of imitation is in some senses the story of the Werkbund. Following some of Schwartz's observations further offers a way of pursuing in more specific detail how the designed domestic object, and its setting in the interior, became the focus for the articulation of a unity of style within the Werkbund.[39]

Identification, consumption and the nation's interior

As has been shown, Schwartz sums up the significance of the concept of *Sachlichkeit* through the idea of a semantic neutralization of the surfaces of objects. In relation to this, he makes the following claim: 'The honest expression of materials, machine production and function all serve – at first – to factor out signification from the design process.'[40] Schwartz reads this non-signification not as the creation of 'mute objects', but rather the removal from the surface of objects of production both 'signs of class' and 'the relations of production'. If *Sachlichkeit* is indeed an attribute still signified by objects, then these other signs are removed in an attempt to show 'the signs of production itself' in the object.[41]

Although signs of class would appear to be removed from the object, such a *sachlich* aesthetic and ethos surrounding the object, as well as its production and consumption, is aimed at the bourgeoisie.[42] The signs of class that are removed are, according to Schwartz, those that are yoked to an outward expression of class through commodity consumption and display, and that are the means by which class position can be manipulated. Yet class as a regulatory social mechanism was still at stake in the shift in emphasis from fashion and the possibilities for class mobility, to style and the givenness of class identity. The question of consumption became figured not as 'how can my possession of this object represent my class aspirations', but rather 'who am I such that this object is not external to me, but is part of my identity?' This latter question gains sense in the regressive register of identification, a register prior to libidinal attachment, or object-choice. In this way, identity is conceived of prior to the social relations of the libido, the sorts of relations that would exploit fashion as a way to class mobility. Here, psychoanalytical concepts, forming in the same historical moment, and, as was shown in Chapter 2, being articulable in relation to the interior's doubled condition, are useful for explaining this Werkbund theorization of consumption. In her theoretical exposition of the concept of identification, Diana Fuss writes: 'Identification is the point where the psychical/social distinction becomes impossibly confused and finally untenable.'[43] This confusion relates to the way in which consumption would generally be understood in terms of object-choice. Fuss suggests that Freud's differentiation between identification and object-choice, or being and having, is itself an untenable distinction:

> Identification is the mechanism Freud summons to keep desire [i.e. object-choice] from overflowing its socially sanctioned borders. But as hard as Freud labours to keep desire and identification from infecting one another, the signs of their fluid exchanges surface everywhere to challenge and to weaken the *cordon sanitaire* erected between them.[44]

Distinctions between style and fashion developed in the Werkbund suffer from the same instability, recalling Wigley's argument that style cannot be produced outside of fashion. Yet the doubleness of the interior, its significance both materially and psychologically for the inhabitant, makes this instability productive. With a theory about the semantic neutralization of the surfaces of consumer objects, consumption does not look like the kind of object-choice where acquisition for social mobility and display are at stake, but rather like an identification, a subject-forming event which is supposedly before or above the vagaries of capital and the marketplace. It is the difference, though subtle, between 'I must possess you' and 'I cannot be without you'. Thus 'bourgeois' becomes not the object of an aspiration that can be achieved materially, but rather the object of an identification whereby such a semantic neutrality is given to the object through a kind of 'natural' affiliation between object and subject. In effect, a blatantly material relation to class and status must be renounced for the value of belonging to the bourgeoisie to be evident. The evidence of class identity is registered not on the surface of the object, but in the relation between an object and a subject who identifies with it.

This sense of a relationality with objects was figured most strongly in the Werkbund's attempt to overcome alienation – theorized in the English Arts and Crafts in terms of production – through the mechanism of consumption. As Schwartz argues: 'alienation – no longer a stable or helpful concept in the rather thin discussion of labour in the Werkbund – disappeared from the assembly line only to reappear at the cash register'.[45] The producer thus had the opportunity of becoming reacquainted with the produced object as a consumer, like all other consumers. The produced object in this argument ranges from the cutlery set to the kettle and light bulb, but also to the turbine engine, the locomotive, and to the factory building itself, especially the factory buildings of Peter Behrens and Walter Gropius, that produced these smaller objects.[46] The interior that encompassed all of these scales of object was literally the interior of the German nation. There is a conceptual thread running through Muthesius's call for each individual to remake their own interior, and the forging of the German nation in terms of its boundedness. Each individual's inhabitation of a domestic interior was doubled by an inhabitation of the interior of the nation. Dal Co comments on this situation in respect of the writings of Hermann Hesse: 'Not only is dwelling essentially "finding a homeland," but the home, as the form of dwelling, is a metaphor for the historical-political concept of homeland.'[47] Through a theoretical sleight of hand, the vagaries of consumption and class become replaced with identification and national spirit.[48] If, as Schwartz believes, 'semantic neutralization' of surfaces and the 'signs of production' can coexist in the object, it is because the object is, at crucial moments where the recognition of these signs can be made, always in an interior. Because of this doubly scaled interior, subjects who relate to objects play out their subjectivity at the level of nation. They become recognized, and recognize themselves, as national, domestic subjects. As Etienne Balibar has suggested: 'external frontiers have to be imagined constantly as a projection and protection of an internal collective personality, which each of us carries within ourselves and enables us to inhabit the space of the state as a place where we have always been – and always will be – "at home".'[49] In Balibar's thinking, individuals do not cede their identity directly to the state. Rather, following Louis Althusser's theory of ideological state apparatuses, Balibar suggests that individuals mutually recognize one another as national subjects; they are 'interpellated' as national subjects within external frontiers that in turn provide the interior of national recognition. For Balibar, national identity is both a mass phenomenon and a phenomenon of individuation, which is why the nation's interior and the domestic interior work in tandem. The Werkbund acts as a state apparatus, in Althusser's sense, for this recognition of identity which constitutes the individual as a national subject. The mechanism of interpellation is congruent with the psychoanalytical concept of identification.[50] Both guarantee recognition in a space of reflection, that is, in an interior.

But this doubling of the interior across two distinct scales had certain other consequences for the relation between subjectivity and inhabitation. Schwartz reads Georg Simmel in order to bring to light Simmel's distinction between subjective and objective culture in relation to what he calls the broadening of consumption, a broadening which resulted in an increasing distance between 'the individual on the one hand and the increasingly estranged products of culture – the material, techno-logical and bureaucratic forms of modern life – on the other'.[51] This is not a gap that could simply be bridged by subjects buying objects. The gap was in some senses the result of this attitude to consumption. Simmel himself says as much when he argues that 'The broadening of consumption, however, is dependent upon the growth of objective culture, since the more objective and impersonal an object is the better it is suited to more people.'[52] Simmel also brought style into this formulation: 'Style is always something general that brings the contents of personal life and creation into a form shared with many and accessible to many.'[53] Here the problem of inhab-itation, as it is framed by consumption, is exposed most fully. It is useful to return to the perspective of Benjamin to see how the creation of an interior through acts of inhabitation might be seen as a compensation against the objectification of culture. Objects were interiorized as an attempt to win them back from objectivity. A mode of organization such as the collection, or the registering of traces of objects in an interior, offers the possibility of conferring a semantic sense to objects shorn of it.[54] This sense was, however, individuated and problematic in its illusoriness, given the focus on the role of consumed objects, and the desire for them to be 'accessible'.

Ultimately, within architectural discourse, the theory of objectivity had to be cast in a way that overcame the interior as a space of retreat. These issues of architectural modernism's relation to turn-of-the-century debates will be taken up in Chapter 5. The next section investigates a different geographically arrayed sense of consumption of the English interior that questions a progressive sense of historical trajectory that usually underpins the relation between English and German domestic design.

Geography and the mobility of consumption

Progressive trajectories

The conventional 'story' of the relations between English and German design around the turn of the twentieth century centres around Muthesius's translation of an English domestic sensibility, perhaps too caught up in an unworkable socialist utopian vision, to a pragmatic programme for the revitalization of German industry. For example, Julius Posener calls Muthesius a 'catalyst' in his being able to see where the potentialities of an English domestic sensibility could be adapted free of socialist ideals (to which Muthesius never refers) and firmly reinscribed within the sphere of the German bourgeoisie.[55] Posener also writes explicitly of the beginnings of the modern movement in architecture as emerging in a counter-attack, in the writings of Adolf Loos, against the lack of a modern sensibility of those who called for a new style, then Muthesius's return from England and the publication of *The English House*, followed by the work of Peter Behrens for AEG, and culminating in the Cologne exhibition of the German Werkbund in 1914, this period before the war looking forward to the developments in the 1920s and 1930s.[56] This is the trajectory made popular by Nikolaus Pevsner in his *Pioneers of Modern Design from William Morris to Walter Gropius*, where he writes that 'the phase between Morris and Gropius is an historical unit'.[57] This 'unit' treats the history of the modern movement as the transfer of an impetus from Britain to Germany via Muthesius, effectively bypassing the influence of Art Nouveau and Jugendstil, and pushing for the objectivity which can be read as explaining the subsequent programmes of industrial manufacture at the Werkbund and the Bauhaus.

Yet Ian Buruma has written of Pevsner's association with England in a way that counters the progressive and causative narrative at the heart of Pevsner's account. As a counterpoint to Pevsner's claim for the roots of the modern movement in England, Buruma muses on the 'reality' of modern England, and more especially London, as largely historicist and anti-modern in architectural character at the time of Pevsner's arrival there in the early 1930s. Buruma argues that Pevsner was an Anglophile, and he describes his love of English national character in terms similar to those used by Muthesius: an emphasis on straightforwardness and common sense, but with a cast of suspicion for the kind of radicality and avant-gardism that provided the modern movement with its impact in Continental Europe. Modernism, as a Continental phenomenon, may well have been treated with suspicion in England for the very reasons an English sensibility presaged its possibilities in Europe. Buruma connects these sorts of difficulties to questions of historical method, more particularly to Pevsner's Hegelianism, and the way in which this progressivist idea of historical method is itself antithetical to appraisals of English culture by the English themselves. And this difficulty bears witness to a shift in Pevsner's historical project vis-à-vis England, a shift evidenced in the difference of trajectory between *Pioneers of Modern Design*, the movement of an English culture out into a European consciousness, and *The Englishness of English Art*,[58] an appraisal of the difference between English and Continental culture manifest through art.[59] The trajectory of exchange in Pevsner's actual writing of *Pioneers of Modern Design* is also important to consider. As Panayotis Tournikiotis observes, Pevsner wrote the book before he left Germany, but it was Pevsner's first in English, and was published in 1936 when he had made his home in England. Tournikiotis adds that Pevsner's history was operative in the sense of providing direction for architects, suggesting that the publication of the work in English was meant to provide an impetus for the development of (Continental) modernism there.[60]

Mobility and fashionized consumption

Thinking geographically about this narrative of translation between England and Germany shows its progressive trajectory to be problematic. This problematic can be understood through fashion, and the way in which it has actively been disavowed in order to construct this progressive trajectory. Wigley has shown how Muthesius's role in debates over fashion and style, and his situation of architecture within a logic of fashion, while crucial to the formation of the narratives of the modern movement, has been effaced from them. As was shown previously, Muthesius articulated *Sachlichkeit* within a logic of the external presentation of cleanliness and hygiene, which he understood through clothing. This articulation presented problems for under-standing how the unity of style might be differentiated from the transitoriness of fashion, but Wigley has argued that the logic of clothing as architecture remained central to the ensuing debates.[61] Clothing's relation to the subject is cast by Wigley in terms of mobility, and it is this sense of mobility or travelling that is the crucial aspect of the way fashion operates within early modernism:

> It is not that certain forms satisfy modern needs; the modern need is for a certain mobility of form. Like [Otto] Wagner, Muthesius sees the very mobility of fashions as matching the basic condition of the modern subject. And thus the structural role of fashion should be acknowledged rather than dismissed or censored.[62]

Wigley argues that the mobility of fashion as a structural question was understood by Muthesius, even as Muthesius would argue against the damaging cultural effects of particular transient fashions. It is this very sense of mobility that informs Muthesius's relation to England, as well as the Barr Smiths' relation to England. This latter relation brings out the problematic of fashion around the turn of the twentieth century very clearly, in that the Barr Smiths consumed the English interior as fashion, as part of a fashionable life, rather than as the possibility for a new unity of style at the level of national culture. The fineness of this difference between the Muthesiuses' and the Barr Smiths' relation to domesticity, and the way in which Wigley's sense of the disavowal of fashion can be seen to operate, is demonstrated in the similarity of their respective photographs of inhabitation. Yet considering this difference within a geohistorical frame, that is, considering the different trajectories of mobility in terms of the geographical relations between England and Germany on the one hand and England and Australia on the other, enables the complexity of this difference to be brought into focus. Part of this complexity revolves once again around labour, which cannot simply be seen in terms of a shift away from the untenable hand-labour practices of many proponents of the English Arts and Crafts and towards mechanized production in Germany. Rather, different conceptions of labour come into play according to particular possibilities in a geographical context of relations.

The look of the modern

At one level, Morris & Co. products, especially carpets, wallpapers and tapestries, involved time-consuming hand labour as an explicit ideological position in relation to the equivalent industrially produced domestic products on the market. The Barr Smiths' fashionized consumption of several of the most labour-intensive, and therefore expensive, products in the Morris & Co. range attests to the paradox in this practice of hand labour,[63] a paradox to which William Morris himself famously referred in his outbursts about having to minister to 'the swinish luxury of the rich'.[64]

Yet this paradox is not one of the untenability of hand labour in relation to the incipient mechanizations of modernism. A sense of labour as execution by the purchaser was a key part of the Barr Smiths' relation with Morris & Co. On the one hand, they bought tapestry sets from Morris & Co., which were executed in Adelaide by the Barr Smiths' daughters.[65] On the other hand, Robert Barr Smith and his architects were given the task of installing the complete interiors whose components were chosen and matched by Morris & Co. designers.[66] This latter example raises the issue of labour and geography explicitly, and can be understood in terms of an argument Tony Fry makes about the arrival of modernity in Australia:

> Australia was first constituted by imposition. The slow progression to self-determination, in conditions of dependency, was bonded to models of the modern drawn from elsewhere – especially Britain and, later, the USA. Modernity was thus not a driving historical condition of transforming social and economical conditions and their cultural consequences. Rather, it was a regime of signs – the arrived appearances of the modern world of metropolitan capitalism. . . . Objects, such as imported machinery and manufactured goods, and images, such as imported illustrated publications, acted to create a typology that registered the look and operation of the modern world.[67]

Modernity arrived as the ready made and totally constituted, without the attendant social and economic conditions that gave rise to this modernity. This has a consequence for the role of designer: 'The designer in such a context has to be named and interrogated not as creative subject but as deployed labourer, as expression of the corporation and commodity.'[68] In this context, the designer as deployed labourer is most aptly the inhabitant, the Barr Smith daughters making their tapestries, and Robert Barr Smith directing his architects as the labourers for the larger-scale work required for fitting out his interiors. These deployed labourers reassembled signs and objects that had been broken down for shipment back into a totality to be experienced through inhabitation.

This sense of labour as deployed after production leverages a similar view held in relation to inhabitation in the Germanic context. Schwarzer writes: 'During the closing decades of the nineteenth century, the user or inhabitant would increasingly be seen as a producer in his or her own right: a producer of useful, comfortable patterns of living.'[69] The consumption practices of Robert and Joanna Barr Smith are a kind of realization of Muthesius's desire for an English interior, the successful re-creation of an interior condition outside of its original territory, or, for the Barr Smiths in particular, the realization that an extension of that territory was possible by the literal buying-in of designed artefacts that would import the look of the metropolitan world. But the consumption practices of the Barr Smiths were a geopolitical impossibility for Muthesius, who found himself having to stage his argument for a national building-art through the concept of an exhibition of representations. In the form of representation, there needed to be a translation from one culturally specific situation to another. The Barr Smiths, on the other hand, were able to think of, and establish, a kind of cultural continuity between London and Adelaide, in which there was no translation, but rather a claim to homogeneity.

For Muthesius, the authenticity of the German bourgeoisie was based on how one made an interior through a conception of style and not fashion. For the Barr Smiths, the nature of their interiors resulted from acts of consumption that were conspicuous in the way they involved distance and travel: the personal ordering of the products and the commissioning of designed interior schemes in London, and the shipping of these interiors as component parts and artefacts between London and Adelaide. There was an almost aristocratic ease to the Barr Smiths' consumption patterns, an ease, and a sense of class distinction, created by great wealth. But what was arriving for them was the *appearance* of metropolitan culture. Though they themselves travelled and participated in the fashionable culture of London, their participation was episodic. The legacy of their consumption practices remained in the geographical distance between London and Adelaide, a distance requiring an importation of appearances, a distance heightening their fashionability. Muthesius, on the other hand, was faced with a situation of a different order, a situation where he intervened in the managing of a set of economic relations that had ramifications for patterns, rather than just instances, of consumption and participation in metropolitan life.

But this is not simply a question of different personal desires. In its doubleness, the interior acted as a mode of organization for relations between design, labour, consumption, culture and economics, a mode of organization within which particular possibilities for agents are figured. And this mode of organization is unthinkable outside a geography that does not simply divide centres from margins. At one level, the Barr Smiths were rendered marginal to a dominant geopolitics of relation between England and Germany, a relation that Muthesius articulated with respect to the revitalization of German industry. The Barr Smiths, on the other hand, were consumers in, and of, the tightly bound economic and cultural exchanges between England and Australia. They were at the physical margin of an imperial centre. But at another level, through what Fry calls 'an appeal to other means',[70] the Barr Smiths enacted a kind of consumption-based freedom because of their position of marginality. But this was a freedom that was consequent upon great wealth, and, in Wigley's terms, it was a freedom that reveals the very structuring of the modern consumption of design through fashion. When the stake for both of these relations to England – that of Muthesius on the one hand, and the Barr Smiths on the other – was the successful translation of an English domesticity, the Barr Smiths' marginality provided them with a more instant and obvious material creation of that fantasy.

Discontinuous modernities

This discussion of the geohistory of relations works in the place of one which would normally position the practices of those on the periphery to be merely the result of a diffusion from centres. Treating two geographical contexts relationally through deploying and interrogating key concepts such as fashion and labour sets up a more nuanced understanding of the differing stakes involved in the uptake of the English interior outside of England around the turn of the twentieth century. This understanding also works to critique the reductive trajectories of historical progression and influence in architecture and design. In considering trajectories of exchange to be multiple and contingent to particular geographical situations, the idea of a single, dominant story of the development of architecture and design from the late nineteenth century onwards becomes an ideology, a fabrication itself tied to the contingencies of a particular geographical context. In terms of Pevsner's own Anglo-German view of the 'success' of the modern movement in Europe in the 1930s, this comment from Taylor rings true, and resonates with Benjamin's critique of the historicism which governed Germanic historical thought:

> behind modernization itself, there is a taken-for-granted geohistorical perspective which combines a Whig history with a diffusionist geography. The former is defined as history whose story celebrates the present. This takes the form of defining important features of contemporary society and tracing their lineage back in time so that the story told is one which culminates in the success of today's society.[71]

In addition, Fry's idea of the agency of the marginal producing one particular version of a multiple modernity questions the taken-for-granted geohistorical perspective of modernization. Thus one does not need to elevate the status of marginal figures such as the Barr Smiths. To do so would only extend the project of universalization in history writing. Rather, the leverage of the marginal raises the issue that, as Taylor suggests:

> Modernity does not just appear as the result of any 'natural' evolution; there are many discontinuities, with both the rise and the development of the modern world creating quite different forms of what it is to be modern. Similarly, the modern does not simply exist as a continuous geographical gradient from high to low: there are discontinuities between core and periphery zones of the system creating quite different forms of what it is to be modern.[72]

Above all, the consideration of different geographical possibilities in relation to *photographs* of the interior shows these multiple relations to be mediated and not simply reducible to one another in a direct, transparent comparison. While both the Muthesiuses and the Barr Smiths might have been 'dreaming of England' in their interiors, the way they acted on this fantasy gave rise to a complex and varied uptake of the English interior in a geography of exchange. The only thing they really had in common was a technology of representation that could provide an externalized picture, a 'proof' of their materialization of this fantasy. Through this technology, both couples constructed and registered the look of the modern. The constructed natural-ness of these scenes would have come into force when, in an idle moment at home, they might have glanced upon these photographs and been given a representation of how they looked when they supposedly were not conscious of 'how they looked at home'. Via a strategic forgetting of the intrusion of the photographic apparatus into their interior, the photographs frame a scene that could be entered by these subjects at will. By entering this frame, a frame within the space of their interior, the inhabitants reiterated their inhabitation of that interior and identified (with) themselves as comfortable, bourgeois domestic subjects. Such an identification worked through a perceptual moment that doubled the reality of the domesticity that surrounded them.

But such an identification, such a securing of a domestic identity, involves both the construction of a domestic scene through photography, and a forgetting that such a scene is a construction. Thus photography veils the complex process of inhabitation, even as this veiling is a part of this very process, inviting viewers to 'enter the frame' of the represented interior. In Chapter 5, this photographic veiling of the interior will be confronted in terms of modernism's construal of the interior as both space and image.

Recognizing the interior

Space and image

Chapter 4 highlighted how interior photographs can render similar discontinuous manifestations of modernity. This photographic veiling disturbs the idea of there being transparent access to a supposedly primary spatial manifestation of the interior. This chapter focuses on how to think about the interactions between the interior as space and as image in various forms. The context for this discussion is the way in which Adolf Loos and Le Corbusier dealt with what Walter Benjamin called the bourgeois interior's liquidation. Considering Loos and Le Corbusier together augments the network of relations surrounding architecture's relation to the interior. Loos was the architect and cultural critic who made one of the most acute contemporary critiques of the German Werkbund,[1] and specifically Hermann Muthesius's goals of 'quality of workmanship and the creation of a style for our times';[2] however, this critique also reveals a shared affinity with and admiration for English domestic architecture and ways of life, about which, as he acknowledges, Muthesius instructed a German readership.[3] Yet in both substance and form, Loos's critique shifted focus away from architecture intervening directly within the world of the commodity and its design and production. He used print media to project his critique,[4] and the visual medium of photography both to critique and to conceptualize an architectural response to the problems of domesticity. The case of Le Corbusier is similarly invested in the role various forms of media play in articulating a modernist sense of spatial organization. He confronted directly the relation between two- and three-dimensional expressions of a spatial conception, grappling with doubleness in the wake of the interior's liquidation.

The pairing of Loos and Le Corbusier engages explicitly with the work of Beatriz Colomina, who has argued that modern architecture – and specifically its domestic manifestations – only became modern in relation to mass media.[5] In responding to Colomina's work, the argument will be made that modern architecture could only link effectively with mass media through the conceptual apparatus of the interior. Rather than appearing to take an explicitly anti-domestic stance, modern architecture exploited the interior's doubleness in new ways.[6]

Loos's photographic effects

In a parody Loos wrote of the Jugendstil artist/architect, a rich man decides to let art into his home as a response to his bourgeois ennui. The man goes to 'a famous architect and says: "Bring Art to me, bring Art into my home. Cost is no object."' The architect, 'who did not wait for him to say it twice',[7] directs all of the interior decoration trades to create an entirely new interior for the man. The rich man is overjoyed, but soon discovers that he has to learn how to live in this new interior, that it is so tightly controlled by the architect's vision of art and an artistic life that there is literally no room for him to accumulate his own belongings and have them placed within the interior. The full impact of what the artist/architect has done to the man is communicated through the presence of his family, who, on the occasion of the man's birthday, for the first time come into the frame as inhabitants of the interior. They present the man with gifts, and the man then summons the architect to help him place the gifts in an appropriate manner. The architect becomes irate, claiming that the man should not accept such 'traces', that through his design of the interior, he has given the man everything, and has 'completed' him. This situation makes the man deeply unhappy, as he comes to the realization that his identity is fixed in place, and is unable to develop further through an ongoing relation to the world of things. The interior spatializes a frozen image of the man, and the actions of his family show at once their exclusion from this image. In Benjamin's terms, at the moment of its total capture by architecture as art, the interior as a space of inhabitation is liquidated.

Loos's writing and architectural practice make a response to this liquidation. Rather than attempt to abandon the interior – as if such a move would really be possible, since part of the historical concept of the interior is that it is additional to architecture, and made as much by inhabitation as by a designer's intent – Loos negotiates a divorce between the interior and the architecture which encloses and makes space for it. In this context, the idea of the inhabitant as naturally and exclusively male is overtaken by an argument about the interior that articulates perspectives on the social and architectural mediation of male and female identity.

Interior, exterior and identity

The domestic interior is conceptualized by Benjamin around the figure of the male inhabitant. It is a space of refuge for him from the public world of the city and its commerce. Yet to avoid the constrictions of his interior, Loos's poor little rich man ends up spending more time at work, attending to his business affairs. This lack of an interior has left the man displaced. Massimo Cacciari has cast this displacement, and Loos's designed response to it, in philosophical terms:

> Like his exteriors, Loos confronts the absence of place head-on: to attempt to reverse its destiny would be to attempt to turn the idea of place into a utopia, and, paradoxically, to reconfirm the very principle of *Entortung* [dislocation] he is attempting to investigate and put into question. In the *Entortung* every 'pure' language of place is a utopia and hence part of the same destiny of uprootedness or displacement that accompanies the *ars aedificandi* of the West. For this reason, Loos'

architecture does not seek the rationalization of 'pure' places, but is aimed at showing the endless contradiction between the thought-out space of calculation, the equivalence of the exteriors, and the possibility of place, the hope of a place.[8]

For Cacciari, the possibility of place is the possibility of the unproductive, the possibility of those things found in the collection, things 'freed from the drudgery of being useful',[9] finding an interior. An interior of unproductivity is needed to counter the rationalization of the metropolis, a rationalization ruled by the exchange value of money. Such a place can only be created within the metropolis, lest it fall into the paradoxical position of simply re-enacting the displacement from which it springs. This situation of the unproductive is characterized by Cacciari with Lou Andreas-Salomé's remembrance of collecting buttons, tokens which, unlike money, have no exchange value, and are collected precisely for this unproductive significance. Cacciari argues that this unproductivity both necessitates and instantiates the interior, and in respect of Loos's interiors, he suggests that this sort of thinking is a facet of 'Loos's profoundly "feminine" side'.[10] It is not that a Loos interior looks feminine in relation to the masculine exterior. Rather, the interior is differentiated from – though enclosed by – the exterior to the extent that the interior is inhabited and not simply seen.

As part of his larger critique of the culture that produced the poor little rich man and his architect, Loos wrote about the way in which clothing mediated male and female identities in the metropolis. Loos begins his 1898 article 'Ladies' Fashion' thus: 'Ladies' fashion! You disgraceful chapter in the history of civilization! You tell of mankind's secret desires.'[11] In this characteristically hyperbolic statement, Loos shows his dismay at the way in which women's clothes are linked to what he terms sensuality. He blames a fashion-conscious culture for forcing women to appeal to men's sensuality through outward display. As masculine tastes towards female sensuality change, so do women's fashions. Ornament and colour as key modes of registering change in fashion link women's clothing to cultural regressiveness. For Loos, modern culture is achieved in the extent to which the desire for ornament is overcome. For those who are modern, clothing is chosen for its appropriateness to particular situations, especially where productive labour is concerned. In writing on men's fashion around the same time, Loos argues that unornamented clothing allows the man to negotiate different public and social situations according to the appropriateness of his attire.[12] The gentleman's suit masks his individuality, which is too strong to be represented directly through clothing. Loos comments: 'In order to be dressed correctly, one must not stand out at *the centre of culture*.'[13] The idea of being inconspicuous means that the man has a certain mobility. Unlike the woman who is a slave to fashion, the man can go about his business unnoticed. If women were modern, they would stand alongside men, dressed in tailored clothes, and appeal to them 'by economic independence earned through work'.[14]

Regardless of what else might be said about it, Loos's position on fashion has a spatial consequence. The anonymity allowed by the mask of the gentleman's suit relates to the equivalence of the exteriors of Loos's domestic buildings, and the way they participate in what Cacciari terms the 'thought-out space of calculation'. As such, they exist in tension with 'the possibility of place', a possibility to be secured in an interior held within but not revealed through the exterior mask, the proper place for the sensual. For Cacciari, the mask is a masculine accoutrement that hides a feminine side, philosophically that part of a masculine identity that seeks an interior place, and manages this place by not revealing its nature to the exterior. At the level of social relations, Janet Stewart has argued:

> The emancipatory promise of modernity which would allow the endless play of difference beneath a veneer of homogeneity fails at the level of sexual equality, and the possibility of social interaction in the bourgeois public sphere is denied to women. . . . Loos maintains that while men occupy the public sphere, a woman's place is in the home.[15]

For Loos, the possibility that women be modernized and join men in the public sphere is predicated on a masculinization of women's clothing, the attainment of a mask. Stewart concludes that there is an 'essentialist distinction between male and female'[16] at play in Loos's thinking.

Stewart's conclusion is, however, somewhat troubling. It provides the way in which one might, at best, condemn Loos intellectually as a product of his time. The essentialism of Cacciari's alignment of the feminine with the interior for putatively 'philosophical' reasons, those that privilege masculine identity in modernity, is equally troubling. And while the arguments of Cacciari and Stewart might be read as being opposed to each other – Stewart's argument against Loos could equally apply to Cacciari – Stewart is still bound to the essentialist thinking she criticizes. Loos may well be thinking gender in terms of essential differences, and the way in which they buy into equally essential differences between the modern and the non-modern or backward in culture. But Stewart confirms an essentialist account of gender by arguing that it is the gender balance, rather than the essentialist framing, which is wrong; however, there is another interpretation of Loos's work which avoids concluding on, and therefore repeating, the essentialist alignment of the feminine and the interior.

Gender is an inextricable aspect of how domesticity is understood, but historically so. In other words, it is through the way in which the bourgeois domestic interior emerged as a doubled condition in the nineteenth century that gender becomes an important question. And the main aspect of this doubled condition that needs emphasizing in relation to Loos's work is how the construction of the photographic image relates to the spatial sense of his interiors.

The feminine masquerade and photography's veil

The mask as a masculine accoutrement of modernity has not been its only designation within modern concepts of identity. Indeed, femininity has been considered a masquerade within a certain strand of psychoanalytical thinking. In 1929, the time Loos was completing his most celebrated houses, Joan Riviere published her seminal study 'Womanliness as a Masquerade'. She argues that womanliness, what might be understood as the recognizability of female identity, is 'put on', is the result of a masquerade.[17] In the male-dominated world of professions and public social interaction, a woman's participation is predicated on both a masculine identification such that participation is desired, and a resultant masquerade as a woman as a defence against the implications for social interaction of such a masculine identification. This masquerade is not a simple case, as it might have been for Loos, of women joining men in tailored clothes. Indeed, it has a much closer relation to Loos's arguments about women's clothing, about their appeal through what he terms sensuality. As Stephen Heath has argued in respect of Riviere's argument: 'In the masquerade the woman mimics an authentic – genuine – womanliness but then authentic womanliness is such a mimicry, *is* the masquerade ([Riviere:] "they are the same thing"); to be a woman is to dissimulate a fundamental masculinity, femininity is that dissimulation.'[18] The Lacanian reiteration of this position is summarized by Heath: 'Adornment is the woman, she exists veiled; only thus can she represent lack, be what is wanted: lack "is never presented other than as a reflection on a veil."'[19]

This reverses the terms of Cacciari's argument. It is a masculinity that is dissimulated through the masquerade, rather than an essential femininity, an essential unproductivity that might be hidden through the masculine mask as exterior blankness. One could work through this reversed position on the mask with respect to Loos's arguments about fashion, that is, in the realm of male and female social relations,[20] and it would be instructive to do so, but this position presents a way of engaging further with Cacciari's designation of Loos's interior as itself feminine, and of testing this association beyond an essentialist alignment.

For Cacciari, the interior is precisely the veiled, the unseen: 'The Loosian difference between seeing and inhabiting, interior and exterior, seeks to preserve yet another place where this [forgotten] dimension [of dwelling] might be collected. This difference is the utmost interior.'[21] Loos might well agree, but on terms that immediately engage with the representation of his interiors in external contexts:

> It is my greatest pride that the interiors which I have created are completely lacking in effect when photographed; that the people who live in them do not recognize their own apartments from the photographs[.] . . . The honour of seeing my works published in the various architectural journals is something I have had to do without. I am denied the satisfaction of my vanity.
>
> Does this perhaps mean I am working in a vacuum? Nothing of mine is known. But this is where the power of my ideas and the rightness of my teachings become apparent. I, the unpublished architect, I, the man working in a vacuum, am the only one among thousands who has real influence.[22]

Loos made these comments in his 1910 article entitled 'Architecture', where he blames representation – drawing in the design phase and photography in the publication phase – for the separation between architect and craftsman that had led to the culturally backward unity of the arts manifest in the poor little rich man's interior. In this particular take on the problem, Loos argues that the rendered drawings of design which are handed to the craftsman/builder for execution force the craftsman to reproduce designed, primarily ornamental, schemes, rather than allowing the craftsman to continue with the traditions of building and manufacture that have given rise to functionally appropriate objects and domestic spaces.

In taking up these issues that Loos raises, Beatriz Colomina links his rejection of representation to his conceptualization of the *Raumplan*, which comes together through an experience and an adjustment to space as it is perceived and felt three-dimensionally in construction.[23] It was not that photography somehow failed Loos. Rather, he was antagonistic towards received notions about the transparency of representation. The doubleness of the interior echoes here. Colomina argues that Loos's interiors involve a complex interaction between representation and spatial condition: 'Looking at the photographs, it is easy to imagine oneself in these precise, static positions, usually indicated by the unoccupied furniture. The photographs suggest that it is intended that these spaces be comprehended by occupation, by using this furniture, by "entering" the photograph, by inhabiting it.'[24] She adds a footnote to this comment, saying that 'the perception of space is produced by its representations; in this sense, built space has no more authority than do drawings, photographs or descriptions.'[25] Colomina comments on Loos's involvement in manipulations of many photographs of his interiors.[26] As such, she argues that photography masks interior spatial experience,[27] ensuring a kind of privacy for the inhabiting subject, but a privacy that is implicated with publicity and publication.

The photograph as unrecognizable is important to think through in this context, and it is useful to turn to concepts called upon by Benjamin to come to grips with the fate of experience in modernity. For Benjamin, the photograph occasions the withering of the aura of what is reproduced. Specifically, it severs the sort of intense, cultic relation to things that is the province of the collector in the bourgeois interior.[28] Benjamin's reading of Proust and Baudelaire coalesces on this point of the withering of the aura, and engages with the sense of modern displacement Cacciari calls up:

> If we think of the associations which, at home in the *mémoire involontaire*, seek to cluster around an object of perception, and if we call those associations the aura of that object, then the aura attaching to the object of a perception corresponds precisely to the experience [*Erfahrung*] which, in the case of an object of use, inscribes itself as long practice. The techniques inspired by the camera and subsequent analogous types of apparatus extend the range of *mémoire volontaire*; these techniques make it possible at any time to retain an event – as image and sound – through the apparatus. Thus they represent important achievements of a society in which long practice is in decline.[29]

The photograph retains the 'event' of the interior, but at the expense of the aura of the objects contained within it, and indeed the aura of the milieu of inhabitation. Culturally, photography surpasses the interior with the decline of long experience. The owners of Loos houses do not recognize their interiors through photography because there is no link to the long experience that the interior should nurture, or allow, in Cacciari's words, as the possibility of the unproductive, the possibility of a place. In becoming an external, circulating image, any association with the *mémoire involontaire*, that special memory of the domestic, is lost. The photograph is a veil which cannot be seen through. It is a point of severance.

But with Loos, the photographs of his interiors are not simply mechanical, subject-less copies. They recapture something of the aura of the unique and unexpected. It is useful to consider some manipulations in two sets of photographs in order to understand how the photograph might simultaneously mask but also manipulate a sense of interior spatial experience. One set shows Loos's Khuner House in Payerbach, Austria (1930), where a picture window is shown with two alternative views (Figures 5.1 and 5.2). The other set shows the music room in Loos's

5.1
**Adolf Loos,
Khuner House,
Payerbach,
Austria, 1930.
View of master's
room**
By permission
Albertina, Vienna.
ALA 2292

5.2
**Adolf Loos,
Khuner House,
Payerbach,
Austria, 1930.
Alternative view
of master's room**
Source: As
published in
Heinrich Kulka
(ed.), *Adolf Loos:
Das Werk des
Architekten*,
Vienna: Löcker,
1930, plate 250

Moller House in Vienna (1928), where a cello appears to sit in a glass cabinet (Figure 5.3), which is otherwise shown with an opaque surface (Figure 5.4). For the Khuner House, the application of a technique such as photomontage or combination printing was most likely a technical necessity. In the practice of interior photography, windows generally provided a direct light source and were not often positioned in shot. If they were, they were likely to appear 'blown out', as luminous light sources rather than

5.3
Adolf Loos, Moller House, Vienna, 1928. View from music room into dining room showing cello in glass cabinet
By permission Albertina, Vienna. ALA 2453

5.4
Adolf Loos, Moller House, Vienna, 1928. Alternative view from music room into dining room showing opaque glass cabinet
Source: As published in Heinrich Kulka (ed.), *Adolf Loos: Das Werk des Architekten*, Vienna: Löcker, 1930, plate 230

as transparent membranes framing a view.[30] Loos and his photographer would have exploited this necessity, choosing two different views for the picture window.[31] For the Moller House, this exploitation of technical possibilities within the medium of photography is taken further with the introduction of the cello into the image. Referring to the photography of Loos's interiors more broadly, Colomina emphasizes the ways in which, through the spaces' interaction with photography, devices such as framing and reflection are played up as part of a pictorial-spatial composition.[32]

The techniques of photographic manipulation developed from the late nineteenth century with the goal of reproducing a more 'natural' scene in the interior.[33] Colomina, on the other hand, argues that Loos's photographs 'draw the viewer's attention to the artifice involved in the photographic process'.[34] These two positions appear to be mutually exclusive, if not antagonistic, but both might in fact be two sides of the same coin if one recalls the idea of the feminine as masquerade. As a compensation for a masculine identification, the masquerade attempts to produce the 'naturally' feminine, but it can only do so in the extent to which the masquerade is the manipulation of artifice. In this way, the photographed interior resonates with the feminine masquerade, doubled between the appearance of 'natural' spatial depth, and the play of the representational surface. This resonance is a productive one to recognize because the stability of identity – what cannot be maintained through the decline in long practice – and especially the stability of gendered domestic subjectivity, is disturbed by it. It is a way to think the feminine that escapes a naturalized recognition and a locatability in a stable, spatial interior.[35] In addition, the interior photograph is a counterpart to the blank façade, a corrective to the idea that anything more than a further masking might be revealed beneath this façade. As such, it disturbs the masking function of the façade in doubling this function at the same time as it denies the façade's assured functioning as a mask. Loos clearly wanted to restrict the circulation of the 'feminine' photographic interior, perhaps, one could infer, because he realized it had the same power of circulability and dissimulation as the gentleman, Herr Loos himself, in his finely tailored English suit.

There is something else going on here. Loos's manipulations of these photographs pull them back within an auratic world of individuated, collectible objects. As much as the interior as the Benjaminian refuge of the collector might be imagined to be its purely spatial sense, the image surface of Loos's photographs obeys this same logic. The technique of photomontage allows the image surface to 'collect' objects and fragments external to it, and through this collection, to interiorize them. The cello in the Moller House is 'freed from the drudgery of being useful' in order to be positioned as a kind of token in the music room. The views through the picture window of the Khuner House, in their very interchangeability, operate as the colportage pictures Benjamin highlighted as belonging to the bourgeois interior, whereby 'The same picture can be copied twenty times without exhausting demand and, as the vogue prescribes, each well-kept drawing room wants to have one of these fashionable *furnishings*.'[36]

Loos is not simply fulfilling bourgeois fancies, however. Through photographic manipulation, he recognizes the doubleness of the interior, that it is at once image and spatial condition. Yet this is a doubleness more complex, more historically bound to the status of culture and experience than Colomina's argument that neither space nor representational image has more authority. What is at stake here is precisely authority, or what Loos called influence. He makes a claim for the 'power of the example', by which he means the power of the embodied experience of built space. But photography is not ignored or rejected in this claim. Its technical parameters are marshalled to support the idea of the power of the example, a power which is ultimately associated with memory and experience.

Loos's photographic manipulations also produce an uncanny effect. They deny photography's transparency by playing with spatial expectation – a cello is seen where it is unexpected, or a picture-window view is substituted for a slightly different one. These discrepancies, the 'ineffectiveness' of these spaces in photographs, create an uncanniness which might trigger recognition as a self-conscious act, an act, as with Freud in his train carriage, which shows the interior's stake in a particularly modern understanding of subjectivity. This recognition would be what Lacan called the orthopaedic locatability of the subject in space, where the veracity of the image is an effect of the subject's ability to recognize themselves as the point of origin for the space which the image constructs. The uncanniness of the image, its constructed nature, shows that this locatability is not natural, but is itself a constructed mastery of space.

This recognition would also be that which attaches to Proust's madeleine. Recognition in this sense is the affiliation of a sense perception with unconscious impulses 'jostling' in the interior of the psyche. The jolt of recognition sparked by an uncanny image would trigger a chain of associations of spatial situations, those things which are unpicturable in not being held in conscious memory, but which might be triggered by pictures. Loos himself might be put in the position of inhabitant, not recognizing a photographed interior, disdaining the very idea of it, but actually working on the photographic surface to produce something like the spark of recognition and memory, something like the *punctum* of the image. Here Loos is describing his own childhood interior, describing precisely what cannot be pictured. It is a memory which a photograph of an interior, in its unrecognizability, in its inadequacy, might prompt:

> Take the table: a crazy jumble of a table with some dreadful metalwork. But *our* table, *our* table! Can you imagine what that meant? Can you imagine what wonderful hours we spent at it? By lamplight! In the evening when I was a little boy I just could not tear myself away from it, and father kept having to imitate the nightwatchman's horn to make me scuttle off in fright into the nursery. My sister Hermine spilled ink on it when she was a little tiny baby. And the pictures of my parents! What dreadful frames! But they were a wedding present from father's workmen. And this old-fashioned chair here! A leftover from grandmother's home. And here an embroidered slipper in which you can hang the clock. Made in kindergarten by my sister Irma. Every piece of furniture, every object, every thing had a story to tell, the story of our family. Our home was never finished, it developed with us, and we with it.[37]

As a refutation of the Jugendstil interior, this memory is centred on childhood and familial experience. For Loos himself, this is a regressive memory, a symptom of his displacement in a modern culture of upheaval. The photographed interior understood through the idea of feminine dissimulation instantiates a lack which produces this symptom. Mary Ann Doane comments that this positioning of the feminine as lack produces a 'mirror-effect by means of which the question of the woman reflects only the man's own ontological doubts'.[38] If the domestic interior is a refuge, it is chimerical, experienced uncannily through its doubled condition.

Le Corbusier's problem with images

One encounters further disjunction in moving from Loos to Le Corbusier. While for Loos the possibilities for an interior are problematized in the wake of Jugendstil, Le Corbusier's houses seem to offer an image of an entirely new domestic condition.[39] While for Loos photography articulates the dislocation at stake in the possibility of an interior, for Le Corbusier photography provides one means for architecture to achieve a kind of 'post-interior' domesticity, where the interior as the provision of soft furnishing, as the covering of an inside space with pliable, impressionable stuff, is seemingly obliterated. In Colomina's terms, this is the moment when modern architecture as mass media emerges.

As was shown in Chapter 1, Benjamin wrote about the possibility of the new in domesticity arising through coming to terms with the poverty of experience. Yet as Francesco Dal Co has noted, this possibility was allied with a 'stereotypical image of the modern – an image given such credence that even Benjamin is deceived by it'.[40] This deception is most evident when Benjamin writes of the emancipatory potential of glass: 'adjustable, movable, glass-covered dwellings of the kind since built by Loos and Le Corbusier'.[41] Benjamin's apparently simplistic account of modern architecture, and misconstrual of Loos, seems to vindicate Loos's argument about the veiling effects of photography, and points to how those effects might contribute to stereotyping the image of the modern.

But there is no deeper, truer beyond of the image. This is not what Loos's arguments were made to suggest. Rather, there is a discrepancy between the imagistic and the spatial. For Loos, this discrepancy illuminates the particularly modern condition within which domesticity finds itself, and Benjamin's problematic clarion call for a glass architecture needs to be seen in this light. In the context of the larger scope of his thinking, Benjamin's more 'programmatic' accounts of the problem of experience, such as the one found in 'Experience and Poverty', reveal an ambivalence about the fate of domesticity in his time.[42] One would do well to hold on to this ambivalence, and consider that the interior is not simply obliterated at the point of its supposed liquidation. Nor does it simply undergo a change of style, from nineteenth-century, to Jugendstil, to modernist. Rather, the doubleness of the interior still carries an interpretive force for thinking through the consequences of this liquidation. There remains a conceptual consistency structured around doubleness that is not about a progression of decorative styles.

Images flat and spatial

Though he might have thought he was – and was thought to be – beyond the problem of the liquidation of the bourgeois interior, that is, beyond the problem of Jugendstil (or, more particularly, Art Nouveau), Le Corbusier was having to deal with a poor little rich man. Maison La Roche, completed in Paris in 1925, was commissioned by banker Raoul La Roche to house his collection of modernist paintings, which included works by Picasso, Braque, Léger, Gris, and several Purist canvases by Le Corbusier and Amédée Ozenfant.[43] The following passage drawn from a letter from La Roche to Le Corbusier, despite its hyperbole, presents the ongoing problem of a 'total art' of the interior:

> Do you recall the origin of my undertaking? 'La Roche, when you have a fine collection like yours, you should have a house built worthy of it.' And my response: 'Fine Jeanneret, make this house for me.' Now what happened? The house, once built, was so beautiful that on seeing it I cried: 'it's almost a pity to put paintings into it!' Nevertheless I did so. How could I have done otherwise? Do I not have certain obligations with regard to my painters, of whom you yourself are one? I commissioned from you a 'frame for my collection'. You provided me with a 'poem of walls'. Which of us two is most to blame?[44]

There is a peculiar confusion here between Le Corbusier as a fine-art painter and as architect and decorator, as constructor and painter of walls. The proximity between these practices sits uneasily with La Roche and with Le Corbusier himself. While his collection of paintings may have instantiated the brief for his house, and necessitated its specific gallery component, La Roche's paintings, and especially the Purist canvases of Le Corbusier and Ozenfant, fulfil an interiorizing function themselves in a way not dissimilar to Loos's manipulated photographs. While they might be described generically as still lifes, conceptually the Purist paintings are interiors in the representational sense given by the term.[45] They appropriate objects that are wrested from their everyday utility, not so much to support the inhabitant's illusions about experience, as might the nineteenth-century collection, but to reorientate the direction of painterly representation. The objects depicted in La Roche's Purist canvases are ones which Le Corbusier celebrated as *objets-types*, objects such as bottles, glasses, pipes and musical instruments. Maison La Roche itself contained furniture *objets-types* such as Le Corbusier's favoured Thonet bentwood chairs, which had supposedly risen by a kind of 'mechanical selection' to a level of universality.[46]

At one level, the paintings encapsulate an interior sensibility of the collection of objects. At another level, they are arrayed in a space that is producing the same sorts of effects as the paintings (Figure 5.5). In discussing the Purism of both Le Corbusier's paintings and the space of Maison La Roche, Rosalind Krauss has described their effects in terms of frontality and rotation.[47] For Krauss, the space of the house allows one to perceive its geometry by moving through and around the space, an effect of rotation. The moments of possible pause in this movement, designated by the interior and exterior balconies of the house, allow a different kind of grasp of the space's composition, one of frontality. Krauss describes this difference

5.5
**Le Corbusier,
Maison La Roche,
Paris, 1925. View
of gallery**
Photograph by
F. R. Yerbury.
© F. R. Yerbury/
Architectural
Association

between frontality and rotation as one between 'ideation and experience. And what Le Corbusier demands of architectural composition is that it should acknowledge the mutual interdependence of the one on the other.'[48] When it comes to Le Corbusier's paintings, Krauss suggests that 'Pictorial space is that which cannot be entered or circulated through; it is irremediably space viewed from a distance, and is therefore eternally resigned to frontality.'[49] For Krauss, here quoting Léger, the relation between frontality and rotation contributed to 'giving order to sensation'. This was an order made manifest in the relation between painting and architecture. Krauss writes: 'Depicted object, painting, room, building: all of them were widening concentric circles in the matrix of sensation; all of them were nested brackets in an equation which was to equal coherence.'[50]

Yet there is evidence to suggest that the discrepancy at the core of the interior's doubleness lurks within this supposed compositional solution in the wake of the interior's liquidation. Le Corbusier himself was distinctly aware of an interference between the paintings and the space in Maison La Roche. It emerged most clearly when he was thinking through the distribution of the paintings around the house. Tim Benton quotes from a letter Le Corbusier sent to Ozenfant over the issue of the hang, one that eventually led to a falling out between the two men. Le Corbusier writes:

> It's about La Roche's paintings: He asked me to take care of the hanging of the pictures in such a way that the arrangement should fit in with the architecture. . . . He insisted on reserving the gallery exclusively for Purism, having himself removed the Picassos which I had hung there. When I dropped in at La Roche's yesterday on a practical matter, I noted the great transformations which you made. Nothing could please me

more than that you should carry out the hanging, but I would like it done by agreement with me – not with the aim of protecting my own interests (since you will have seen that I kept a good place for you) – but simply with the intention of ensuring that the La Roche house should not take on the look of a house of a (postage-stamp) collector. I insist that certain parts of the architecture should be entirely free of paintings, so as to create a double effect of pure architecture on the one hand, and pure paintings on the other.[51]

This concern over the paintings becoming 'decorative' can be read in light of Christopher Reed's argument that the 'heroic' avant-gardes, and Le Corbusier in particular, defined modernism as the antithesis of the domestic.[52] And Benton suggests that around the time of completing Maison La Roche, Le Corbusier began 'to prioritize architecture, and architectural values, over those of painting'.[53] Yet there is not a simple prioritization of architecture, or a fear of the domestication of his art, at stake here. Le Corbusier is attempting to direct the contribution to the interior of specifically chosen paintings, their arrangement being the province of the architect and not the inhabitant. This would be the continuation, conceptually, of Jugendstil/Art Nouveau's 'total design' ethos. In a stylistic sense at this point in time, Le Corbusier was clearly not an Art Nouveau architect.[54] Yet conceptually, he was negotiating the fallout of the liquidation of the interior, a fallout which had to do with how the doubleness of the interior, its existence through spatial and image-based conditions, was handled. In Le Corbusier's figuring of this problem, transformed conceptions of space and image merge in a diachronic experience. In this way, Le Corbusier describes the Maison La Roche as

> an *architectural promenade*. You enter: the architectural spectacle at once offers itself to the eye. You follow an itinerary and the perspectives develop with great variety, developing a play of light on the walls or making pools of shadow. Large windows open up views of the exterior where the architectural unity is reasserted. . . . Here, reborn for our modern eye, are historic architectural discoveries: the pilotis, the long windows, the roof garden, the glass façade. Once again we must learn at the end of the day to appreciate what is available.[55]

While Le Corbusier might write of historic architectural discoveries, they are ones nonetheless involved with a revolution in perception and experience, based implicitly on what is no longer available in a supposed historical continuity of architectural production, but what can be 'reborn' for modern eyes.[56] In this situation, Le Corbusier gives the image a cinematic value. He writes: 'Architecture is judged by eyes that see, by the head that turns, and the legs that walk. Architecture is not a synchronic phenomenon but a successive one, made up of pictures adding themselves one to another, following each other in time and space, like music.'[57] The interior is not simply obliterated by an architecture of transparency and movement. Rather, an interior is formed in a particular perceptual mode, rather than being identifiable in terms of enclosure and encasing. For Colomina, this condition means that the house is not simply experienced like cinema, but itself becomes a kind of movie camera.[58] Thus rather than the transparency of glass dissolving boundaries, the window performs in relation to a particular sort of moving image capture within the interior.

Theodor Adorno's thoughts on the bourgeois domestic interior, thoughts which Benjamin referenced in *The Arcades Project*, become important here. Adorno used the interior as a metaphor to discuss the structuring of Søren Kierkegaard's philosophical thinking, particularly his idea that the world is given space for thought through semblance. Semblance is given in reflection, just as the exterior is reflected inside by the window mirrors, called 'spies', of the bourgeois interior:

> The window mirror is a characteristic furnishing of the spacious nine-teenth century apartment. . . . The function of the window mirror is to project the endless row of apartment buildings into the isolated bourgeois living room; by the mirror, the living room dominates the reflected row at the same time as it is delimited by it[.][59]

In the Maison La Roche, the exterior delimits the interior through the image capture effected by the horizontal window, a window dimension that encapsulates the broad-ness of view that the window mirror gave to the vertical window. For the peripatetic eye, and in terms of Le Corbusier's architectural claims, this becomes a mechanism to 'reassert the architectural unity'. It is also a way for the interior to be delimited. The horizontal window frames and flattens a world which is held at a distance, a world which is split from the interior world created in the house, but whose semblance delimits it.[60]

Yet the perceptual experience of the Maison La Roche, and a supposed new unity of architecture and the interior, is not so neatly resolved. The paintings figure forth a different perceptual problem. Krauss's argument about the nesting of Purist frames of painting and house, experienced through frontal and rotational perceptual modes, breaks down in the face of Le Corbusier's concern over the hang. His concern reveals that the paintings' flatness as images disturbs the three-dimensionality of space formed like a cinematic succession, one that brooks no pauses for a frontal appreciation of the paintings.[61] One plan for overcoming the actual presence of the paintings on the walls involved installing an exhibition cabinet in the gallery, where paintings might be stored and engaged with in much the same way as trinkets or books, being taken out when needed for contemplation.[62] In this way, the paintings and the space might truly have been separated, and therefore would have doubled each other in a way that reinforced the claims of each to Purist experi-mentation.[63] Unlike the horizontal windows, which allowed for a genuine architectural novelty, the presence of the paintings reveals that Le Corbusier was still dealing with the interior as the space of the collection, and that his attempts to refigure it in a Purist sense echo the crisis of the interior at the point of its (now seemingly long-drawn-out) liquidation.

Interior urbanism
In attempting to reassert a distinctly architectural unity, architecture laid claim to the expertise of the interior in a way that translated a bourgeois comfort – or oppression,

take your pick – into a professedly more 'healthy' sense of movement and openness. But the mechanism for this translation was the interior's doubleness, a particular construal of, but also problem with, the relation between a spatial and an image-based condition. What is interesting to consider here, finally, is how this modernist engagement with the interior's doubleness leverages a larger issue, one to do with how architecture claims its disciplinary role within the industrialized metropolis. In *The Modulor*, Le Corbusier's definition of architecture as a phenomenon experienced in movement was coupled with an expanded definition of architecture to encompass the infrastructural. The modulor grid would act as a regulating net spreading out from the vision of a modulor man in motion, encompassing an urbanized field.[64] Le Corbusier's speculative urban schemes, from, for example, the Ville Contemporaine (1922), to the Obus plans for Algiers (1932–42), show a desire to link the organization of movement and the organization of dwellings. Benjamin has a compelling interpretation of such plans:

> Le Corbusier's 'contemporary city' is yet another settlement along a highway. Only the fact that now its precincts are travelled over by autos, and that aeroplanes now land in its midst changes everything. An effort must be made to secure a foothold here from which to cast a productive glance, a form-and-distance-creating glance, on the nineteenth century.[65]

In the Obus plans, fragments of the old city of Algiers were to be rearticulated within a scheme that would see architecture-become-urbanism give a new visual and perceptual identity to the city. The sinuous lines of the plans concretize an image of the unifying *promenade architecturale* at the urban level. Manfredo Tafuri has seen the failure of such plans, and the conception of architecture's agency they embody, in terms of architecture's utopian thinking. At one level, the failure had to do with the image of totality that the plans portrayed, and the subsequent difficulty in realizing this image as architecture. For Tafuri, the desire for such a 'total' realization stemmed from a misconstrual of architecture's disciplinary agency in the face of the external forces that drove urban planning.[66]

But with the Maison La Roche, there is a more subtle and perhaps more compelling realization of the *promenade architecturale* as an urban condition. It was a promenade effected as an interior condition, but where this was made coextensive with the existing city. And it was a promenade that eventually gave way to the reality that there needed to be pictures on walls. From its completion, Maison La Roche was open Tuesday and Friday afternoons for public viewing of the La Roche collection. While it may have been a very select public that had their names recorded in La Roche's golden visitor's book,[67] the promenade acted as a continuation of the experience of the urban field. The architectural unity asserted at its end was one of relation between interior and urban field, a recognition of their interdependence spatially and experientially.

The interior archaic and new

For Benjamin, what was new in the architecture and urbanism of Le Corbusier was precisely the vantage it offered on the past. Thus Le Corbusier's promenades offered a view not so much of the city purified and made coherent architecturally, but of the disjunction between the new and the newly archaic. What might catch the eye of the wanderer in this urban scape would be 'those few images that might have a positive effect in the present',[68] those images being illuminated precisely at the moment where disjunction is grasped as critical. Here the interior's 'positive effect' might be determined. Its historical emergence, cast in archaic terms, is illuminated at the point its obliteration is supposedly carried out. Yet what might come after this obliteration can only be conceived in terms of what is crucial about the interior's emergence, which is its doubleness. Thus the force of the interior in the particular 'present' of its illumination is how its doubleness is the pivot for reorienting domesticity, how the liquidation of its 'overstuffed', constricting bourgeois form gives way to, but conceptually is still present within, something like the *promenade architecturale*.

Here, an ambivalence about the interior's fate – whether it is just that easy to reorient domesticity – parallels an ambivalence about the fate of experience. Is the interior done away with by the *promenade architecturale*, just as one would have to trade in a 'portion of the human heritage . . . for the small change of "the contemporary"'?[69] Or is one's longing for how the values of such a heritage might be preserved only accentuated when threatened in this way? In which direction does illumination lead? The interior was a particularly charged site for these considerations, and Benjamin's 'difficulty in reflecting on dwelling' might be recalled to underline this: on the one hand, dwelling's eternal aspect, and on the other, its conditions of exis-tence as short-lived, as those of the nineteenth century now viewed as the archaic past.[70]

Architecturally, this situation was more unstable than what might be shown in a simple stereotypical image that Le Corbusier did much to promote, and that in some instances Benjamin seems to have been taken in by. In articulating the 'strange interplay between reactionary theory and revolutionary practice' that he found in the work of Karl Kraus, Loos's other 'I',[71] Benjamin was wary of the society 'that perpetrates the political radioscopy of sexuality and family, of economic and physical existence, . . . a society that is in the process of building houses with glass walls, and terraces extending far into the living rooms that are no longer living rooms'.[72] This delineation of the new includes a sense of wariness about how certain norms and forms of the nineteenth century – those of sexuality and the family, and their interlinking – can become subject to new regimes of oppression. In writing about Kraus, Benjamin argued that the private must be protected, but as a condition in ruins. In its clearest image, the value of the bourgeois domestic interior is illuminated at the point of its social and political impossibility. As such, it sheds light on conditions, problematically, beyond its own historically inscribed existence.

In 'Experience and Poverty', Benjamin articulated most clearly the direction of illumination, despite his ambivalence about what might be lost in taking such steps into the future. Benjamin wrote of the poverty of experience as a 'total absence of illusion about the age and at the same time an unlimited commitment to it'.[73] The loyalty was towards an age prepared to 'begin construction' on a perpetually undefined future without recourse to the past as authority. Yet this orientation was an effect of the past's work on the present. The glance in travelling towards the future was always a backward one,[74] one that perceived ruins that would speak 'in the foreign and stony tongue of untimely epitaphs.'[75]

At this point, Colomina's work and the issues surrounding what might be called its own 'direction of view' return. Loos and Le Corbusier have been discussed in terms of how they dealt with the so-called 'liquidation of the interior'. The very terms by which each responds to the specific, historically inscribed problems of modernity come from the interior's doubleness, the conceptual apparatus of the interior's historical emergence. Thus the conditions for modern architecture's emergence in terms of the mass media are sown approximately a century before modern architecture realizes itself through and ultimately as media, and this realization is only possible in the extent to which architecture re-engages with the interior as that which emerged separately from it a century previously. Thus the idea of modern architecture as mass media is not simply reducible to technological newness and its perceptual and experiential effects offered by photography, mass publication and circulation, new spatialities, and materials and modes of architectural construction that figure newness. Rather, the potential of the technologically new is only articulable architecturally in the extent to which architecture finds ways of dealing with its relation to the interior. Effectively, this is done by utilizing the terms of the interior's emergence to structure architecture's becoming media. The bourgeois form of the interior may be problematized (Loos), and outwardly and antagonistically destroyed (Le Corbusier), but the structuring it bequeaths remains crucial for modern architecture.

Modern architecture as mass media is made possible by what it renders, notwithstanding certain ambivalences, socially and politically untenable. Thus the question of modernism is one of history. It is not a progressive choice of the present about its dwelling; rather, it is about how present conditions are focused by a critical understanding of the historical conditions of dwelling, and, more particularly, of the historical emergence of the interior. To deny this historical emergence means being prey to illusions of the eternal in dwelling. To think that the interior simply progresses stylistically is to make the same mistake.

Conclusion

Mediatized domesticity

Considering the emergence of the interior has meant dealing with a range of contexts and sites where this emergence has had significant effects. Walter Benjamin marked out the contours of the interior's 'short historical life' as part of an 'interiorized' historiography that harboured revolutionary effects. Sigmund Freud's theory and practice were enmeshed within the interior's social and cultural norms, yet what emerged from these norms was a revolutionary account of the subject. In an architectural context through the nineteenth century, the interior enabled an articulation of domestic arrangements through the technique of the plan. It figured architecture's participation in questions surrounding the reform of design and industry in a geographically diverse context. And it became the site for the articulation of a self-consciously modern architecture, its doubleness presenting both problems and opportunities for this articulation.

Yet throughout these involvements, the interior has eluded a direct grasp, its emergence being seen as an effect of other circumstances, discourses and occurrences. In this light, the book's chapters might be summarized in a different way: the interior is the elusive figure organizing an unfinished history of the nineteenth century; it is the site, forever lost, of the subject's memory of themselves, and the spatiality for an always alienated re-membering; it is the future possibility projected from but always put off by the inscription of domesticity in architectural plans; it comes to realization in different ways geographically disjunct from a certain idealized cultural source; and any sense of its supposed spatial essence escapes the means by which it is represented and circulated. In these terms, the interior is pervasive yet disjunct, emergent yet outmoded, vital yet contingent, untimely yet of the nineteenth century.

In what way, then, is it possible to say that the interior emerged historically at the beginning of the nineteenth century? There was certainly a shift in the meaning of interior and *intérieur* around that time, and from this shift came the doubled, domestic sense of the term. But this shift did not deliver a new condition, fully formed, where previously nothing had existed. Rather, it allowed a new way of thinking about domesticity and directed a particular comportment towards the material realities of domestic life, realities which were beginning to be fashioned in ways that were themselves effects of this semantic development. But understanding the interior in a way that also recognizes its elusiveness means that many of the certainties that are usually associated with the term and its material manifestations are questioned. These are the certainties of a continuous, developing history of the interior, a simplified, affirming psychology of the interior, and a sense that the interior is subservient to architecture as the primary 'space provider' in culture. Considering the emergence of the interior means entertaining the idea that it is not what 'we' know it to be. The effects of its emergence have been more diffuse, yet more pervasive, than those highlighted when it is defined in terms of what is already assumed, or what seems to be essential.

It is perhaps most useful to understand these certainties not as what this account of the interior has ideologically opposed, but rather to understand that they are themselves effects of the interior's emergence, points of stability which attempt to counter the uncertainty and disjunction at the core of this emergence. The critical potential of recognizing the interior's emergence is shown here. Rather than simply being seen as one among many cultural and social phenomena, the interior can be treated as a critical tool for understanding key formations of the modern of which it is inextricably a part.

None of this is to propose that 'we' change our ways by embracing some other condition of the interior and a domesticity it might support, as if there was simply a choice to be made. Rather, it is the very framing in terms of 'we', the naturalization of the (bourgeois) domestic subject as the pre-requisite and assumed centre of consideration, that needs to be questioned as a final stage in this study of the interior's emergence. To pursue this idea, examples of architectural and social-scientific literature will be investigated to see how they deal with changes in domesticity brought about by the presence of electronic media.[1] These considerations extend the discussion of the relation between domesticity and the media from Chapter 5,[2] the focus in this instance being placed on how the subjectivities and formations of the interior might be rethought through new media and technology.

Un-privacy

In his survey of late-twentieth-century architectural design for houses, Terence Riley has identified a condition of the 'un-private house' consequent upon the infiltration of electronic media. To support this claim, Riley develops a conception of domestic privacy through accounts such as *A History of Private Life*, and Witold Rybczynski's *Home: A Short History of an Idea*. Following these, he argues that the house has been associated with privacy since the seventeenth century. He also recognizes that the house does not cut the public world off from the private. Indeed, various media form a link between them, and in the nineteenth century, the development of rooms such as the study and the library became the context for the bourgeoisie to engage with the media in the form of books, newspapers and magazines.[3] The presence of such media in the private house is consistent with the idea that it is the interior, itself a concept involving the sense of its mediation in images, that provides the context for this presence as one of its defining characteristics. Yet Riley's historical account leads towards the characterization of a contemporary situation where the boundaries of the private are put in dispute via the presence of media in new, electronic form: 'Today, the private house has become a permeable structure, receiving and trans-mitting images, sounds, text and data.'[4] Riley makes the distinction between the effects of electronic versus 'traditional' media via Martin Heidegger's account of how electronic media produce a profound 'distancelessness' between people and things, an idea that suggests this relation cannot be defined in terms of either far or near.[5] Riley invokes the figure of the cyborg, itself a hybrid of human and thing which con-founds conventional relationships, in order to give a figure to the possible inhabitant of this new, un-private house. He quotes Donna Haraway's 'A Cyborg Manifesto': 'No longer structured by the polarity of public and private, the cyborg defines a technological polis based partly on a revolution of social relations in the *oikos*, the household.'[6] Yet Riley is uneasy about this position, suggesting that 'The implications of Haraway's manifesto for everyday life are difficult to grasp, much less idealize.'[7] Electronic media threaten the supposed purity of the domestic, and its innate 'human' quality of privacy, and figures forth the cyborg as an impure, uncanny and unthinkable inhabiting subject.

Questions of identity in their relation to boundaries have also been con-cerns of the social-scientific study of electronic media in the domestic environment. In his synthetic account of studies in this field, David Morley claims that the home has become an 'electronic landscape',[8] a place where claims to identity across different scales are managed: 'These [media and communications] technologies must be understood as both transgressing the boundaries of the household – bringing the public world into the private – and simultaneously producing the coherence of broader social experience, through the sharing of both broadcast time and ritual.'[9] In a way similar to Riley, the idea of the purity of identity is crucial in this argument, in that Morley's concern with mediated identity as it is 'played' through the electronic landscape-cum-home has to do with analysing 'the attempt to expel alterity beyond the boundaries of some ethnically, culturally or civilizationally purified homogeneous enclave, at whatever level of social or geographical scale'.[10]

Infiltration is, however, key to the social-scientific method. Morley sug-gests: 'I have, in effect, taken the single concept of home as my central focus and worked by attempting to identify and articulate the different discourses which pass through that conceptual space.'[11] The idea of discourses 'passing through' is akin to the action of media on the physical corollary to that conceptual space, where each discourse would draw a boundary around that space according to different disciplinary perspectives. Yet this is where a problem surfaces within Morley's account, and with the empirical perspectives it calls upon. Even though its boundaries might be extended through the idea of the electronic landscape of dwelling, a con-ventional domesticity, carried by the term 'home', is the basis for analysis. Media come to disturb this as a pre-existing, non-mediated condition. The impurity of the cyborg, the very figuration of electronic media's effects on subjectivity, still has no place.

It is important to remember, however, that a sense of mediation is present within the very concept of the interior, and has been present through the way the interior has organized modern domesticity from its emergence. There is, as both

Morley and Riley would recognize, undoubtedly a close correlation between many popular media images taking the domestic as their content, and the domestic setting of their consumption. This correlation is at the core of a contemporary fascination with lifestyle,[12] which might be defined as the way in which domesticity is formed and experienced through its mediation in images. Yet it is precisely this fascination, this ease with domestic media consumption, and consumption of media about the domestic, which reveals mechanisms of the media as constitutive of the interior as the site of domesticity's modern formation, a formation Morley, Riley (and Heidegger) would consider to be disturbed by the newness of electronic media. At this point there is no need to distinguish between electronic and older forms of media which still persist in their own right, and interact with electronic media formats.[13]

It is instructive to take a current snapshot of media images in and about the domestic sphere to see how this argument plays out. There is a range between the ominously but aptly named Martha Stewart Living Omnimedia, and the reality TV of *Big Brother*. Framed conventionally, these examples might seem to be polarized around normalizing versus perverting images of the domestic. Yet their mechanisms of mediation actually unite them, revealing the latent aspects of control and training that have been constitutive of domesticity since the nineteenth century. *Big Brother* doesn't bear witness to the collapse of an ideal domesticity so much as it tests, quite literally, powers of suggestion in a new mutation of the domestic beyond the nuclear family. The phenomenon of Martha Stewart belongs in the same category of the production of the domestic through regimes of control that direct self-fashioning, though her regime is perhaps more insidious in that the voice of Big Martha speaks through an illusion of individual choice. The ten-month incarceration to which Stewart was sentenced in 2004 for misleading an investigation into her business affairs – half of which was spent under 'house arrest' – does not represent the irony of the supposed collapse of her vision of the domestic into that of *Big Brother*. Rather, it shows how they are intertwined from the start: Stewart's incarceration time will have reacquainted her with the mechanism of her own success. Unlike Morley's and Riley's 'disturbed' domestic, this is a contemporary version of the very configuration of the domestic. But this is not simply a stable configuration, as if Martha Stewart and *Big Brother* are repeating Robert Kerr's or Freud's linkage with the interior in the name of a normalizing regime, only with added electronic technology. Technologies of the image as they bear on the interior are not simply subject to a progressive sense of development, as if images of the interior transmitted via the television screen or the internet are simple progressions from the watercolour, the plan drawing or the photograph.

From the representational to the machinic image

In a different framing of domesticity's relation to media, Christopher Hight has argued that there is a shift from a representational to a machinic or productive sense of the image in the way spatialities of domesticity are constructed via contemporary media technologies. He makes this argument in an analysis of the television series *24*, and the way its particular storyline and montage techniques relate to television as a domestic technology par excellence. Hight's argument is worthy of an extended consideration because of the way in which it reconstitutes many of the key terms that have been discussed in this book, including the family, the city, geography, subjectivity and the image.

While the storyline of *24* – a group of counter-terrorist operatives attempt to foil a complex assassination plot within the space of 24 hours – belongs to the hybrid genre of the action thriller, Hight argues that the characters' relations to one another are entirely oedipalized, in this way replicating a family structure. This structuring takes place at the scale of the city: *24* constructs an image of the suburbanized metropolis, in this case Los Angeles, as a network of interiors. This network is imaged through the way in which action takes place in discrete interiorized locales which give no indication of an exterior. As Hight suggests:

> Throughout the programme, the *oikos* no longer possesses a formal organic unity; instead, domesticities are continually divided into smaller pockets of space orchestrated by the interaction between various members. Although each of these spaces is coded as domestic, the characters orbit each other in an escalating claustrophobic estrangement. In each episode, characters move through half a dozen or more social networks, each time folding one into another and multiplying connections.[14]

This condition is articulated not as the loss of a previously secure and discrete sense of the interior, nor as its simple expansion, but as a condition of suburbanization. This articulates a shift in how the interior is constructed through media transmission and reception. The multiplying connections between the programme's characters are enabled by communications technologies such as mobile phones and the internet. The crucial characteristic of the connectivity between the discrete, interiorized locales of action – and the structural conceit of the television programme – is its simultaneity. This simultaneity impacts upon how the suburbanism of Los Angeles is understood spatially, or, rather, it points towards a metropolitan organization where relations conventionally defined by distance are overwritten by the simultaneity of mediated relations. Hight notes how Los Angeles is never depicted in its suburban vastness. The mobile interiors of the Chevy Suburban SUVs that transport characters between the different scenes of action serve as locales of communication, where telephone calls and data transfers deliver information, circumventing the need for actual movement. Indeed, the spatial movement of these vehicles is factored out of the programme's 24-hour conceit. As Hight suggests, if the characters had to be delivered to geographically separated locations for action to take place, the entire 24 hours of the programme would be taken up in travel time, and nothing would actually happen. Instead, interactions via communications technologies construct these characters as true cybernetic organisms, their interior being the 'static vehicle'.[15]

All of these relationships are communicated by the programme's montage:

> *24*'s montage regularly breaks into multiple split screens with as many as seven separate frames. Sometimes a character in one frame communicates (either in person or by electronic device) to one in another frame,

or two different narratives are juxtaposed. In other cases, the same narra-tive is shown from multiple camera angles. Often all of these possibilities are mixed in a single moment.[16]

He likens these effects to the multiple open application windows of personal com-puters, windows which are organized without hierarchy, and where movement and information exchange between them can be made at will. These multiple screens and windows also form major components of the sets in *24*, creating an interiorized loop between the setting for the programme's plot, the means of its advancement and multiplication via communications technologies, and the communication of this network to suburban interiors as the television programme. The effects of this montaging are claimed by Hight as machinic rather than representational. They do not reflect a given reality, but rather offer 'concepts of spacing and organization with which to engage the suburban metropolis'.[17] The effect of these concepts is to displace the humanist subject as the centre of space and its organization. This occurs through the way in which perception can be understood to be located in matter. Apropos Gilles Deleuze and Bruno Latour, Hight suggests:

> [*24*'s] mixed networks of things and subjects, technologies and sensation, are matter-content assemblages that create a montage universe in which human reception is merely another component. This is not to say that they are unproblematic, but we cannot understand what may or may not be at work by naturalizing terms and concepts of space simply because they are more familiar.[18]

This is the point at which one can distinguish most sharply the perspective on elec-tronic media and domesticity given by Riley and Morley from the conceptualizations offered by Hight. From a humanist perspective, Riley and Morley investigate the effects of electronic media infiltration in the domestic sphere, a sphere which pre-exists such an infiltration, and as such offers the essential qualities of privacy, purity and stability, no matter how the formation of these qualities relies to a large extent on the presence of 'traditional' media. The uptake of electronic media is then about the ways in which they threaten these qualities, or might themselves be naturalized and accommodated to this conception of domesticity. Hight, on the other hand, argues how a television series such as *24* does not simply infiltrate the domestic space of its reception, or become accommodated to it. Rather, it offers material by which to reconceptualize the relations between spatial configurations of domesticity and the effects of electronic, and specifically montage, media. These concepts are directed towards the yet to come, hence they are not about the representation of existing conditions, no matter how grounded these concepts are in technologies and themes that are already ubiquitous. And it is because of this very ubiquity that a reconceptualization of what are taken to be stable and naturalized concepts and their material manifestations is both possible and necessary. *24* offers the portal on to that reconceptualization, one that is conveniently home-delivered.

As a way towards this reconceptualization, it is worth considering how the doubleness of the interior might be rearticulated in terms of electronic media.

First, as Riley and Morley recognize, this would involve the idea that the interior is implicated in both the reception and the transmission of electronic media. But what is crucial here is the idea that the interior is also something transmissible. This does not simply mean that images of interiors are the content of media transmissions, though in many instances they are. Rather, taking up the idea of the image as machinic, the interior is not simply represented by the image, but is actually constituted through a condition of transmission and reception. Such a condition can produce a spatialized interior in locales such as SUVs and open-plan offices. These interiors are not different in kind – and do not necessarily replace – the more recognizable domestic interiors of the suburban metropolis. Indeed, interiors can be constituted in this way at these more conventional locales. As Hight has shown, the production of interiors through electronic media does not rely on, or merely corrupt, conventional concepts or manifestations of domesticity. Rather, it produces new ones.[19]

But this condition of newness is not simply the next in line in domestic developments. In the way architecture's engagement with mass media was understood in Chapter 5, it is a condition illuminated in relation to what it appears to render outmoded. This sense of illumination is carried by a conceptual consistency which has been dealt with throughout this book: the interior in its doubleness. Such a conceptual consistency does not imply the continuity of forms or experiences of the interior. It can cope with discontinuity in the movement of historical time, and does not have recourse to categories such as style, or notions such as the progressive development of essential domestic qualities. In the context of these concluding thoughts, such a conceptual consistency actually makes it impossible to think about the interior in a conventional way as something infiltrated by electronic media, and thereby having sacrificed its 'naturally domestic' qualities. And in the way new modes of domesticity and the interior's formation become thinkable through electronic media, such a conceptual consistency highlights how certain qualities of domesticity have in fact become naturalized.

Even though the interior is still a current and pervasive concept, this does not simply mean that its bourgeois or even its modernist manifestations are recognizable today, or are simply different options to be chosen, though at the level of consumer culture, the interior is indeed imaged in terms of such 'styles'. Rather, that it is still possible to speak of the interior means that one's thinking is organized around the interior's doubleness: the interior is constituted by and recognized through the relation between image and space. These images and spaces do not have any essential characteristics. As such, it is possible to shift between different concepts of the image, and to consider different spatialities that might link to these. Throughout this book, the image has been considered in terms of either imaginal or representational concepts. In considering current questions, the machinic offers itself as a particularly useful conceptualization of the image, one that can deal with new formations of the interior, and the forms of life they might structure. The spatiality of the interior, never wholly separate from such imagistic considerations, never simply the three-dimensional reality of the interior, might be conceived of in a conventional enclosed sense, or wholly outside of such an architecturally based designation. While the interior's relation to architecture has been a major concern of the book, one might begin to think of its relation to different concepts and instances of spacing and structuring. What the idea of the interior's historical emergence might reveal, in the end, is a sense of how one might be able to think differently about the history and future orientation of what has come to be known as domesticity.

Notes

Introduction

1   Charles Baudelaire, 'The Twofold Room', in Francis Scarfe (ed.), *The Poems in Prose, with La Fanfarlo*, London: Anvil Press, 1989, p. 37.

2   Baudelaire, 'The Twofold Room', p. 39.

3   Compare Walter Benjamin's drug-induced reverie: 'During my second experiment with hashish. Staircase in Charlotte Joël's studio. I said: "A structure only habitable by wax figures. I could do so much with it plastically; Piscator and company can just go pack. Would be possible for me to change the lighting scheme with tiny levers. I can transform the Goethe house into the Covent Garden Opera; can read from it the whole of world history. I see, in this space, why I collect colportage images. Can see everything in this room – the sons of Charles III and what you will."' Walter Benjamin, *The Arcades Project*, Cambridge, MA: The Belknap Press of Harvard University Press, 1999, p. 216 [I2a,1]. Compare also Xavier de Maistre's two stories about imaginal travelling: 'A Journey around my Room' (1794), and 'A Nocturnal Expedition around my Room' (1825), in Xavier de Maistre, *A Journey around my Room*, London: Hesperus, 2004. Benjamin links de Maistre's schema to Søren Kierkegaard's philosophical reflections on domesticity through the idea of a flâneur going for a walk in a room as if on a city street. See Benjamin, *The Arcades Project*, p. 421 [M2a,2]. References to material in the convolutes of *The Arcades Project* are given via page number and the alpha-numerical code that orders the material.

4   Charles Baudelaire, 'The Painter of Modern Life', in Jonathan Mayne (ed.), *The Painter of Modern Life and Other Essays*, London: Phaidon, 1964, pp. 1–40.

5   Compare, for example, Edgar Allan Poe, 'The Philosophy of Furniture', in Clarence Stedman and George Woodberry (eds), *The Works of Edgar Allan Poe*, Chicago: Stone & Kimball, 1894, pp. 174–82, a 'sketch' of an interior displaying refined taste.

6   'interior', 'interior decoration', in *The Oxford English Dictionary*, available HTTP: <http://dictionary.oed.com/>.

7   The 4th edition of the *Dictionnaire de L'Académie française* (1762) is the first to suggest a meaning and usage for *intérieur* that has an association with the domestic: 'Il se dit figurément Des choses les plus cachées. Il connoît l'intérieur de cette maison, de cette famille' ('Figuratively one can speak of things that are the most hidden. *He knows the interior of that house, of that family*'); however, this domestic usage is not repeated in the *Jean-François Féraud dictionnaire critique de la langue française* of 1787–8. The sense is a little more specific in the 5th edition of the *Dictionnaire de L'Académie française* (1798), uniting the prevalent 'personal' meaning with the interior as a placeholder for this meaning: 'On dit qu'*Un homme est gai, triste, malheureux dans son intérieur*, pour dire, Dans l'intérieur de sa maison'. (It is often said that *a man is happy, sad, or unhappy in his interior*, that is to say, in the interior of his house.) Interestingly, this edition slightly rewrites the domestic sense of the 4th edition, removing 'maison': 'Il se dit figurément Des choses les plus cachées. Il connoît l'intérieur de cette famille'. The 6th edition (1832–5) is the first to mention a meaning in the image-based sense: 'En termes de Peinture, *Tableau d'intérieur*, ou simplement, *Intérieur*, Tableau de genre qui a pour objet principal la représentation de l'architecture et des effets de lumière à l'intérieur des maisons, des édifices. Il se dit également d'*Un tableau qui représente quelque scène de la vie domestique, dans l'intérieur d'une maison*.'

(With reference to painting, *interior painting*, or simply, *interior*, genre painting which has as its principal object the representation of the architecture and effects of light in the interior of houses and other buildings. Equally one could speak of a painting which represents scenes of domestic life in the interior of a house.) Available HTTP: <http://portail.atilf.fr/dictionnaires/onelook.htm>. The *Trésor de la langue française* dates *tableau d'intérieur* to 1829. Available HTTP: <http://atilf. atilf.fr/tlf.htm>. German derives its usage for *interieur* from the French, recognizing its meaning in the post-nineteenth-century sense of the interior of a room, its decoration, and its sense as a representation of such conditions. The more particular sense given by the *Duden Wörterbuch* for *interieur* as image is as follows: '(bild Kunst) *einen Innenraum darstellendes Bild, besonders in der niederlandischen Malerei des 17. Jh.s.*' ((art image) *the inner room as a representational image, particularly in Dutch painting of the seventeenth century*). *Duden. Das große Wörterbuch der deutschen Sprache*, Mannheim: Duden Verlag, 1999. This suggests that the naming of the domestic scenes of Dutch seventeenth-century painting was a nineteenth-century occurrence. See Chapter 1 for a discussion of the place of Dutch painting in relation to the history of the interior.

8   The concept of interior decoration gave rise to a profession that by the late nineteenth century had emerged in its own right and largely seized control of the interior's treatment. See Peter Thornton, *Authentic Décor: The Domestic Interior, 1620–1920*, New York: Viking, 1984, pp. 10–12. For the impact of the interior's emergence in the context of literary description, see Charlotte Grant, 'Reading the House of Fiction: From Object to Interior, 1720–1920', *Home Cultures*, vol. 2, no. 3, 2005, pp. 233–49.

9   The domestic interior gives a spatial and representational sense to a subjective notion of interiority that, according to Carolyn Steedman, arose with prominence in the late eighteenth century through the figure of the child, and the idea of childhood for the bourgeoisie. Childhood took hold into the nineteenth century as the history of the self, a history which then became theorized by Freud around the turn of the twentieth century through the unconscious. Thus the personal history that a child embodied came to define an adult concept of interiority. See Carolyn Steedman, *Strange Dislocations: Childhood and the Idea of Human Interiority, 1780–1930*, Cambridge, MA: Harvard University Press, 1995, p. 4. In her study of paintings of bourgeois interiors, Susan Sidlauskas emphasizes 'two different kinds of interiors: the body and the inner chamber of the house', where 'the imaginative relation between the body and its surroundings must always be in doubt'. Susan Sidlauskas, *Body, Place and Self in Nineteenth-Century Painting*, Cambridge: Cambridge University Press, 2000, p. 2, emphasis in original. Further on, she argues that 'Subjectivity became interiority when it was staged in the space that was identified with its most intense, authentic expression: the domestic interior' (p. 19). Here Sidlauskas recognizes the mutual implication and inseparability of subjectivity and interiority – as well as subject and interior – with the rise of the bourgeois domestic interior: 'Subjectivity was not simply pictured within the domestic interior; it was here that it *came into being*' (p. 20, emphasis in original).

10 Peter Gay, *The Bourgeois Experience: Victoria to Freud*, 5 vols, Oxford: Oxford University Press, 1984–99, vol. 1, p. 43. In a seminal article, John Lukacs has laid out the historical characteristics of what he calls the bourgeois spirit, which is not reducible to the sociologically verifiable characteristics of a class. He sees that this spirit reached its apogee in the nineteenth century through the way in which domestic arrangements carried crucial significations of bourgeois life. Yet his account suggests that the domestic interior was the prerequisite for such an amplification of domesticity, rather than being historically emergent in relation to the newly articulated domestic needs of the bourgeoisie, as this book will argue. See John Lukacs, 'The Bourgeois Interior', *American Scholar*, vol. 39, no. 4, 1970, pp. 616–30.

11 While it is important to realize the difference between spatialities, decorative styles and modes of inhabitation of interiors in different European centres of culture, this study emphasizes the concept of the interior as one which, in an interpretive sense, is mobile across these differences. See, for example, the way in which Donald Olsen describes the difference between domestic

interiors in London, Paris and Vienna, as well as the sense of interest and critique of these differing conditions sustained by the citizens of these cities because of a shared bourgeois identification. Donald Olsen, *The City as a Work of Art: London, Paris, Vienna*, New Haven: Yale University Press, 1986, pp. 89–131.

12 Several literary studies of the domestic refer to architecture and use architectural terms. See especially: Fredric Jameson, 'The Realist Floor-Plan', in Marshall Blonsky (ed.), *On Signs*, Baltimore: Johns Hopkins University Press, 1985, pp. 373–83; Victoria Rosner, *Modernism and the Architecture of Private Life*, New York: Columbia University Press, 2005; and Sharon Marcus, *Apartment Stories: City and Home in Nineteenth-Century Paris and London*, Berkeley: University of California Press, 1999. The method of this book could be cast in reverse: there is often recourse to literature and literary theory while focus is maintained on architecture, especially in Part 2 of the book.

13 It should be noted that 'space' as a specifically architectural concept denoting three-dimensional volume only became conceptualized towards the end of the nineteenth century, and it could be argued that it owes its conceptualization to the cultural significance of the bourgeois domestic interior. One of the key theorizers of space was August Schmarsow, who tied his concep-tualization to the comfortableness of the interior: 'the true artistic expression of our particular sense of space will certainly be greeted with pleasure and enjoyed with gratitude in all those enduring places where the work of our civilisation is carried on, right down to the domestic seclusion and cosy setting of our private lives.' August Schmarsow, 'The Essence of Architectural Creation', in Harry Francis Mallgrave and Eleftherios Ikonomou (eds), *Empathy, Form and Space: Problems in German Aesthetics, 1873–1893*, Santa Monica: Getty Center for the History of Art and the Humanities, 1994, p. 296. Similarly, one might read Gottfried Semper's mid-nineteenth-century attempt to provide a foundational theory for architecture in his four elements as one concerned with claiming the interior as foundational for architecture. His theory gives priority to the hearth-surrounding woven enclosure as the primary element in architectural creation. Supporting structure, what might be thought to be properly architectural, is rendered secondary. See Gottfried Semper, *The Four Elements of Architecture and Other Writings*, Cambridge: Cambridge University Press, 1989, pp. 101–10.

14 While interested in particular theories of the relations between subjects and objects, envi-ronmental psychology tends to universalize preferred theories, and hence the domesticity wherein they go to work, losing sight of the historical formation, and thus the contingency, of psychology's relation to the domestic. See especially: Clare Cooper Marcus, *House as a Mirror of Self: Exploring the Deeper Meaning of Home*, Berkeley: Conari Press, 1995; and Mihaly Csikszentmihalyi and Eugene Rochberg-Halton, *The Meaning of Things: Domestic Symbols and the Self*, Cambridge: Cambridge University Press, 1981. Note also the way in which Gaston Bachelard's *The Poetics of Space*, Boston: Beacon Press, 1994 [1964], has become emblematic of an approach that essen-tializes and universalizes the relations between subjects and domesticity. For an example of how psychology and its relation to domesticity can be treated historically, and, as such, critically, see Jacques Donzelot, *The Policing of Families*, Baltimore: Johns Hopkins University Press, 1997; Nikolas Rose, *The Psychological Complex: Psychology, Politics and Society in England, 1869–1939*, London: Routledge & Kegan Paul, 1985; idem, *Inventing Ourselves: Psychology, Power, and Personhood*, Cambridge, Cambridge University Press, 1996; and idem, *Governing the Soul: The Shaping of the Private Self*, London: Free Association Books, 1999.

15 See the account of the nineteenth-century 'cult' of domesticity in Hilde Heynen, 'Modernity and Domesticity: Tensions and Contradictions', in Hilde Heynen and Gülsüm Baydar (eds), *Negotiating Domesticity: Spatial Constructions of Gender in Modern Architecture*, London: Routledge, 2005, pp. 6–9.

16 In his discussion of classical notions of domesticity in the Renaissance treatises of Alberti, Mark Wigley has argued that ideas about family, household and gender are unable to be located at an orginary historical point, one which a classical term such as *oikos* (household) might suggest. He

suggests that Alberti's treatise on the family 'is strangely suspended between the classical arguments it appropriates and those identified with the nineteenth century'. Mark Wigley, 'Untitled: The Housing of Gender', in Beatriz Colomina (ed.), *Sexuality and Space*, New York: Princeton Architectural Press, 1993, p. 342.

17 The most prominent example of this tendency is Witold Rybczynski, *Home: A Short History of an Idea*, Harmondsworth: Penguin, 1987. For more recent examples, see Akiko Busch, *Geography of Home: Writings on Where We Live*, New York: Princeton Architectural Press, 1999; and Peter King, *Private Dwelling: Contemplating the Use of Housing*, London: Routledge, 2004. The use of the term home is also strongly associated with social-scientific studies of domesticity. See, for example: David N. Benjamin (ed.), *The Home: Words, Interpretations, Meanings, and Environments*, Aldershot: Avebury, 1995; Irene Cieraad (ed.), *At Home: An Anthropology of Domestic Space*, Syracuse: Syracuse University Press, 1999; and Daniel Miller (ed.), *Home Possessions: Material Culture Behind Closed Doors*, Oxford: Berg, 2001. In his own contribution to the volume, Miller gives a useful outline of the literature and history of social-scientific studies of the home. See Miller, 'Behind Closed Doors', in *Home Possessions*, pp. 1–19. Even though there is a degree of variability and criticality in the sorts of studies discussed, for Miller they need to be underpinned by a sense of 'empathy' between researcher and the subjects of research. While not falling into the same category as the universalisms of Rybczynski, Busch and King, such an appeal to empathy reveals a flaw in such a human-centred research paradigm. Conversely, this book appeals to a sense of estrangement from how 'we' 'normally' associate with the home in delineating the historical emergence of the interior, and, as such, how such notions of domestic empathy are constructed through this historical emergence.

18 On the threat to domesticity posed by avant-garde art and architectural movements, see Christopher Reed, 'Introduction', in Christopher Reed (ed.), *Not at Home: The Suppression of Domesticity in Modern Art and Architecture*, London: Thames & Hudson, 1996, pp. 7–17. For a critique of Reed's argument, see Heynen, 'Modernity and Domesticity', pp. 4, 15.

19 See Hilde Heynen, *Architecture and Modernity: A Critique*, Cambridge, MA: MIT Press, 1999, pp. 14–24.

20 The most influential essays, especially in schools of architecture, are: Martin Heidegger, 'Building, Dwelling, Thinking', and 'Poetically Man Dwells', in *Poetry, Language, Thought*, New York: Harper & Row, 1975, pp. 143–61, 213–29.

21 See the way in which King misunderstands and misrepresents Benjamin's argument about the 'eternal' aspects of dwelling, in King, *Private Dwelling*, p. 60. David Morley criticizes Benjamin's account of the bourgeois domestic interior because it 'is far from being a universal experience'. David Morley, *Home Territories: Media, Mobility, Identity*, London: Routledge, 2000, p. 29. Once again, this is to misunderstand the intent of Benjamin's account.

1 Irrecoverable inhabitions: Walter Benjamin and histories of the interior

1 Walter Benjamin, 'Paris, Capital of the Nineteenth Century (exposé of 1939)', in *The Arcades Project*, Cambridge, MA: The Belknap Press of Harvard University Press, 1999, p. 20.

2 Graeme Gilloch suggests that the constrictions of the interior mean that 'The vitality of the living and the integrity of the dead are simultaneously denied in this space. As a result it becomes lifeless, sterile and inhuman. Although the site of the "murder scene," the interior is not so much a space of death as itself "dead space."' Graeme Gilloch, *Myth and Metropolis: Walter Benjamin and the City*, Cambridge: Polity Press, 1996, pp. 82–3.

3 Benjamin, *The Arcades Project*, p. 218 [I3,1]. References to material in the convolutes of *The Arcades Project* are given via page number and the alpha-numerical code that orders the material.

4 Benjamin, *The Arcades Project*, p. 406 [L1,5], [L1a,1]. On the relations between interior and exterior in Benjamin, see Tom Gunning, 'The Exterior as *Intérieur*: Benjamin's Optical Detective', *boundary 2*, vol. 30, no. 1, 2003, pp. 105–29; and Gilloch, *Myth and Metropolis*, pp. 125–6.

5 Benjamin, *The Arcades Project*, p. 220 [I4,4].

6 For a discussion of the status of the two exposés in Benjamin's conception of *The Arcades Project*, see Pierre Missac, *Walter Benjamin's Passages*, Cambridge, MA: MIT Press, 1995, pp. 139–45.

7 Walter Benjamin, 'Experience and Poverty', in *Selected Writings*, 4 vols, Cambridge, MA: The Belknap Press of Harvard University Press, 1996–2003, vol. 2, p. 731.

8 Benjamin, 'Paris, Capital of the Nineteenth Century', p. 19.

9 Christoph Asendorf, *Batteries of Life: On the History of Things and their Perception in Modernity*, Berkeley: University of California Press, 1993, p. 3.

10 Asendorf, *Batteries of Life*, p. 5. See also Martin Jay, 'Experience without a Subject', in *Cultural Semantics: Keywords of our Time*, London: Athlone, 1998, pp. 47–61.

11 Asendorf, *Batteries of Life*, p. 6.

12 Karl Marx, *Capital: A Critique of Political Economy*, New York: International Publishers, 1975, vol. 1, p. 172. Quoted in Asendorf, *Batteries of Life*, pp. 5–6.

13 Another way to describe momentary experiences would be to call them the commodification of experience, their packaging as multiple, discrete, non-continuous but rapidly and continuously produced 'events'.

14 Susan Stewart, *On Longing: Narratives of the Miniature, the Gigantic, the Souvenir, the Collection*, Baltimore: Johns Hopkins University Press, 1984, pp. 164–5.

15 Stewart, *On Longing*, p. 155.

16 Stewart, *On Longing*, p. 166.

17 See Stewart, *On Longing*, p. 160.

18 See Walter Benjamin, 'Unpacking my Library', in *Selected Writings*, vol. 2, pp. 486–93.

19 See Howard Eiland, 'Reception in Distraction', *boundary 2*, vol. 30, no. 1, 2003, pp. 62–3.

20 Benjamin, *The Arcades Project*, p. 211 [H4a,1].

21 Benjamin, *The Arcades Project*, p. 205 [H1a,5].

22 Benjamin, *The Arcades Project*, p. 206 [H2,3]. Benjamin casts this somewhat differently in 'Unpacking my Library': 'ownership is the most intimate relationship that one can have to things. Not that they come alive in him; it is he who lives in them. So I have erected before you one of his dwellings, with books as the building stones; and now he is going to disappear inside, as is only fitting'. Benjamin, 'Unpacking my Library', p. 492.

23 Benjamin, *The Arcades Project*, p. 211 [H5,1].

24 See Stewart, *On Longing*, p. 151.

25 Benjamin, *The Arcades Project*, pp. 220–1 [I4,4].

26 Walter Benjamin, 'One-Way Street', in *Selected Writings*, vol. 1, pp. 446–7.

27 Here is Benjamin's own gnomic note to this effect: 'Multiplication of traces through the modern administrative apparatus.' Benjamin, *The Arcades Project*, p. 225 [I6a,4]. In his investigation of the trace in criminological uses of photography and in detective fiction, Tom Gunning emphasizes the major effect of modernity as a change in experience brought about through mobility. Specifically in relation to the use of the photograph as evidence, its indexical quality is overtaken by its ability to be detached and to circulate separately from its referent. See Tom Gunning, 'Tracing the Individual Body: Photography, Detectives and Early Cinema', in Leo Charney and Vanessa R. Schwartz (eds), *Cinema and the Invention of Modern Life*, Berkeley: University of California Press, 1995, pp. 15–45. In this context, Benjamin's invocation of detective fiction in relation to the traces left in the interior speaks of the experience of modernity as the ambivalence between a stabilization of one's identity in the interior, and the possibility of one's traces themselves becoming mobile, and being treated within the frame of criminality. On experience and detective fiction, see my 'Evidence, Experience and Conjecture: Reading the Interior through Benjamin and Bloch', *Home Cultures*, vol. 2, no. 3, 2005, pp. 285–97.

28 Walter Benjamin, 'On Some Motifs in Baudelaire', in *Selected Writings*, vol. 4, p. 316.

29 Benjamin, 'On Some Motifs in Baudelaire', p. 317.

30 Benjamin writes about the way in which the photographic plate similarly registers traces that fall beneath conscious perception. As such, photography is one of the 'important achievements of a society in which long practice is in decline'. Benjamin, 'On Some Motifs in Baudelaire', p. 337.

31 Benjamin, 'On Some Motifs in Baudelaire', p. 315.

32 Marcel Proust, *In Search of Lost Time*, 6 vols, London: Vintage, 1996, vol. 1, pp. 50–1.

33 Benjamin, 'On Some Motifs in Baudelaire', p. 315.

34 Benjamin, *The Arcades Project*, p. 866 [Q,7].

35 Benjamin, 'Paris, Capital of the Nineteenth Century', p. 20.

36 Asendorf, *Batteries of Life*, p. 129.

37 Asendorf, *Batteries of Life*, p. 130. See also Gilloch, *Myth and Metropolis*, pp. 78–83, on the link between eroticism and commodity fetishism in the interior.

38 Benjamin, 'Experience and Poverty', p. 731.

39 Gilloch describes Benjamin's upbringing in a 'prosperous, upper-middle-class assimilated Jewish family. . . . The Benjamins resided in [Berlin's] comfortable, desirable West End District, and Walter's childhood was a period of relative affluence'. Gilloch, *Myth and Metropolis*, p. 55. See Gilloch's account of how childhood influenced Benjamin's recollection and reading of the city, and how this revealed Benjamin's ambivalence about the way in which the bourgeois interior shaped domesticity and experience (pp. 55–92). See Benjamin's own recollections in 'Berlin Childhood around 1900', in *Selected Writings*, vol. 3, pp. 344–86.

40 Mario Praz, *An Illustrated History of Interior Decoration from Pompeii to Art Nouveau*, London: Thames & Hudson, 1964, p. 17.

41 Praz, *An Illustrated History of Interior Decoration*, p. 18.

42 Charlotte Gere, *Nineteenth-Century Interiors: An Album of Watercolours*, London: Thames & Hudson, 1992, p. 14. Peter Thornton puts this argument thus: 'It was fashionable, from about 1815 to about 1840, to draw and paint views of interiors. Grand people instructed a draughtsman to make pictures of their favourite rooms; the less grand did it themselves.' Peter Thornton, *Authentic Décor: The Domestic Interior, 1620–1920*, New York: Viking, 1984, p. 217. Gere recognizes that there are precedents for interior view painting in examples from the eighteenth century. She suggests that these earlier examples were either isolated representations that were informational sources in relation to the rooms they depicted (rather than having 'artistic' merit, which would define a genre in Gere's terms), were representations of well-known houses in periodicals and other publications, or were representations produced to accompany visits to well-known houses. Thornton argues that the practice of allowing these visits, and producing the attendant publications, ceased around 1840, when the interior shifted from being a space for the display of taste and wealth, to being the space of familial privacy and the cultivation of domestic virtues. See Thornton, *Authentic Décor*, p. 210.

43 Praz, *An Illustrated History of Interior Decoration*, p. 25.

44 T. B. Macauley, *History of England from the Accession of James II*, London, 1848, vol. 1, ch. 111. Quoted in Thornton, *Authentic Décor*, p. 8.

45 Thornton, *Authentic Décor*, p. 8.

46 See Thornton, *Authentic Décor*, p. 8.

47 Praz, *An Illustrated History of Interior Decoration*, p. 25. He does remark at this point that the Benjaminian phantasmagorical interior is far less revealing of the character of its inhabitant than supposedly more transparent examples, but he misses the point that this very opacity of the interior is what launched it conceptually.

48 Witold Rybczynski, *Home: A Short History of an Idea*, Harmondsworth: Penguin, 1987, p. 43. See also Praz, *An Illustrated History of Interior Decoration*, pp. 50–5.

49 Heidi de Mare, 'Domesticity in Dispute: A Reconsideration of Sources', in Irene Cieraad (ed.), *At Home: An Anthropology of Domestic Space*, Syracuse: Syracuse University Press, 1999, p. 14. This argument would also seem to put in dispute the idea that bourgeois culture and society themselves, as particularly 'domestic' manifestations, were born in seventeenth-century Holland.

For this perspective, see John Lukacs, 'The Bourgeois Interior', *American Scholar*, vol. 39, no. 4, 1970, pp. 616–30. As discussed in the introduction, the German meaning for *interieur* as an image references seventeeth-century Dutch painting. De Mare's argument reinforces the idea that this meaning would have occurred as a nineteenth-century projection of values on to this art.

50   De Mare. 'Domesticity in Dispute', p. 14.

51   De Mare. 'Domesticity in Dispute', p. 20.

52   Martha Hollander, *An Entrance for the Eyes: Space and Meaning in Seventeenth-Century Dutch Art*, Berkeley: University of California Press, 2002, p. 3.

53   Hollander, *An Entrance for the Eyes*, pp. 3–4.

54   Victor Stoichita, *The Self-Aware Image: An Insight into Early Modern Meta-Painting*, Cambridge: Cambridge University Press, 1997, pp. 44–53.

55   See also de Mare, 'Domesticity in Dispute', pp. 20, 26–9.

56   Rybczynski, *Home*, p. 69.

57   See Stoichita, *The Self-Aware Image*, pp. 157–73, and Hollander, *An Entrance for the Eyes*, pp. 119–29.

58   Robin Evans, 'The Developed Surface: An Enquiry into the Brief Life of an Eighteenth-Century Drawing Technique', in *Translations from Drawing to Building and Other Essays*, London: Architectural Association, 1997, pp. 200–3. On this drawing technique, see also Laura Jacobus, 'On "Whether a Man Could See Before Him and Behind Him Both at Once": The Role of Drawing in the Design of Interior Space in England, c. 1600–1800', *Architectural History*, no. 31, 1988, pp. 148–65.

59   Evans, 'The Developed Surface', pp. 210–14, 222. In terms of the occupation of such rooms, Evans suggests that 'The peripheral ring of chairs in particular was a long-established formation. In Daniel Marot's well-known designs for the furnishing of a palace, published in the 1690s, a ring of chairs is to be found in nearly every room. With Chippendale, Hepplewhite and Adam furniture, the seventeenth-century bulk is quite gone, allowing de facto freedom to escape this arcane arrangement, but the magnet of convention is still strong. When the room is empty, the furniture reverts to the wall. During the last three decades of the eighteenth century, a brief equilibrium was achieved between house planning, the method of representing interiors, and the distribution of furniture' (p. 214).

60   Evans, 'The Developed Surface', pp. 214–15. Emphasis in original. Evans suggests that this was a belated uptake of the example of variety in occupying rooms visible in Paris from the 1750s.

61   The adequacy of representation was not necessarily measured in an architectural sense. In Evans's argument, adequacy relates primarily to the interior being able to be represented as an entire spatial ensemble. As Evans suggests, 'Insufficient by itself, incapable (because of the extremity of its flatness) of incorporation with perspective, the developed surface was now a positive hindrance to comprehension.' Evans, 'The Developed Surface', p. 222.

62   Evans, 'The Developed Surface', p. 219. Emphasis in original.

63   This point is made most clearly when Praz discusses three different representations of 'Saint Jerome in his Study'. Given the continuity of subject matter, the variance in representational styles and preoccupations has more to say about those styles and preoccupations than it does about the universally desirable qualities Praz writes about, such as *Stimmung*. See Praz, *An Illustrated History of Interior Decoration*, pp. 98–9.

64   Benjamin, 'Paris, Capital of the Nineteenth Century', p. 19.

65   Michelle Perrot (ed.), *A History of Private Life*, Cambridge, MA: The Belknap Press of Harvard University Press, 1990, vol. 4. See also Norbert Elias, *The Civilizing Process: The History of Manners*, Oxford: Basil Blackwell, 1978.

66   Michelle Perrot and Roger-Henri Guerrand, 'Scenes and Places', in *A History of Private Life*, vol. 4, p. 354.

67   Perrot and Guerrand, 'Scenes and Places', p. 354.

68 Perrot and Guerrand, 'Scenes and Places', p. 356.

69 There is a distinction to be made here between decoration as a means to self-expression, and even class mobility, and the understanding of display as the display of wealth. Alain Corbin notes this difference when he states: 'The thirst for public esteem in the obsession with decorations often exceed the desire for riches, and the difficulties faced by the parvenu show that social mobility was not merely a matter of wealth.' Alain Corbin, 'Backstage', in *A History of Private Life*, vol. 4, p. 503.

70 Perrot and Guerrand, 'Scenes and Places', p. 369.

71 Corbin, 'Backstage', p. 487.

72 See especially Corbin, 'Backstage', pp. 479–502, 519–47.

73 Michelle Perrot, 'Introduction', in *A History of Private Life*, vol. 4, p. 3.

74 Perrot, 'Introduction', p. 5.

75 Perrot, 'Introduction', p. 4.

76 Georges Duby, 'Foreword', in Paul Veyne (ed.), *A History of Private Life*, Cambridge, MA: The Belknap Press of Harvard University Press, 1987, vol. 1, p. viii.

77 Duby, 'Foreword', p. viii.

78 Emmanuel Le Roy Ladurie, 'The "Event" and the "Long Term" in Social History: The Case of the Chouan Uprising', in *The Territory of the Historian*, Hassocks: The Harvester Press, 1979, p. 123.

79 Michel Foucault, 'Nietzsche, Genealogy, History', in Paul Rabinow (ed. and trans.), *The Foucault Reader*, Harmondsworth: Penguin, 1984, p. 87.

80 Foucault, 'Nietzsche, Genealogy, History', p. 88.

81 Foucault, 'Nietzsche, Genealogy, History', p. 88.

82 See Walter Benjamin, 'On the Concept of History', in *Selected Writings*, vol. 4, pp. 380–411. See also Gilloch, *Myth and Metropolis*, pp. 107–8.

83 Benjamin, 'Experience and Poverty', p. 734.

84 While Benjamin's notational thinking on the interior is not confined to Convolute I, it does offer the most intense coalescence of thinking and sources on the interior.

85 See Gilloch, *Myth and Metropolis*, pp. 100–1.

86 Rolf Tiedemann, 'Dialectics at a Standstill: Approaches to the *Passagen-Werk*', in *The Arcades Project*, p. 931.

87 Gilloch, *Myth and Metropolis*, p. 94.

88 Howard Eiland and Kevin McLaughlin, 'Translators' Foreword', in *The Arcades Project*, p. xi.

89 Eiland and McLaughlin, 'Translators' Foreword', p. xi. Compare also Eiland's account of a distracted reading that the structure of *The Arcades Project* encourages in Eiland, 'Reception in Distraction', pp. 62–6.

90 Benjamin, *The Arcades Project*, p. 406 [N4a,6].

91 Susan Buck-Morss, *The Dialectics of Seeing: Walter Benjamin and the Arcades Project*, Cambridge, MA: MIT Press, 1989, p. 6.

92 Buck-Morss, *The Dialectics of Seeing*, p. 6.

93 Buck-Morss, *The Dialectics of Seeing*, p. 59.

94 Benjamin, 'Paris, Capital of the Nineteenth Century', p. 20.

95 Gilloch, *Myth and Metropolis*, p. 100. He also gives a useful account of the fitful development of the project, and its relation to Benjamin's other published pieces (pp. 95–100).

96 Missac, *Walter Benjamin's Passages*, p. 136.

97 Benjamin, 'One-Way Street', p. 462.

98 Benjamin, *The Arcades Project*, p. 212 [I1,1].

99 Benjamin, *The Arcades Project*, p. 212 [I1,3].

100 Benjamin, *The Arcades Project*, p. 213 [I1,6].

101 Benjamin, *The Arcades Project*, p. 215 [I2,3].

102 Benjamin, *The Arcades Project*, p. 216 [I2,6].

103 Benjamin, *The Arcades Project*, p. 221 [I4,4].

104 Benjamin, *The Arcades Project*, p. 222 [I5,2].

105 Benjamin, *The Arcades Project*, p. 225 [I6a,4].

106 Gilles Deleuze and Félix Guattari, 'The Plane of Immanence', in *What Is Philosophy?* New York: Columbia University Press, 1994, p. 38.

107 Benjamin, *The Arcades Project*, p. 463 [N3,1].

108 Michael W. Jennings, *Dialectical Images: Walter Benjamin's Theory of Literary Criticism*, Ithaca: Cornell University Press, p. 38.

109 See Gilloch, *Myth and Metropolis*, p. 114.

110 For a discussion of Benjamin's thoughts on dwelling and modernity, see Hilde Heynen, *Architecture and Modernity: A Critique*, Cambridge, MA: MIT Press, 1999, pp. 107–19.

2 Lost objects: Sigmund Freud's psychoanalytical interior

1 Gilles Deleuze, 'Foreword: The Rise of the Social', in Jacques Donzelot, *The Policing of Families*, Baltimore: Johns Hopkins University Press, 1997, p. xvii.

2 Nikolas Rose, *Inventing our Selves: Psychology, Power and Personhood*, Cambridge: Cambridge University Press, 1998, p. 186.

3 Rose, *Inventing Our Selves*, p. 172.

4 Deleuze, 'The Rise of the Social', p. ix.

5 Donzelot, *The Policing of Families*, p. xxv.

6 Donzelot, *The Policing of Families*, p. xxiv.

7 See Michel Foucault, *The History of Sexuality*, Volume 1: *An Introduction*, London: Allen Lane, 1978, pp. 120–31.

8 Foucault, *The History of Sexuality*, p. 47.

9 Foucault, *The History of Sexuality*, p. 46.

10 On the relations between Freud's theory of dream interpretation and Walter Benjamin's historical analysis of the interior, see my 'Evidence, Experience and Conjecture: Reading the Interior through Benjamin and Bloch', *Home Cultures*, vol. 2, no. 3, 2005, pp. 292–3.

11 Sigmund Freud, 'The Interpretation of Dreams', in James Strachey (ed.), *The Standard Edition of the Complete Psychological Works of Sigmund Freud*, 24 vols, London: The Hogarth Press, 1953–74, vol. 5, p. 346.

12 See Freud, 'The Interpretation of Dreams', p. 214, n. 2.

13 Freud, 'The Interpretation of Dreams', p. 354.

14 Freud, 'Introductory Lectures on Psychoanalysis. Lecture XIX: Resistance and Repression', in *The Standard Edition*, vol. 16, pp. 295–6. Note also the analogy between the psyche and an optical device, described as a microscope or a telescope in Freud, 'The Interpretation of Dreams', pp. 536–7; the analogy between the movement of mental processes from an unconscious to a conscious state and the developing of a photograph from negative to positive in Freud, 'Introductory Lectures on Psychoanalysis. Lecture XIX', p. 295; and the analogy between repression, the unconscious and the conscious, and the situation of a lecture hall in Freud, 'Five Lectures on Psychoanalysis: Second Lecture', in *The Standard Edition*, vol. 11, p. 25. Diana Fuss has referred to the 'highly analogical descriptions of psychoanalysis', in particular, Freud's reliance on literary tropes. See Diana Fuss, *Identification Papers*, London: Routledge, 1995, p. 5.

15 Freud, 'Fragment of an Analysis of a Case of Hysteria', in *The Standard Edition*, vol. 11, p. 18.

16 Freud, 'Fragment of an Analysis of a Case of Hysteria', pp. 109

17 For an account of Dora's mother's obsessional behaviour, which Freud dubbed 'housewife's psychosis', see Hannah S. Decker, *Freud, Dora, and Vienna 1900*, New York: Free Press, 1991, pp. 54–5. See also Freud, 'Fragment of an Analysis of a Case of Hysteria', p. 20.

18 Freud, 'Fragment of an Analysis of a Case of Hysteria', p. 122.

19 See Lisa Appignanesi and John Forrester, *Freud's Women*, London: Weidenfeld & Nicolson, 1992, pp. 146–7. For a discussion of the construction of health and sickness within the milieu of the two families, see Robin Tolmach Lakoff and James C. Coyne, *Father Knows Best: The*

Use and Abuse of Power in Freud's Case of Dora, New York: Teachers College Press, 1993, pp. 30–1.

20 Appignanesi and Forrester, *Freud's Women*, p. 160.

21 See Appignanesi and Forrester, *Freud's Women*, pp. 161–2.

22 Peter Stallybrass and Allon White, *The Politics and Poetics of Transgression*, Ithaca: Cornell University Press, 1986, pp. 163, 168.

23 See Appignanesi and Forrester, *Freud's Women*, 147.

24 Diana Fuss, 'Freud's Ear', in *The Sense of an Interior*, London: Routledge, 2004, p. 78. Fuss also emphasizes the 'carefully staged orientalist scene' of the consulting room proper, and the 'sexual overtones of the famous couch' (p. 90). For a psychoanalytical account of the fetishistic aspects of the collection in a bourgeois context, see Emily Apter, 'Cabinet Secrets: Fetishism, Prostitution and the Fin-de-Siècle Interior', *Assemblage*, no. 9, 1989, pp. 7–19.

25 Fuss, 'Freud's Ear', p. 81. On the spatial location of Freud's mirror, see also Beatriz Colomina, *Privacy and Publicity: Modern Architecture as Mass Media*, Cambridge, MA: MIT Press, 1994, pp. 80–2.

26 Fuss, 'Freud's Ear', p. 92.

27 Freud, 'Group Psychology and the Analysis of the Ego', in *The Standard Edition*, vol. 18, p. 126. This work, published in 1921, would have been written in Freud's Berggasse study. Part of this passage is quoted in Fuss, 'Freud's Ear', p. 102.

28 See Lynn Gamwell, 'A Collector Analyses Collecting: Sigmund Freud on the Passion to Possess', in Stephen Barker (ed.), *Excavations and their Objects: Freud's Collection of Antiquity*, Albany: State University of New York Press, 1996, p. 2. For an analysis of Freud's collection, see Lynn Gamwell and Richard Wells (eds), *Sigmund Freud and Art: His Personal Collection of Antiquities*, Binghamton and London: State University of New York and The Freud Museum, 1989.

29 Kenneth Reinhard, 'The Freudian Things: Construction and the Archaeological Metaphor', in *Excavations and their Objects*, p. 57.

30 Reinhard, 'The Freudian Things', p. 58. Reinhard distinguishes his interpretation of the archaeological metaphor from that of Donald Kuspit, who draws more literal relations between psychoanalysis and archaeology. Reinhard takes issue with Kuspit's claim that psychoanalysis can recover fully knowledge that had remained hidden, and in this way surpass the limits of the practice of archaeology, which can never recover whole objects and their true meaning. See Donald Kuspit, 'A Mighty Metaphor: The Analogy of Archaeology and Psychoanalysis', in *Sigmund Freud and Art*, pp. 133–52, and Reinhard, 'The Freudian Things', pp. 59–60. Reinhard's argument aids the present argument in an 'interiorized' reading of the archaeological metaphor, rather than the more straightforward art-historical approach of Kuspit.

31 Reinhard, 'The Freudian Things', p. 61. In respect of Benjamin's reading of the historical past in the layers of the city, time is not simply past time unearthed in the present, but also time past, the time that renders direct access to past time impossible through time's own transformative work. Yet this transformative work allows for the illuminative and redemptive potential of the past's fragments. See Graeme Gilloch, *Myth and Metropolis: Walter Benjamin and the City*, Cambridge: Polity Press, 1996, pp. 70–8.

32 Reinhard, 'The Freudian Things', p. 63.

33 Reinhard, 'The Freudian Things', p. 64.

34 Reinhard, 'The Freudian Things', p. 77.

35 See Reinhard, 'The Freudian Things', pp. 68–70.

36 Reinhard, 'The Freudian Things', p. 70.

37 Reinhard, 'The Freudian Things', p. 70.

38 See Walter Benjamin, 'On Some Motifs in Baudelaire', in *Selected Writings*, 4 vols, Cambridge, MA: The Belknap Press of Harvard University Press, 1996–2003, vol. 4, p. 317. On the relation between conceptions of *Erinnerung* and *Gedächtnis* in psychoanalysis, see Reinhard, 'The Freudian Things', passim.

39 See Reinhard, 'The Freudian Things', pp. 78–9.

40 Reinhard, 'The Freudian Things', p. 71.

41 Fuss, 'Freud's Ear', p. 102.

42 Compare Fuss: 'a principle of photographic likenesses, of double exposures and exposed doubles, animates and reanimates the transferential scene. Insofar as the mechanism of transference works precisely by means of a double exposure – a superimposition of one figure onto another – the process of psychoanalysis can be seen to operate as a form of photographic development. Like photography, the technology of transference performs a kind of spirit work in which the phantoms of missing or lost others come back to life in the person of the analyst.' Fuss, 'Freud's Ear', pp. 103–4.

43 See Reinhard, 'The Freudian Things', p. 76.

44 See *20 Maresfield Gardens: A Guide to the Freud Museum*, London: Serpent's Tail, 1998, p. 2; and Fuss, 'Freud's Ear', p. 104.

45 *20 Maresfield Gardens* suggests: 'After Freud's death in 1939, his wife Martha made no changes to the study during the rest of her life and Anna Freud, the youngest of Freud's six children, subsequently kept it just as it was in her father's lifetime. She herself lived and practised psychoanalysis at 20 Maresfield Gardens for over 40 years' (p. 3). Photographs of this space, now part of the Freud Museum in London, appear in the guidebook. In being able to visit this space, however, one must also forget that 'this is how it was'.

46 See Yosef Hayim Yerushlami, 'The Purloined Kiddush Cups: Reopening the Case on Freud's Jewish Identity', supplement to *Sigmund Freud and Art*, n.p., for a discussion of evidence provided by Engelman's photographs.

47 Fuss, 'Freud's Ear', p. 72.

48 Fuss, 'Freud's Ear', p. 73.

49 Fuss does argue that the photographs 'have themselves *become* the museum – miniature sites of preservation and display', Fuss, 'Freud's Ear', p. 73.

50 Reinhard, 'The Freudian Things', p. 77.

51 Anthony Vidler, *The Architectural Uncanny: Essays in the Modern Unhomely*, Cambridge, MA: MIT Press, 1996.

52 Vidler, *The Architectural Uncanny*, p. 3.

53 Vidler, *The Architectural Uncanny*, p. 3.

54 Vidler, *The Architectural Uncanny*, p. 11.

55 A similar focus on the representation of spaces of unease occurs in Susan Sidlauskas's reading of the interior paintings of Degas, Sargent, Vuillard and Sickert. She explores the way in which 'the signs of subjectivity [were] . . . embedded directly in the lineaments of compositional structure'. Susan Sidlauskas, *Body, Place and Self in Nineteenth-Century Painting*, Cambridge: Cambridge University Press, 2000, p. 13. She uses theories of empathy between a spectator and a painting to explore the way in which a spectator might experience 'a visceral response [to a painting], a bodily empathy, for the discomfort of their protagonists' (pp. 2–3). Like Vidler, Sidlauskas escapes the sense of representation being transparent to the material evidence of an interior, and instead looks at the ways in which the techniques of depiction give on to a reading of domestic subjectivity itself. But she too reads space solely within representation, even as she writes about a viewer's bodily empathy. Sharon Marcus's analysis of the textual representation of the interior is engaged with a similar methodological problematic as Vidler and Sidlauskas. Marcus analyses the negotiation of private and public realms in the context of nineteenth-century Paris and London: 'My focus throughout is on discourses about apartment houses, not on apartment houses themselves', the novel being treated as a privileged site of discourse about nineteenth-century domesticity. Sharon Marcus, *Apartment Stories: City and Home in Nineteenth-Century Paris and London*, Berkeley: University of California Press, 1999, p. 9. Here again there is a desire to focus interpretation within representation. Marcus's concept of a topography of narration emphasizes this: 'By topography I mean the ways that narration itself (and not simply

the events narrated) inscribes spatial relations – the ways that narration established zones as exterior and interior, mobile and fixed, global and local, publicly open and privately opaque' (p. 10).

56 Vidler, *The Architectural Uncanny*, p. 11. Emphasis in original. Slightly later, he describes buildings acting as 'representations of estrangement' (p. 12).

57 Vidler, *The Architectural Uncanny*, p. 12. Sarah Kofman underpins this position when she argues: '[Freud's essay] "The Uncanny" establishes differences between real experience and works of fiction concerning the arousal of the feeling of uncanniness. In fiction, the uncanny is much fuller and richer than in real life; it embraces real life and includes as well things which do not occur under real life conditions. "The realm of imagination depends for its effect on the fact that its content is not submitted to reality testing." The author can multiply the effects imagination can have by creating events which do not occur in reality; the reader goes along with him because "when belief makes him happy, he has to take the acceptance of quite a considerable number of improbable occurrences into the bargain."' Sarah Kofman, *The Childhood of Art: An Interpretation of Freud's Aesthetics*, New York: Columbia University Press, 1988, p. 139. Kofman is quoting, in turn, Freud, 'The "Uncanny"', in *The Standard Edition*, vol. 17, p. 249; and idem, 'Delusions and Dreams', in *The Standard Edition*, vol. 9, p. 18.

58 See Vidler, *The Architectural Uncanny*, pp. 12–14. In his introduction to a subsequent collection of essays, Vidler proposes a more spatial reading of psychological affect: 'Space, in these various iterations [from Romanticism to Modernism], has been increasingly defined as a product of subjective projection and introjection, as opposed to a stable container of objects and bodies. From the beginning of the [twentieth] century, the apparently fixed laws of perspective have been transformed, transgressed and ignored in the search to represent the space of modern identity'. Anthony Vidler, *Warped Space: Art, Architecture and Anxiety in Modern Culture*, Cambridge, MA: MIT Press, 2000, p. 1. Vidler's ultimate concern, however, is still to do with the way in which spatial affect produces shifts in representation. This is undoubtedly an important area of research, but one that does not get closer to the specificity of the interior experienced in its doubleness.

59 Ernst Bloch, 'A Philosophical View of the Detective Novel', in *The Utopian Function of Art and Literature: Selected Essays*, Cambridge, MA: MIT Press, p. 245. Vidler cites this passage from Bloch at the beginning of his account of the uncanny. Apropos Bloch, he suggests that 'the vicarious taste for the uncanny has been a constant in modern culture, only intensified by shifts in media'. Vidler, *The Architectural Uncanny*, p. 4. For a comparative discussion of Bloch and Benjamin on the interior, see my 'Evidence, Experience and Conjecture'.

60 The 'shock' of this encounter can be related to a connection Tom Gunning has made between the railway carriage and the cushioning and protection offered by the Benjaminian domestic interior: 'Encased within an upholstered environment, the inhabitant of the *intérieur* is cushioned, like the railway passenger for whose comfort Wolfgang Schivelbusch claims the modern shock-absorbing techniques of upholstered furniture were first designed'. Tom Gunning, 'The Exterior as *Intérieur*: Walter Benjamin's Optical Detective', *boundary 2*, vol. 30, no. 1, 2003, p. 106. See also Wolfgang Schivelbusch, *The Railway Journey: The Industrialization of Time and Space in the 19th Century*, Leamington Spa: Berg, 1986, pp. 123–5.

61 Freud, 'The "Uncanny"', p. 248, n. 1.

62 Jean Pierre Vernant distinguishes between an image or likeness and the double in his discussion of the figure of the double in ancient Greek thought: 'A double is not at all the same thing as an image. It is not a "natural" object, but nor is it simply a product of the mind. It is not an imitation of a real object or an illusion of the mind or a creation of thought. The double is something separate from the person who sees it, something whose peculiar character sets it in opposition, even in appearance, to familiar objects in life's ordinary setting. It exists on two contrasting planes at the same time: at the very moment that it shows itself to be present it also reveals itself to be not of this world and as belonging to some inaccessible, other sphere'. Jean Pierre Vernant, 'The Representation of the Invisible and the Psychological Category of the Double: The Colossos', in *Myth and Thought amongst the Greeks*, London: Routledge & Kegan Paul, 1983, pp. 308–9.

63 Elizabeth Grosz, 'Space, Time, and Bodies', in *Space, Time, and Perversion: Essays on the Politics of Bodies*, London: Routledge, 1995, p. 86.

64 Grosz, 'Space, Time and Bodies', p. 87.

65 Grosz, 'Space, Time and Bodies', p. 90.

66 Jacques Lacan, 'The Mirror Stage as Formative of the Function of the I as Revealed in Psychoanalytic Experience', in *Écrits: A Selection*, New York: W. W. Norton, 1977, p. 4.

67 Freud, 'The "Uncanny"', pp. 235–6.

68 See Fuss, *Identification Papers*, pp. 27–8.

69 See Freud, 'Group Psychology and the Analysis of the Ego', pp. 105–10. Fuss has outlined the two main models for understanding identification as the interiorization of the other, either through the ingestion or oral incorporation of the other, or through being invaded or infected by the other. These two models explain the 'difference between an active and a passive relation to the Other: to seize the Other, or to be seized by the Other'. Fuss, *Identification Papers*, p. 41. Fuss explains that Freud developed the term identification over a long period of time, but never arrived at a systematic exposition of it. Fuss has tracked the term through Freud's writings in *Identification Papers*, pp. 21–56. In addition, identification as a relation to objects in the register of what one wants to be, needs to be distinguished from libidinal attachment to objects, or what one wants to have. Fuss discusses this distinction between being and having in terms of 'identification's relation to its theoretical other, desire', where desire is the register of object-choice, or having. Fuss, *Identification Papers*, p. 11. Despite describing, in Freud's terms, the theoretical impossibility of both identifying with and desiring the same object, Fuss discusses how this distinction is open to question (pp. 11–13, 45–6).

70 See Freud, 'Group Psychology and the Analysis of the Ego', p. 109.

71 Kaja Silverman, *World Spectators*, Stanford: Stanford University Press, 2000, p. 78.

72 Silverman, *World Spectators*, p. 88.

73 Silverman, *World Spectators*, p. 89. Diana Fuss defines subjectivity in a Freudian sense in a way that aligns identification with this struggle of looking: 'What Freudian psychoanalysis understands by "subjectivity" is precisely this struggle to negotiate a constantly changing field of ambivalent identifications; indeed, subjectivity can be most concisely understood as *the history of one's identifications*.' Fuss, *Identification Papers*, p. 34. Emphasis in original.

74 Marcel Proust, *In Search of Lost Time*, 6 vols, London: Vintage, 1996, vol. 1, pp. 49–55.

75 Proust, *In Search of Lost Time*, p. 53.

76 Proust, *In Search of Lost Time*, p. 52.

77 Proust, *In Search of Lost Time*, pp. 53–4.

3 Imagining the interior: Plan and comfort

1 Robert Kerr, *The Gentleman's House, or How to Plan English Residences from the Parsonage to the Palace; with Tables of Accommodation and Cost, and a Series of Selected Plans*, 3rd revised edn, London: John Murray, 1871 [1864], p. 111; quoted in Peter Thornton, *Authentic Décor: The Domestic Interior 1620–1920*, New York: Viking, 1984, p. 10.

2 Jill Franklin, *The Gentleman's Country House and its Plan, 1835–1914*, London: Routledge & Kegan Paul, 1981. See also Mark Girouard, *The Victorian Country House*, New Haven: Yale University Press, 1979; and idem, *Life in the English Country House: A Social and Architectural History*, New Haven: Yale University Press, 1978, pp. 267–98. On the relation of Kerr's ideas on planning to the furnishing of interiors, see Thornton, *Authentic Décor*, pp. 218–21.

3 Franklin, *The Gentleman's Country House*, p. 1.

4 Robin Evans, 'Figures, Doors and Passages', in *Translations from Drawing to Building and Other Essays*, London: Architectural Association, 1997, p. 57.

5 Franklin, *The Gentleman's Country House*, p. 129.

6 For a broader argument about the emergence of comfort as a domestic sensibility in the Anglo-American context from the eighteenth century, see John Crowley, 'The Sensibility of Comfort',

American Historical Review, vol. 104, no. 3, 1999, pp. 749–82. Crowley's argument will be discussed below with a closer examination of the value of comfort.

7 This approach forms a kind of dialogue with William Taylor's analysis of Kerr's treatise, which develops a concept of characterization to discuss how the plan relates an imagined subject to a calibrated inhabitational environment. While the sources each use to develop a sense of the 'imaginative inhabitation' of the plan differ, as do the scope and context of each inquiry, the critical intent behind the projects is very similar. See William Taylor, *The Vital Landscape: Nature and the Built Environment in Nineteenth-Century Britain*, Aldershot: Ashgate, 2004, pp. 151–73, and idem, 'Characterizing the Inhabitant in Robert Kerr's *The Gentleman's House*, 1864', *Design Issues*, vol. 18, no. 3, 2002, pp. 27–42. On character as an architectural concept, see Colin Rowe, 'Character and Composition; or Some Vicissitudes of Architectural Vocabulary in the Nineteenth Century', in *The Mathematics of the Ideal Villa and Other Essays*, Cambridge, MA: MIT Press, 1976, pp. 60–87.

8 Kerr, *The Gentleman's House*, p. 70.

9 In his investigation of flow lines on plans, which includes work on Kerr, Paul Emmons has written: 'A flow line drawn on a plan can be a meandering doodle that invites imaginative inhabitation in order to view a future realm of rich experience.' Paul Emmons, 'Intimate Circulations: Representing Flow in House and City', *AA Files*, no. 51, 2005, p. 48; however, he does not explore how this imaginative inhabitation might actually operate in relation to techniques of planning.

10 Another essay by Evans is useful in considering the relation between imagination and orthographic projection. See Robin Evans, 'Architectural Projection', in Eve Blau and Edward Kaufman (eds), *Architecture and its Image: Four Centuries of Architectural Representation. Works from the Canadian Centre for Architecture*, Montreal: Canadian Centre for Architecture, 1989, pp. 19–35.

11 Elaine Scarry, *Dreaming by the Book*, Princeton: Princeton University Press, 1999, p. 11.

12 Scarry, *Dreaming by the Book*, p. 14.

13 Scarry, *Dreaming by the Book*, p. 14.

14 Scarry, *Dreaming by the Book*, p. 31.

15 Compare Taylor's account of Kerr's use of literary techniques of identification between reader and inhabitant in *The Vital Landscape*, pp. 164–5.

16 Scarry, *Dreaming by the Book*, p. 31.

17 Scarry, *Dreaming by the Book*, p. 4.

18 Scarry, *Dreaming by the Book*, p. 6.

19 A note on the structuring of *The Gentleman's House* is useful at this point. The book is divided into six thematic parts. The first is titled: 'A Sketch of the History and Development of the Domestic Plan in England', the second: 'The Principles of Plan as Now Established', the third part is on site and grounds, the fourth on architectural style, the fifth on accommodation and cost, and the sixth, as an appendix, is a critical commentary on the plates of plans printed in the volume. The first two parts relate quite directly to one another, 'The Principles of Plan as Now Established' being a direct summation of Kerr's historical observations.

20 Kerr, *The Gentleman's House*, p. 69.

21 On Kerr's relation to the nineteenth-century debate about style, see Taylor, *The Vital Landscape*, pp. 155–6.

22 Kerr, *The Gentleman's House*, p. 62.

23 Kerr, *The Gentleman's House*, p. 50. Emphasis in original.

24 Kerr, *The Gentleman's House*, pp. 50–1.

25 Kerr, *The Gentleman's House*, pp. 56–7.

26 An expanded discussion of these plans is given in the section of 'Critical Notes on the Plates'. See Kerr, *The Gentleman's House*, pp. 430–1.

27 Kerr, *The Gentleman's House*, p. 57.

28 Kerr, *The Gentleman's House*, p. 58.

29 Kerr draws a sharper distinction between these two plans in his separate discussion of the individual plates, praising Balmoral over Osborne. See Kerr, *The Gentleman's House*, pp. 431–3. He begins his discussion of Osborne by lamenting that 'the aid of a proper architect was not had in this plan. Mr Cubitt (the eminent builder) was perhaps as near an approach to an architect as any man not an architect could be' (p. 431). He then suggests in a footnote that the builder should employ an architect himself. Franklin lists Osborne as being by Thomas Cubitt and Prince Albert, with Prince Albert and Queen Victoria as clients. Franklin, *The Gentleman's Country House*, p. 265. It is unclear, then, why Osborne would be represented in an engraving on the title page of *The Gentleman's House*. Kerr's criticism of the plan seems to be made from the angle that Cubitt was not an architect.

30 Kerr, *The Gentleman's House*, p. 60.

31 The difference between Kerr's principles as outlined in *The Gentleman's House*, and the reactions of some of his clients vis-à-vis the houses he built are documented by Franklin. The book seems to have been good publicity for Kerr, but his houses were not seen to match its guiding principles of planning. See Franklin, *The Gentleman's Country House*, pp. 120, 122, 245.

32 On this point, compare Taylor: 'Kerr reinterpreted the now well-trodden clash of architectural styles in terms of each simply being a different way of configuring rooms. In *The Gentleman's House* the neo-Classical and the Gothic appeared as variations on the same theme of suitable habitat. Irrespective of which style clothed the exterior of a building, an organic unity of spatial experience was presumed indoors.' Taylor, *The Vital Landscape*, p. 156. The present argument is, however, that Kerr develops a marked preference for the Gothic due to its perceptible qualities of asymmetry mapping more easily on to the contemporary demands of comfort, convenience and privacy.

33 Kerr, *The Gentleman's House*, p. 61. On the way in which the landscape and the environment, through ideas of aspect and prospect, bear on Kerr's thoughts on internal arrangement, see Taylor, *The Vital Landscape*, pp. 159–61.

34 Kerr, *The Gentleman's House*, p. 63.

35 Kerr, *The Gentleman's House*, p. 65.

36 Kerr, *The Gentleman's House*, p. 69.

37 Along with comfort, Kerr discusses such principles as privacy, convenience, spaciousness, compactness, light and air, salubrity, aspect and prospect, all of which flow from the consideration of the relation of rooms to each other, and the compromises and adjustments necessary to fit a plan together. See Kerr, *The Gentleman's House*, p. 67.

38 Kerr, *The Gentleman's House*, p. 70.

39 This double condition of the plan can usefully be situated in relation to the argument Robin Evans makes about the relation between drawing and building. I would agree with Evans when he argues that 'Drawing in architecture is not done after nature, but prior to construction; it is not so much produced by reflection on the reality outside the drawing, as productive of reality that will end up outside the drawing'. Robin Evans, 'Translations from Drawing to Building', in *Translations from Drawing to Building and Other Essays*, p. 165. I would add to this argument by saying that the plan drawing enables the production of two 'realities' outside the drawing: on the one hand, 'the building', and on the other, the interior inserted into the inside space provided by the building. This play of doubles multiplies: the condition of the interior as insertion is both material and immaterial, in relation to both the imagining of inhabitation with the plan (where the plan provides the material for imagining), and the modes of inhabitation that negotiate built space.

40 The principle of privacy impinges upon Kerr's notion of scale when he suggests that in larger dwellings, planning for and maintaining privacy becomes a more comprehensible task, and he is able to advocate the provision of separate entrances, stairs and corridors for servants and the family. See Kerr, *The Gentleman's House*, p. 69.

41 Kerr, *The Gentleman's House*, p. 69. See also Girouard, *Life in the English Country House*, p. 285.

42 Crowley, 'The Sensibility of Comfort', p. 751. Sigfried Giedion appears to support this shift in

meaning, by suggesting that in the West after the eighteenth century comfort comes to be aligned with convenience, replacing its earlier Latinate sense as strength. Yet in expanding upon this shift after the eighteenth century, Giedion contrasts Eastern notions of comfort as control and physical self-support with Western notions of the body needing to be supported in its repose. In the second half of the nineteenth century, he sees comfort taking a new turn with the idea of readily movable furniture. See Sigfried Giedion, *Mechanization Takes Command: A Contribution to Anonymous History*, New York: W. W. Norton, 1969.

43 Crowley, 'The Sensibility of Comfort', p. 752. Crowley explicitly argues that comfort is not a natural desire, but exists as a term within a nexus of other terms, including luxury, commodity, convenience and decency, which shift and are adopted for different usages, the borrowing of terms between English and French being of special significance. He singles out Peter Thornton, *Seventeenth-Century Interior Decoration in England, France and Holland*, New Haven: Yale University Press, 1978, and Witold Rybczynski, *Home: A Short History of an Idea*, Harmondsworth: Penguin, 1986, as historians of the domestic who assume comfort as a natural response and desire in relation to the progressive changes to physical environments. Crowley, 'The Sensibility of Comfort', p. 753. See also idem, *The Invention of Comfort: Sensibilities and Design in Early Modern Britain and Early America*, Baltimore: Johns Hopkins University Press, 2001, pp. ix–xi, for his framing of a non-essentialist history of comfort.

44 J.-F. Blondel, *Architecture françoise ou recueil des plans, élévations, coupes et profils*, vol. 1, Paris, 1752, p. 26. Quoted and translated in Adrian Forty, *Words and Buildings: A Vocabulary of Modern Architecture*, London: Thames & Hudson, 2000, p. 190.

45 J. C. Loudon, *An Encyclopaedia of Cottage, Farm and Villa Architecture*, London: Longman, 1833, p. 1114. Quoted in Forty, *Words and Buildings*, p. 190.

46 Forty, *Words and Buildings*, p. 190. In his analysis of Kerr's treatise, Taylor distinguishes between comfort and convenience, the former relating to the perception and experience of the immediate environment, and the latter to the arrangement of 'component parts' in plan. See Taylor, 'Characterizing the Inhabitant', pp. 34–5.

47 Tomás Maldonado, 'The Idea of Comfort', in Victor Margolin and Richard Buchanan (eds), *The Idea of Design*, Cambridge, MA: MIT Press, 1995, pp. 248–56.

48 Maldonado, 'The Idea of Comfort', p. 250.

49 Maldonado, 'The Idea of Comfort', p. 254.

50 J. J. Stevenson, *House Architecture*, 2 vols, London: Macmillan, 1880. The first volume, 'Architecture', gives an account of the development and application of the historical styles, with an emphasis on their suitability for producing good domestic architecture. The second volume is entitled 'House-planning' and deals with the 'practicalities' of house design, although its first chapter is devoted to a history of house planning.

51 Franklin, *The Gentleman's Country House*, p. 2.

52 Girouard, *The Victorian Country House*, p. 69.

53 See Girouard, *The Victorian Country House*, pp. 69–70.

54 Stevenson, *House Architecture*, vol. 2, pp. 3–4.

55 Stevenson, *House Architecture*, vol. 2, pp. 47–51.

56 This situation can be compared to Evans's conviction that nineteenth-century domesticity attests to a caveat on the proximity of bodies. His evidence for the emergence of objects and furnishings as mediators of sensibility and identity comes from his reading of visual representations. But as I shall argue in relation to Stevenson, a different sort of picturing, one not able to deliver the sort of verifiable evidence Evans is after, tells a different story. See Evans, 'Figures, Doors and Passages', pp. 79–84. One might conclude that Evans's findings are very much a result of his method of reading representations and plans together, just as the present findings come from the particular attention to the relation between plans and the instructional texts in which they were presented.

57 Stevenson, *House Architecture*, vol. 2, p. 79.

58 Stevenson recognizes that at this time, servants no longer relied on the family. Serving was a job-option among many, and hence comfort and better conditions were being demanded. See Stevenson, *House Architecture*, vol. 2, pp. 110–13.

59 Stevenson, *House Architecture*, vol. 2, p. 80.

60 W. J. T. Mitchell's hybrid concept of the imagetext is a useful one to compare to Scarry's division between verbal and visual arts along 'imaginary' lines. Mitchell discusses ekphrasis as one example of an imagetext. He outlines three moments of ekphrasis: first, ekphrastic hope, where a text would have the capacity to 'give voice' to a mute visual object; second, ekphrastic fear, where the difference between verbal and visual representation might actually disappear; and third, ekphrastic indifference, where it is deemed impossible for words to conjure up satisfactorily a visual object. See W. J. T. Mitchell, *Picture Theory*, Chicago: University of Chicago Press, 1994, pp. 151–82. Scarry's division between the verbal and visual arts would seem to come out of this notion of ekphrastic indifference, where the difference between the verbal and the visual is seen to be too great for any useful conjunction to be made. Mitchell's account of the three moments of ekphrasis does, however, allow for indifference to be read against the two extremes of hope and fear: that to be indifferent about the relation between verbal and visual representation might be a way through one's oscillation between hope of a unification, and fear that this might lead to the capitulation of one into the other.

61 For an account of the way the imagination works on and through matter, see Michael Carter, 'Notes on Imagination, Fantasy and the Imaginary', in John Macarthur (ed.), *Imaginary Materials: A Seminar with Michael Carter*, Brisbane: IMA Publishing, 2000, pp. 48–53. As a case for this theoretical account, Carter has discussed the impact of oil paint as a particular artistic material in the history of picturing, suggesting oil paint's capacity to enfold the imagination within depiction, so that it represents a deepening of one's ability to imagine the world. He goes so far as to speak of oil paint having an imagination of its own. See Michael Carter, *Putting a Face on Things: Studies in Imaginary Materials*, Sydney: Power Publications, 1997, pp. 225–70.

62 Stevenson, *House Architecture*, vol. 2, p. 59. There is an echo here of Humphry Repton's 'Old Cedar Parlour', an example which he used to differentiate between the single occupation of a room in a house whose plan consisted of the arrangement of many rooms of different variety, and the possibilities for a variety of occupation within any given room, what Stevenson champions with the idea of the hall. Robin Evans has given an account of Repton's example: 'The circle of chairs [around a room] had to be broken, redolent as it was, he [Repton] said, of dull, obsequious, outmoded conversation directed at one senescent, overbearing figure, the matriarch, whose domineering presence was symbolized by a portrait in his drawing of "the Old Cedar Parlour."' Evans, 'The Developed Surface: An Enquiry into the Brief Life of an Eighteenth-Century Drawing Technique', in *Translations from Drawing to Building*, p. 215. In Stevenson's description, the radial presentation of books on the round table might stand in for the radial arrangement of chairs around a room.

63 Stevenson, *House Architecture*, vol. 2, p. 130.

64 Stevenson ends the volume on house planning by considering town houses, and other forms of dwelling such as mansions, by which he means town-based, multi-level and multi-dwelling buildings. But he concludes that these types, while representing particular problems but also opportunities for the development of plan technique, are not what is meant by the 'English home'. Stevenson, *House Architecture*, vol. 2, pp. 154–5.

65 Stevenson, *House Architecture*, vol. 2, p. 133.

66 Note Taylor on the factors influencing inhabitation: 'For the social theorist, the Victorian home was a site where powers governed at a local or intimate level. It was a place where medical, psychiatric and educational theories informed a range of bodily and building practices. One must be mindful, however, that the Victorian home was also a place for imagining what it meant to be a unique person, to be blessed with autonomy and personal freedom.' Taylor, *The Vital Landscape*, p. 173.

4 Consuming the interior: Geography and identity

1 See Peter Taylor, *Modernities: A Geohistorical Approach*, Cambridge: Polity Press, 1999, pp. 11–12.

2 The Barr Smiths are mentioned in Charlotte Gere, *Nineteenth-Century Decoration: The Art of the Interior*, New York: Harry N. Abrams, 1989, p. 292.

3 Anna Muthesius was a dress designer and published a book on dress reform titled *Das Reformkleid* in 1903. She also designed department store window displays with Lilly Reich, and participated with her on other design projects. Mark Wigley suggests that Hermann Muthesius consulted her on the interior aspects of his own domestic architectural designs, and that her critique of fashion and dress would have influenced Muthesius's thoughts on fashion and clothing. See Mark Wigley, *White Walls, Designer Dresses: The Fashioning of Modern Architecture*, Cambridge, MA: MIT Press, 1995, pp. 138–41, 151. Their son, Eckart Muthesius, says that Anna befriended Margaret McDonald Mackintosh and Jessie Newbery while the Muthesiuses were in England, and that they both contributed to *Das Reformkleid*. See Eckart Muthesius, 'Muthesius', in *Hermann Muthesius, 1861–1927*, London: Architectural Association, 1979, pp. 4–5.

4 J. J. Stevenson, *House Architecture*, 2 vols, London: Macmillan, 1880, vol. 2, p. 59.

5 Julia Hirsch, *Family Photographs: Content, Meaning, and Effect*, Oxford: Oxford University Press, 1981, p. 43. On the photography of English domestic interiors around this time, see Nicholas Cooper, *The Opulent Eye: Late Victorian and Edwardian Taste in Interior Design*, London: Architectural Press, 1976, p. 2. For the American context, see William Seale, *The Tasteful Interlude: American Interiors through the Camera's Eye, 1860–1917*, 2nd revised edn, Nashville: American Association for State and Local History, 1981, pp. 26–7. On the development of portrait photography in relation to a nineteenth-century understanding of portrait painting, see Walter Benjamin, 'Little History of Photography', in *Selected Writings*, 4 vols, Cambridge, MA: The Belknap Press of Harvard University Press, 1996–2003, vol. 2, pp. 507–30. A more detailed discussion about technical aspects of photographing interiors takes place in Chapter 5.

6 Christopher Menz, *Morris & Company, Pre-Raphaelites and the Arts & Crafts Movement in South Australia*, Adelaide: Art Gallery Board of South Australia, 1994, p. 42. See also Fayette Gosse (ed.), *Joanna and Robert: The Barr Smiths' Life in Letters, 1853–1919*, Adelaide: Barr Smith Press, 1996, p. xxii.

7 Many of the furnishings and objects bought by the Barr Smiths are held in the collection of the Art Gallery of South Australia, Adelaide, which continues to collect Morris & Co. objects and furnishings. For a full catalogue of holdings, see Christopher Menz, *Morris & Co.*, Adelaide: Art Gallery of South Australia, 2002.

8 Robert Barr Smith's family came from the village of Lochwinnoch, near Glasgow, and Joanna Barr Smith's family, the Elders, came from Kirkcaldy, near Edinburgh. For details on their early lives in Scotland, and their travels between Scotland, England and Australia, see Ken Preiss and Pamela Oborn, *The Torrens Park Estate: A Social and Architectural History*, Adelaide: K. Preiss & P. Oborn, 1991, pp. 57–66.

9 Robert Barr Smith initially employed London architect Neville Ashbee (no relation to Arts and Crafts architect C. R. Ashbee) to give advice as to the installation of the Morris & Co. interiors. Installation work was supervised first by John Grainger in Adelaide, and then by the firm Henderson & Marryat. Some of the installation work involved structural changes to the inside spaces of the houses. See Menz, *Morris & Company*, pp. 46–9.

10 Hermann Muthesius, *The English House*, London: Crosby Lockwood Staples, 1979.

11 Manfredo Tafuri and Francesco Dal Co note the possibility of a different side to Muthesius's presence in England: 'There was some basis for [English Arts and Crafts architect] William Lethaby's accusation in 1916 that Muthesius carried on industrial espionage in England in the interests of the expansionist German capitalism.' Manfredo Tafuri and Francesco Dal Co, *Modern Architecture*, New York: Harry N. Abrams, 1979, p. 93.

12 Hermann Muthesius, *Style-architecture and Building-art: Transformations of Architecture in the Nineteenth Century and its Present Condition*, Santa Monica: Getty Center for the History of Art and the Humanities, 1994. The work consolidated at the turn of the twentieth century several decades of discussion in the Germanic world which proposed that architecture be appraised in accordance with the opportunities and limitations accorded by material and technology, rather than by an appeal to the reanimation of historical styles. See Harry Francis Mallgrave, 'From Realism to *Sachlichkeit*: the Polemics of Architectural Modernity in the 1890s', in Harry Francis Mallgrave (ed.), *Otto Wagner: Reflections on the Raiment of Modernity*, Santa Monica: Getty Center for the History of Art and the Humanities, 1993, p. 306. Stanford Anderson's edited and translated text of *Style-architecture and Building-art* is an amalgamation of its two editions of 1901 and 1903. He has charted subtle but significant changes in the text between the two editions, which can be seen to be linked to Muthesius's continued reassessment of contemporary artistic developments over that period. The first edition was witness to the height of activity in the Viennese Secession, and Jugendstil and Art Nouveau design. Anderson detects that Muthesius remained sceptical of the profundity of such movements and tendencies, but saw that any new tendencies of significance would inevitably arise from such beginnings. The 1903 edition bears witness as much to the actual decline of these movements as it does to Muthesius's reconsideration of them, and strengthening of his own position. The largest change between the two editions of *Style-architecture and Building-art* was an expansion of the section entitled 'The New Interior', in which he distinguished between what was promising in contemporary developments in Europe, and what had merely developed into (architectural) style. See Stanford Anderson, 'Style-architecture and Building-art: Realist Architecture as the Vehicle for a Renewal of Culture', in Hermann Muthesius, *Style-architecture and Building-art*, p. 26. Mark Wigley has characterized Muthesius's reassessment of Jugendstil between the two editions in terms of Jugendstil's abuse by 'commercial interests'. Wigley, *White Walls, Designer Dresses*, p. 147.

13 In the German-language context of the late nineteenth and early twentieth centuries, Mitchell Schwarzer has shown how the development of architectural theory was wedded to its involvement in a broader cultural and industrial context. His conception of cultural exchange in an international context is particularly important. At one level he wants to critique the accepted wisdom that there was a transfer of impetus between England and Germany around the turn of the century. In elucidating the arguments of important German-language architectural theorists, Schwarzer instead proposes a more complex structure of the consolidation of national identities and differences in an increasingly international context, a context created principally in the nineteenth century by the international expositions, and the crucial role design played in representing the cultural identity and economic strength of various nations. See Mitchell Schwarzer, *German Architectural Theory and the Search for Modern Identity*, Cambridge: Cambridge University Press, 1995, pp. 128–66.

14 Muthesius, *Style-architecture and Building-art*, pp. 79–80. Wigley discusses this passage in terms of the aesthetic or look of the machine as the actively produced look of the modern. See Wigley, *White Walls, Designer Dresses*, pp. 176–7. His discussion is situated in the context of an argument about fashion's role in modernism, and Muthesius's crucial but forgotten contribution to debates on fashion, style and architecture in the early twentieth century that informed modernism's particular fashioned 'look'. These debates will be discussed in more detail below.

15 Muthesius, *Style-architecture and Building-art*, p. 80.

16 Wigley, *White Walls, Designer Dresses*, p. 144.

17 Muthesius, *Style-architecture and Building-art*, p. 96.

18 *Style-architecture and Building-art* is divided into two sections, the first being a critical history of architecture which aimed to show whether, in broadly defined periods, architecture had been a unifying force for the applied arts and thus a shaper of culture. Greek antiquity and the Nordic Middle Ages were held up as examples where culture and artistic production were unified. The most recent manifestation of a suitable relation between culture and art was the Biedermeier

period of the early nineteenth century, while the more recent 'battle of the styles' or *Gründerzeit* had debased the idea of a unification of artistic production and culture. The second section of *Style-architecture and Building-art* then appraises the present condition in Germany in terms of these principles of culture and artistic production established historically. Schwarzer has accounted for the tendency in nineteenth-century German-language architectural theory to assess history in terms of a present context and need through the lineage of historicism. See Schwarzer, *German Architectural Theory*, pp. 10–12.

19 For an account of the influence of English applied art and architecture in the Germanic world, see Schwarzer, *German Architectural Theory*, pp. 138–46. He also outlines the Germanic admiration for American production processes. Schwarzer identifies Robert Dohme, and his 1888 publication *The English House*, as the first to situate the Germanic admiration for English design in an account of English domesticity. On Dohme see also Mallgrave, 'From Realism to *Sachlichkeit*', pp. 290–1.

20 Muthesius, *Style-architecture and Building-art*, p. 82.

21 See Stanford Anderson, '*Sachlichkeit* and Modernity, or Realist Architecture', in *Otto Wagner*, pp. 323–60, for a wider survey and set of examples of interiors in relation to the theme of objectivity.

22 Muthesius, *Style-architecture and Building-art*, pp. 82–3.

23 Muthesius, *Style-architecture and Building-art*, p. 83.

24 Muthesius, *Style-architecture and Building-art*, p. 83.

25 Muthesius, *Style-architecture and Building-art*, p. 84.

26 Muthesius, *Style-architecture and Building-art*, p. 86.

27 Muthesius, *Style-architecture and Building-art*, p. 86.

28 Walter Benjamin, 'Paris: Capital of the Nineteenth Century (exposé of 1939)', in *The Arcades Project*, Cambridge, MA: The Belknap Press of Harvard University Press, 1999, pp. 19–20.

29 Muthesius, *Style-architecture and Building-art*, p. 84.

30 Muthesius, *Style-architecture and Building-art*, p. 97.

31 On the international exhibition of architecture and design as a means of design's international exchange, see Schwarzer, *German Architectural Theory*, pp. 128–66.

32 For further discussion of these terms and their interrelation see Anderson, '*Sachlichkeit* and Modernity', pp. 323–60.

33 Frederic Schwartz, *The Werkbund: Design Theory and Mass Culture before the First World War*, New Haven: Yale University Press, 1996, p. 42. Emphasis in original.

34 Wigley, *White Walls, Designer Dresses*, p. 152. On the relation of fashion and style in Germanic architectural and cultural debates, see also Janet Stewart, *Fashioning Vienna: Adolf Loos's Cultural Criticism*, London: Routledge, 2000, pp. 98–130.

35 Francesco Dal Co, *Figures of Architecture and Thought: German Architecture Culture, 1880–1920*, New York: Rizolli, 1990, p. 201.

36 Schwarzer, *German Architectural Theory*, p. 146.

37 Schwarzer, *German Architectural Theory*, p. 146.

38 Schwarzer, *German Architectural Theory*, p. 147.

39 The general outline for the role of domestic design in relation to the revitalization of German design and industry has been provided by Schwarzer in terms of the place of historicism in nineteenth-century German architectural theory, whereby the collection, study and display of historical artefacts could be deployed as a productive impetus for change in present design. The role of applied art museums, and the discourse of art and architectural historians and theorists in the late nineteenth century, contributed to the promotion of reform in architecture and the applied arts. See Schwarzer, *German Architectural Theory*, pp. 112–27. For a general history of the Werkbund, see Joan Campbell, *The German Werkbund: The Politics of Reform in the Applied Arts*, Princeton: Princeton University Press, 1978. For a series of thematic papers addressing various aspects of the Werkbund's activities, and also making reference to the Austrian and Swiss Werkbunds, see Lucius Burckhardt (ed.), *The Werkbund: Studies in the History and Ideology of the Deutscher Werkbund, 1907–1933*, London: Design Council, 1980.

40 Schwartz, *The Werkbund*, p. 42.

41 Schwartz, *The Werkbund*, p. 43. This argument can be seen against the background of debates within the Werkbund about the development of objects as 'types'. Muthesius and Henry Van de Velde were the key figures in these debates. See 'Muthesius/Van de Velde: Werkbund Theses and Antitheses', in Ulrich Conrads (ed.), *Programs and Manifestoes on 20th-Century Architecture*, Cambridge, MA: MIT Press, 1997, pp. 28–31, and Stanford Anderson, 'Deutscher Werkbund – the 1914 debate: Hermann Muthesius versus Henry Van de Velde', in Ben Farmer and Hentie Louw (eds), *Companion to Contemporary Architectural Thought*, London: Routledge, 1993, pp. 462–7. Wigley has argued for a closer relation between Muthesius and Van de Velde than is normally given in discussions on this debate. See Wigley, *White Walls, Designer Dresses*, pp. 71–2, 146–7. For a discussion of 'standard' (as opposed to standardization) in production, and the relation between objects and consumers in the English context, see C. R. Ashbee, 'The Essential Need of Standard and its Protection', in *Craftsmanship in Competitive Industry. Being a Record of the Workshops of the Guild of Handicraft, and Some Deductions from their Twenty-One Years' Experience*, London: Essex House Press, pp. 91–111.

42 See Frederic J. Schwartz, 'Ornament and Spirit, Ornament and Class', *Harvard Design Magazine*, no. 11, 2000, pp. 76–84.

43 Diana Fuss, *Identification Papers*, London: Routledge, 1995, p. 10.

44 Fuss, *Identification Papers*, pp. 45–6. One of the major ways of explaining identification is through a trope of consumption, the ingestion or oral incorporation of the object of identification as a way of interiorizing it within the subject. This sense of identification was developed by Freud in relation to the idea of the totem meal, where the primal horde of brothers killed and ate their father, putting an end to the father's domination of them, and allowing each brother to gain something of his strength by ingesting him. See Sigmund Freud, 'Totem and Taboo', in James Strachey (ed.), *The Standard Edition of the Complete Psychological Works of Sigmund Freud*, 24 vols, London: Hogarth Press, 1953–74, vol. 13, pp. 1–161. For a discussion of identification as incorporation, see Fuss, *Identification Papers*, pp. 32–6. Though she does not explicitly deal with identification, or the identification/object-choice binary, see Rachel Bowlby's discussion of the way in which Freudian psychoanalysis has impacted on theories of marketing and consumption, especially its 'economic' model of the psyche, in Rachel Bowlby, *Shopping with Freud*, London: Routledge, 1993, pp. 114–19.

45 Schwartz, *The Werkbund*, p. 51.

46 For an account of the industrial buildings of Behrens and Gropius, and their relation to the Werkbund debate on production and labour, see Schwartz, *The Werkbund*, p. 56.

47 Dal Co, *Figures of Architecture and Thought*, p. 23. Compare also Schwarzer on Robert Dohme's advocacy for the detached, asymmetrically planned English house in a country setting: 'The house expanded over its terrain into a mirror image of its occupants' relationship to their land.' Schwarzer, *German Architectural Thought*, p. 140. The wider context for the discussion of dwelling and home-land in Germany in the late nineteenth century involved the opposed concepts of *Gesellschaft*, as the civilization of the progressive, industrial city and its attendant cosmopolitan nationalism, and *Gemeinschaft*, as the culture of rural dwelling, and its attendant conservative nationalism. On these terms and their meanings, see Schwarzer, *German Architectural Thought*, pp. 9–10, 147–8; and Dal Co, *Figures of Architecture and Thought*, pp. 23–7.

48 See Schwartz, 'Ornament and Spirit, Ornament and Class.'

49 Etienne Balibar, 'The Nation Form: History and Ideology', in Geoff Eley and Ronald Grigor Suny (eds), *Becoming National*, Oxford: Oxford University Press, 1996, p. 139. For a discussion of the specifically German concept of *Heimat* as home or homeland in the context of nineteenth-century German nationality and provincialism, and especially in relation to the significance of borders, see Celia Applegate, *A Nation of Provincials: The German Idea of Heimat*, Berkeley: University of California Press, 1990, pp. 1–19.

50 See Louis Althusser, 'Ideology and Ideological State Apparatuses', in *Lenin and Philosophy and Other Essays*, London: New Left Books, 1971, pp. 166–8.

51 Schwartz, *The Werkbund*, p. 52.

52 Georg Simmel, *The Philosophy of Money*, 2nd enlarged edn, London: Routledge, 1990, p. 455.

53 Georg Simmel, 'The Psychology of Ornament', in K. H. Wolff (ed.), *The Sociology of Georg Simmel*, New York: Free Press, 1950, p. 341. Quoted in Schwartz, *The Werkbund*, p. 70. Simmel is concentrating his argument on the form of objects themselves, but it was through the presentation and representation of commodities – their mediation in advertisements or shop windows – that subjects engaged with the objective world. See Schwartz, *The Werkbund*, pp. 96–105, 164–91.

54 See the discussion of Benjamin in Schwartz, *The Werkbund*, pp. 219–21. K. Michael Hays sees these issues of subjectivity, style and objective culture to be 'most intensified in the specialized spatial realm of the bourgeois interior and its household objects, the realm where an autonomous individualism is clung to most desperately and symbolized most completely.' K. Michael Hays, *Modernism and the Posthumanist Subject: The Architecture of Hannes Meyer and Ludwig Hilberseimer*, Cambridge, MA: MIT Press, 1992, p. 56.

55 See Julius Posener, 'Muthesius in England', in *From Schinkel to the Bauhaus: Five Lectures on the Growth of Modern German Architecture*, London: Lund Humphries for the Architectural Association, 1972, p. 20.

56 Julius Posener, 'Hermann Muthesius', in Trevor Dannat (ed.), *Architects' Year Book 10*, London: Elek Books, 1962, pp. 45–51.

57 Nikolaus Pevsner, *Pioneers of Modern Design from William Morris to Walter Gropius*, London: Penguin, 1991 [1936], p. 39. The 1936 first edition bore the title *Pioneers of the Modern Movement from William Morris to Walter Gropius*. The title was changed and revisions made in 1960. See Panayotis Tournikiotis, *The Historiography of Modern Architecture*, Cambridge, MA: MIT Press, 1999, p. 273, n. 9.

58 Nikolaus Pevsner, *The Englishness of English Art*, Harmondsworth: Penguin, 1976 [1956].

59 See Ian Buruma, *Anglomania: A European Love Affair*, New York: Random House, 1998, pp. 242–3. What modern architecture there was in England at that time was largely an imported European and colonial phenomenon. Paul Walker has cited David Saunders' summation of English modernism thus: '"In the year 1930, the English Modern Movement was, apparently, entirely represented by seven men and only two of them were Englishmen. Even one of these two, Serge Chermayeff, was of Russian Family." These seven men were Chermayeff, Colin Lucas (the other Englishman), Amyas Connell and Basil Ward (New Zealanders), Berthold Lubetkin (Russian), Wells Coates (Canadian), and Raymond McGrath (Australian).' Paul Walker, 'Mapping New Zealand Architecture: Local Histories and International Exchange', in Maryam Gusheh (ed.) *Double Frames: Proceedings of the First International Symposium of the Centre for Asian Environments*, Sydney: Faculty of the Built Environment, University of New South Wales, 2000, p. 29, n. 18. Walker is quoting David Saunders, 'So I Decided to Go Overseas', *Architecture Australia*, vol. 66, no. 1, 1977, p. 23.

60 Tournikiotis, *The Historiography of Modern Architecture*, pp. 21–7.

61 Further, Wigley argues that the *Neue Sachlichkeit* of the 1920s and 1930s, presented most notably by Sigfried Giedion as the result of pure constructional and functional concerns, continues this logic of clothing, with its white surfaces and literal transparencies producing the look of modernism. A disavowal of the transitoriness of fashions, and the proclamation of 'the new' as that which surpasses the transitory, is, nonetheless, part of the logic of fashion, a logic which, Wigley argues, Muthesius was consistent in expounding into the 1920s. On Muthesius's conception of fashion and the Modern Movement, see Wigley, *White Walls, Designer Dresses*, pp. 175–80. On Wigley's project to recover Muthesius, and the concept of fashion, as figures erased from the narratives of the Modern Movement, see Wigley, *White Walls, Designer Dresses*, pp. xxiv–vi.

62 Wigley, *White Walls, Designer Dresses*, p. 177.

63 In the mid-1880s, the Barr Smiths decorated the drawing-room of their Adelaide home, Torrens Park, with Morris & Co.'s most expensive wallpaper design, 'St James', originally designed by

Morris for St James's Palace in 1881. Because of the design's complexity, it was made to order. They also ordered several very large hand-knotted Morris & Co. Hammersmith carpets which were used in their Adelaide houses. See Menz, *Morris & Company*, pp. 49–52. The Barr Smiths' taste for the most recent and most expensive designs, and especially the ordering of a 'royal' design, suggests a consumption well beyond the ordinarily bourgeois.

64 See Gosse, *Joanna and Robert*, p. 57. She does not comment, however, on the implication of the Barr Smiths themselves as being those to whose 'swinish luxury' Morris was ministering.

65 See Menz, *Morris & Company*, pp. 50–1.

66 The importation of domesticity, in the form of interiors and whole houses, is the history of colonial architecture in Australia. Portable, prefabricated houses were shipped to Australia from England from the earliest days of settlement, and this practice has been recorded as continuing through the nineteenth century. In an account of the portable house in Australia, Miles Lewis argues that in the middle period of the nineteenth century 'Britain was the major prefabricator and Australia the largest importer. Prefabrication – as opposed to mass production, modular building, and the manufacture of specialized elements off-site – makes sense economically when labour is cheaper at the point of origin than at the point of destination. Conditions are particularly propitious when the recipient market is already importing building materials, so that labour and know-how simply need to be added to the existing package.' Miles Lewis, 'The Portable House', in Robert Irving (ed.), *The History and Design of the Australian House*, Melbourne: Oxford University Press, 1985, p. 275. It is significant to note that Thomas Elder, Robert Barr Smith's business partner in Elder Smith & Co., imported to Adelaide two two-storeyed prefabricated houses from the United States as an investment around 1880. See Lewis, 'The Portable House', p. 287. In a wider sense from the early twentieth century, mail order houses from Sears Roebuck & Co. unfolded across the north-east and mid-west of the United States because of the extensive rail network. Here the mail-order catalogue, techniques of prefabrication which included elements of standardization and repetition, but also differentiation between a vast array of models, transportation, the provision and use of materials, individual financing, and the labour of assembly combined in a nexus of spatialized relations to enable a particular type of object – the whole house – to be bought and consumed. On Sears Roebuck houses, see Katherine Cole Stevenson and H. Ward Jandl, *Houses by Mail: A Guide to Houses from Sears, Roebuck and Company*, Washington, DC: The Preservation Press, 1986; and *Homes in a Box: Modern Homes from Sears Roebuck*, Altgen, PA: Schiffer Publishing, 1998. The latter publication is a facsimile reprint of the 1911 Sears Roebuck Modern Homes catalogue. On the mail-order catalogue as an agent in the dissemination of modernity, with a special focus on Sears Roebuck catalogues at the turn of the twentieth century, see Alexandra Keller, 'Disseminations of Modernity: Representation and Consumer Desire in Early Mail-Order Catalogues', in Leo Charney and Vanessa R. Schwartz (eds), *Cinema and the Invention of Modern Life*, Berkeley: University of California Press, 1995, pp. 156–82; and Thomas J. Schlereth, 'Country Stores, County Fairs and Mail-Order Catalogues: Consumption in Rural America', in Simon J. Bronner (ed.), *Consuming Visions: Accumulation and Display of Goods in America, 1880–1920*, New York: W. W. Norton, 1989, pp. 339–75.

67 Tony Fry, 'A Geography of Power: Design History and Marginality', *Design Issues*, vol. 6, no. 1, 1989, pp. 24–5.

68 Fry, 'A Geography of Power', p. 24.

69 Schwarzer, *German Architectural Theory*, p. 112. Francesco Dal Co extends this idea in a philosophical sense by invoking Emmanuel Levinas: 'Labour is the very *energy* of acquisition. It would be impossible in a being that had no dwelling.' Dal Co, *Figures of Architecture and Thought*, p. 36.

70 Fry, 'A Geography of Power', p. 16.

71 Taylor, *Modernities*, p. 11. See also Walter Benjamin, 'On the Concept of History', in *Selected Writings*, vol. 4, pp. 380–411.

72 Taylor, *Modernities*, p. 12.

5 Recognizing the interior: Space and image

1 See Adolf Loos, 'Surplus to Requirements', in *Ornament and Crime: Selected Essays*, Riverside, CA: Ariadne Press, 1998, pp. 154–6.

2 Adolf Loos, 'Cultural Degeneration', in *Ornament and Crime*, p. 163. See Mitchell Schwarzer, *German Architectural Theory and the Search for Modern Identity*, Cambridge: Cambridge University Press, 1995, pp. 238–47, 255–60, for a more detailed appraisal of Loos's position vis-à-vis the Werkbund and the idea of a unification of architecture, the applied arts and industry.

3 For a discussion of Loos's anglophilia, see Jules Lubbock, *The Tyranny of Taste: The Politics of Architecture and Design in Britain, 1550–1960*, New Haven: Yale University Press, 1995, pp. 301–9.

4 Part of Loos's involvement in these debates was through the medium of his own short-lived cultural journal *Das Andere* (The Other), subtitled 'a journal for the introduction of Western culture to Austria'. For a discussion of this journal in the context of Loos's advocacy for English domesticity in Austria, see Schwarzer, *German Architectural Theory*, pp. 145–6; and Janet Stewart, *Fashioning Vienna: Adolf Loos's Cultural Criticism*, London: Routledge, 2000, pp. 42–72.

5 Beatriz Colomina, *Privacy and Publicity: Modern Architecture as Mass Media*, Cambridge, MA: MIT Press, 1994.

6 See Christopher Reed (ed.), *Not at Home: The Suppression of Domesticity in Modern Art and Architecture*, London: Thames & Hudson, 1993. In arguing against this framing of modernism, I am also arguing against Reed's attempts to recuperate a supposedly more 'domestic' sense of modernism with the Bloomsbury group in Britain. See idem, *Bloomsbury Rooms: Modernism, Subculture, and Domesticity*, New Haven: Yale University Press, 2004. The problem is not whether various modern artists and architects were pro- or anti-domestic, but rather how the interior, in its doubleness, might be articulated in relation to self-consciously modern ideas and practices.

7 Adolf Loos, 'The Poor Little Rich Man', in *Spoken into the Void: Collected Essays, 1897–1900*, Cambridge, MA: MIT Press, 1982, p. 125.

8 Massimo Cacciari, *Architecture and Nihilism: On the Philosophy of Modern Architecture*, New Haven: Yale University Press, 1993, p. 172.

9 Walter Benjamin, 'Paris, Capital of the Nineteenth Century', in *The Arcades Project*, Cambridge, MA: The Belknap Press of Harvard University Press, 1999, p. 19.

10 Benjamin, 'Paris, Capital of the Nineteenth Century', p. 182.

11 Adolf Loos, 'Ladies' Fashion', in *Spoken into the Void*, p. 99.

12 Adolf Loos, 'Men's Fashion', in *Spoken into the Void*, p. 11.

13 Loos, 'Men's Fashion', p. 12. Emphasis in the original. For Loos, writing in 1898, the centre of culture was London.

14 Loos, 'Ladies' Fashion', p. 103. For further analysis on Loos's writings on fashion and social relations, see Jules Lubbock, 'Adolf Loos and the English Dandy', *Architectural Review*, no. 1038, 1983, pp. 43–9.

15 Stewart, *Fashioning Vienna*, p. 121.

16 Stewart, *Fashioning Vienna*, p. 121.

17 Joan Riviere, 'Womanliness as a Masquerade', in Victor Burgin, James Donald and Cora Kaplan (eds), *Formations of Fantasy*, London: Routledge, 1986, pp. 35–44.

18 Stephen Heath, 'Joan Riviere and the Masquerade', in *Formations of Fantasy*, p. 49.

19 Heath, 'Joan Riviere and the Masquerade', p. 52.

20 In thinking about the social construction of identity, Heath compares the feminine masquerade to masculine identity built on presentation: 'To the woman's masquerade there thus corresponds male display (*parade* is Lacan's term)[.] . . . All the trappings of authority, hierarchy, order, position make the man, his phallic identity: "if the penis was the phallus, men would have no need of feathers or ties or medals. . . . Display [*parade*], just like the masquerade, thus betrays a flaw: no one has the phallus."' Heath, 'Joan Riviere and the Masquerade', pp. 55–6.

21 Cacciari, *Architecture and Nihilism*, p. 183.

22 Adolf Loos, 'Architecture', in *On Architecture*, Riverside, CA: Ariadne Press, 2002, p. 78.

23 See Colomina, *Privacy and Publicity*, p. 269.

24 Colomina, *Privacy and Publicity*, p. 234.

25 Colomina, *Privacy and Publicity*, p. 369, n. 3.

26 Colomina, *Privacy and Publicity*, pp. 270–1.

27 See Colomina, *Privacy and Publicity*, p. 31.

28 See Walter Benjamin, 'The Work of Art in the Age of its Technological Reproducibility', in *Selected Writings*, 4 vols, Cambridge, MA: The Belknap Press of Harvard University Press, 1996–2003, vol. 4, pp. 251–83; and idem, 'Little History of Photography', in *Selected Writings*, vol. 2, pp. 507–30.

29 Walter Benjamin, 'On Some Motifs in Baudelaire', in *Selected Writings*, vol. 4, p. 337.

30 The late-nineteenth-century photographic advice of Frederick Mills goes further into the technicalities of setting up a good interior scene for the photograph, and dealing with windows as light sources. Mills specifically mentions Henry Peach Robinson's method of combination printing, which enabled the printing of one image from two different negatives exposed over the same scene. The combination print could combine elements of the image requiring different foci, or enable the combination of parts of a picture requiring different exposure times or aperture settings. See Frederick Mills, *Exterior and Interior Photography*, London: Dawbarn & Ward, 1895, pp. 28–9; idem, *The Art and Practice of Interior Photography*, London: Simpkin, Marshall, Hamilton, Kent & Co., 1890, p. 18; and Henry Peach Robinson, *Art Photography in Short Chapters*, London: Hazell, Watson & Viney, 1890, pp. 48–51, 52–6. On photographic theory and practice during the Weimar period, see Claire Zimmerman, 'Photographic Modern Architecture: Inside "The New Deep,"' *Journal of Architecture*, vol. 9, no. 3, 2004, pp. 331–54.

31 Based on other photographs of the house, Figure 5.2 appears to show what would be the actual view through the picture window. Other photographs of the Khuner House suggest that the alternative view is a different aspect of the surrounding landscape. Figures 5.2 and 5.4 were published in Heinrich Kulka (ed.), *Adolf Loos: Das Werk des Architekten*, Vienna: Löcker, 1930, while Figures 5.1 and 5.3 belong to the Adolf Loos Archive at the Albertina in Vienna, suggesting that the Kulka photographs are 'real' and the Albertina ones are 'doctored'.

32 See Colomina, *Privacy and Publicity*, p. 271.

33 See especially Nicholas Cooper's description of the interior photographic practice of English photographer H. Bedford Lemere, who was active from 1881 to 1941, in Nicholas Cooper, *The Opulent Eye: Late Victorian and Edwardian Taste in Interior Design*, London: The Architectural Press, 1976, p. 2; and also applications of interior flash photography in Robert Slingsby, *A Treatise on Magnesium Flash-Light Photography for Various Subjects with Methods for its Application Practically Considered*, London: Marion & Co., 1890, pp. 3–5.

34 Colomina, *Privacy and Publicity*, p. 271.

35 See Laura Mulvey, 'Pandora: Topographies of the Mask and Curiosity', in Beatriz Colomina (ed.), *Sexuality and Space*, New York: Princeton Architectural Press, 1992, pp. 53–71, for a discussion of the feminine, the mask and the spatiality of the interior in the context of the cinematic image.

36 Benjamin, *The Arcades Project*, p. 218 [I2a,7], quoting a French literary account of the 1870s. Emphasis in the original.

37 Adolf Loos, 'The Interiors in the Rotunda', in *Ornament and Crime: Selected Essays*, Riverside, CA: Ariadne Press, 1998, p. 58.

38 Mary Ann Doane, 'Film and the Masquerade: Theorizing the Female Spectator', in Kate Conboy, Nadia Medina and Sarah Stanbury (eds), *Writing on the Body: Female Embodiment and Feminist Theory*, New York: Columbia University Press, 1997, p. 177.

39 In moving from Loos to Le Corbusier, Colomina notes: 'In the houses of Le Corbusier, the reverse condition of Loos's interiors may be observed.' Colomina, *Privacy and Publicity*, p. 283.

40 Francesco Dal Co, *Figures of Architecture and Thought: German Architecture Culture, 1880–1920*, New York: Rizolli, 1990, p. 15. For a thorough account of Benjamin's relation to modern archi-

tecture, see Detlef Mertins, 'The Enticing and Threatening Face of Prehistory: Walter Benjamin and the Utopia of Glass', *Assemblage*, no. 29, 1996, pp. 7–23.

41 Walter Benjamin, 'Experience and Poverty', in *Selected Writings*, vol. 2, p. 733. Compare Benjamin on the political implications of such an architecture, prompted by his visit to Moscow in 1926–7: 'To live in a glass house is a revolutionary virtue par excellence. It is also an intoxication, a moral exhibitionism, that we badly need. Discretion concerning one's own existence, once an aristocratic virtue, has become more and more an affair of petty-bourgeois parvenus.' Walter Benjamin, 'Surrealism', in *Selected Writings*, vol. 2, p. 209. See also idem, 'Moscow', in *Selected Writings* vol. 2, pp. 22–46. On the effect of this visit on Benjamin's thinking, see Graeme Gilloch, *Myth and Metropolis: Walter Benjamin and the City*, Cambridge: Polity Press, 1996, pp. 49–54.

42 See Hilde Heynen, *Architecture and Modernity: A Critique*, Cambridge, MA: MIT Press, 1999, pp. 117–18.

43 As well as contributing to his collection, Le Corbusier also helped La Roche buy other modernist (Cubist and Purist) paintings to augment his collection. See Tim Benton, *The Villas of Le Corbusier*, New Haven: Yale University Press, 1987, pp. 54, 65–7.

44 Raoul La Roche quoted in Benton, *The Villas of Le Corbusier*, p. 67.

45 Kurt W. Forster argues the opposite, suggesting that the interior is a still life. See Kurt W. Forster, 'Antiquity and Modernity in the La Roche–Jeanneret Houses of 1923', in K. Michael Hays (ed.), *Oppositions Reader*, New York: Princeton Architectural Press, 1998, pp. 471–5. See also Thomas Schumacher, 'Deep Space', *Architectural Review*, no. 1079, pp. 37–42, for an analysis of photographic composition in Le Corbusier's oeuvre.

46 See Stanislaus von Moos and Arthur Ruegg (eds), *Le Corbusier before Le Corbusier: Applied Arts, Architecture, Painting, Photography, 1907–1922*, New Haven: Yale University Press, 2002, pp. 254–7.

47 Rosalind Krauss, 'Léger, Le Corbusier, and Purism', *Artforum*, vol. 10, no. 8, 1972, pp. 50–3. These terms are the same employed by Kenneth Frampton in his formalist criticism of projects by the New York Five group of architects. See Kenneth Frampton, 'Frontality vs. Rotation', in *Five Architects: Eisenman, Graves, Gwathmey, Hejduk, Meier*, New York: Oxford University Press, 1975, pp. 9–13. The spoken text from which this piece derives was delivered in 1969. Krauss does not refer to Frampton, but the relationship between the rereading of modernism around this time and the argument that will be touched upon below, about the problems of architecture's autonomy, is notable.

48 Krauss, 'Léger, Le Corbusier, and Purism', p. 52.

49 Krauss, 'Léger, Le Corbusier, and Purism', p. 52.

50 Krauss, 'Léger, Le Corbusier, and Purism', p. 52.

51 Le Corbusier, *Oeuvre Complète*, 6 vols, Zurich: Les Éditions Girsberger, 1957–63, vol. 1, p. 60, quoted in Benton, *The Villas of Le Corbusier*, p. 67.

52 See Reed, *Bloomsbury Rooms*; and idem, 'Introduction', in *Not at Home*, pp. 7–17. Reed falls back on an essentialism regarding the domestic interior, regarding 'heroic' modernist avant-gardism as an anti-domestic aberration within the continuity of (nineteenth-century) domesticity.

53 Benton, *The Villas of Le Corbusier*, p. 70.

54 Or, to go along with the editorial intent of von Moos and Ruegg's *Le Corbusier before Le Corbusier*, one can see that the Maison La Roche was one of the first completed commissions that allowed Le Corbusier to shed his earlier arts and crafts/Art Nouveau training.

55 Le Corbusier quoted in Benton, *The Villas of Le Corbusier*, p. 43.

56 See Forster, 'Antiquity and Modernity', for an argument about Le Corbusier's debt to antiquity in Maison La Roche.

57 Le Corbusier, *The Modulor: A Harmonious Measure to the Human Scale Universally Applicable to Architecture and Mechanics*, London: Faber & Faber, 1961, pp. 72–3.

58 Colomina, *Privacy and Publicity*, p. 134. Colomina later argues that 'The house is a system for taking pictures. What determines the nature of the picture is the window' (p. 311).

59 Theodor Adorno, *Kierkegaard: Construction of the Aesthetic*, Minneapolis: University of Minnesota Press, 1989, p. 42. On the relation between these thoughts and Benjamin's conception of the interior, see Tom Gunning, 'The Exterior as *Intérieur*: Benjamin's Optical Detective', *boundary 2*, vol. 30, no. 1, 2003, pp. 106–10. Benjamin cites Adorno's thoughts on the interior articulated through Kierkegaard in *The Arcades Project*, pp. 219–20, 461, 542, 548.

60 Colomina uses Krauss's argument about Purist paintings to describe the way in which an interior might be delimited by the horizontal window. Krauss argues that 'distance or depth in the painting becomes no longer a matter of representing the space separating one object from another in the real world. Instead distance is transformed into a representation of the caesura between the *appearance* of the object and the object itself.' Krauss, 'Léger, Le Corbusier, and Purism', p. 53. Emphasis in original. Quoted in Colomina, *Privacy and Publicity*, p. 133.

61 Rather than moments of pause for an appreciation of frontality, the balconies in the Maison La Roche maintain the movement of the eye through a space that the body cannot walk. See the account of the relations between image, perception and experience at the Maison La Roche in John Macarthur, 'The Image as an Architectural Material', *South Atlantic Quarterly*, vol. 101, no. 3, 2002, pp. 684–5.

62 See Jacques Sbriglio, *Le Corbusier: The Villas La Roche-Jeanneret*, Basle: Birkhauser, 1997, p. 96.

63 From 1926, the gallery underwent a series of renovations, mostly to do with heating, flooring and insulation. Charlotte Perriand and Le Corbusier designed and installed a fixed table in the gallery, as well as strip lighting to offer both direct and indirect light. The idea of a cabinet for the paintings was considered during these renovations. See Sbriglio, *The Villas La Roche-Jeanneret*, pp. 93–7. F. R. Yerbury's photograph (Figure 5.5) shows the gallery in its pre-renovated state.

64 Le Corbusier, *The Modulor*.

65 Benjamin, *The Arcades Project*, p. 407 [L1a,5].

66 Manfredo Tafuri, *Architecture and Utopia: Design and Capitalist Development*, Cambridge, MA: MIT Press, 1976, pp. 125–49. See also the account of the development of the Obus plans in Mary McLeod, 'Le Corbusier and Algiers', in *Oppositions Reader*, pp. 489–519.

67 See Sbriglio, *The Villas La Roche-Jeanneret*, p. 102.

68 Michael W. Jennings, *Dialectical Images: Walter Benjamin's Theory of Literary Criticism*, Ithaca: Cornell University Press, 1987, p. 38.

69 Benjamin, 'Experience and Poverty', p. 735.

70 Benjamin, *The Arcades Project*, p. 220 [I4,4].

71 On the relation between Loos and Kraus, see Schwarzer, *German Architectural Theory*, pp. 239–44.

72 Walter Benjamin, 'Karl Kraus', in *Selected Writings*, vol. 2, p. 438.

73 Benjamin, 'Experience and Poverty', p. 733.

74 See Benjamin, 'On the Concept of History', in *Selected Writings*, vol. 4, p. 392.

75 Kenneth Reinhard, 'The Freudian Things: Construction and the Archaeological Metaphor', in Stephen Barker (ed.), *Excavations and their Objects: Freud's Collection of Antiquity*, Albany: State University of New York Press, 1996, p. 61.

Conclusion: Mediatized domesticity

1 The power of nostalgia as a way of dealing with change is made clear in Akiko Busch, *Geography of Home: Writings about Where We Live*, New York: Princeton Architectural Press, 1999. She suggests, without critical intent, that 'For all the lures of the electronic hearth, the real hearth continues to have a sustaining appeal in our collective memory.' This sentiment culminates in the following claim: 'It occurs to me that the bedroom, the kitchen, and the basement reflect the three basic realms of home: the private and necessary sanctuary, the place of nourishment and community, the area where things get made. So long as the places we live can accommodate these three very different human activities, it might be called home' (pp. 23–4).

2 Note the way in which issues of the media opened in Colomina's work on Loos and Le Corbusier have come to inform a much wider conception of the media's relation to domesticity in her work. Of significance here is her attempt to think the architecture of the twentieth century through the relations between the media and the house, in Colomina, 'The Media House', *Assemblage*, no. 27, 1995, pp. 55–66; and her reconsideration of the Eameses' design practice in terms of multimedia production, where architecture and furniture design are one aspect of this output, in ead., 'Enclosed by Images: The Eameses' Multimedia Architecture', *Grey Room*, no. 2, 2001, pp. 6–29. See also Beatriz Colomina, Annmarie Brennan and Jeannie Kim (eds), *Cold War Hothouses: Inventing Postwar Culture, from Cockpit to Playboy*, New York: Princeton Architectural Press, 2004.

3 Terence Riley, *The Un-Private House*, New York: Museum of Modern Art, 1999, p. 11.

4 Riley, *The Un-Private House*, p. 11.

5 Riley, *The Un-Private House*, pp. 11–12. He is referring to Martin Heidegger, 'The Thing', in *Poetry, Language, Thought*, New York: Harper & Row, 1975, pp. 163–86.

6 Donna Haraway, 'A Cyborg Manifesto: Science, Technology, and Socialist-Feminism in the Late Twentieth Century', in *Simians, Cyborgs and Women: The Reinvention of Nature*, London: Free Association Books, 1991, p. 151. Quoted in Riley, *The Un-Private House*, p. 13.

7 Riley, *The Un-Private House*, p. 13. Riley seems to miss that the implications of Haraway's manifesto are entirely of the 'everyday' in the sense of how an emancipatory feminism might be given a figure. On cyborgs and domesticity, see also Andrew Benjamin, 'Housing the Future: The Architecture of Blade Runner', in *Architectural Philosophy*, London: Athlone, 2000, pp. 161–6; Christopher Hight, 'Subjects, Boundaries, Negotiations, aka Gettin' Jiggy in da *Oikos*', in +RAMTV, *Negotiate My Boundary! Mass Customization and Responsive Environments*, London: Architectural Association, 2002, pp. 16–19; and Anthony Vidler, 'Homes for Cyborgs', in *The Architectural Uncanny: Essays in the Modern Unhomely*, Cambridge, MA and London: MIT Press, 1992, pp. 147–64.

8 David Morley, *Home Territories: Media, Mobility, and Identity*, London: Routledge, 2000, p. 3.

9 Morley, *Home Territories*, p. 3. See also Roger Silverstone and Eric Hirsch (eds), *Consuming Technologies: Media and Information in Domestic Spaces*, London: Routledge, 1992, an earlier study of electronic media and domesticity.

10 Morley, *Home Territories*, p. 3.

11 Morley, *Home Territories*, p. 7.

12 See Edward Mitchell, 'Lust for Lifestyle', *Assemblage*, no. 40, 1999, pp. 80–8.

13 A useful guide in understanding relationships between different media forms is Jay David Bolter and Richard Grusin, *Remediation: Understanding New Media*, Cambridge, MA: MIT Press, 1999.

14 Christopher Hight, 'Inertia and Interiority: *24* as a Case Study of the Televisual Metropolis', *Journal of Architecture*, vol. 9, no. 3, 2004, p. 373.

15 See Paul Virilio, 'The Last Vehicle', in Dietmar Kamper and Christoph Wulf (eds), *Looking Back on the End of the World*, New York: Semiotext(e), 1989, pp. 106–19.

16 Hight, 'Inertia and Interiority', pp. 374–5.

17 Hight, 'Inertia and Interiority', p. 371.

18 Hight, 'Inertia and Interiority', p. 380. On the relation between the body and electronic media, see also Ron Burnett, *How Images Think*, Cambridge, MA: MIT Press, 2004; and Mark B. N. Hansen, *New Philosophy for New Media*, Cambridge, MA: MIT Press, 2004.

19 See the way in which the development of responsive environments has been articulated through new generations of design software and new materializations of computing components, in +RAMTV, *Negotiate My Boundary!*; and Vincente Guallart (ed.), *Media House Project: The House Is the Computer, the Structure Is the Network*, Barcelona: IaaC, 2004. See also the critical account of issues surrounding Bill Gates's 'smart house' in Adi Shamir Zion, 'New Modern: Architecture

in the Age of Digital Technology', *Assemblage*, no. 35, 1998: pp. 63–79; and Fiona Allon, 'An Ontology of Everyday Control: Space, Media Flows and "Smart" Living in the Absolute Present', in Nick Couldry and Anna McCarthy (eds), *Mediaspace: Place, Scale and Culture in a Media Age*, London: Routledge, 2004, pp. 253–74.

Bibliography

Ábalos, Iñaki, *The Good Life: A Guided Visit to the Houses of Modernity*, Barcelona: Editorial Gustavo Gili, 2001.

Adorno, Theodor, *Kierkegaard: Construction of the Aesthetic*, trans. Robert Hullot-Kentor, Minneapolis: University of Minnesota Press, 1989.

Althusser, Louis, *Lenin and Philosophy and Other Essays*, trans. Ben Brewster, London: New Left Books, 1971.

Anderson, Stanford, 'The Legacy of German Neoclassicism and Biedermeier: Behrens, Tessenow, Loos and Mies', *Assemblage*, no. 15, 1991, pp. 63–85.

Appignanesi, Lisa and John Forrester, *Freud's Women*, London: Weidenfeld & Nicolson, 1992.

Applegate, Celia, *A Nation of Provincials: The German Idea of Heimat*, Berkeley: University of California Press, 1990.

Apter, Emily, 'Cabinet Secrets: Fetishism, Prostitution and the Fin-de-Siècle Interior', *Assemblage*, no. 9, 1989, pp. 7–19.

Ariès, Philippe and Georges Duby (eds), *A History of Private Life*, 5 vols, Cambridge, MA: The Belknap Press of Harvard University Press, 1987–94.

Asendorf, Christoph, *Batteries of Life: On the History of Things and their Perception in Modernity*, trans. Don Reneau, Berkeley: University of California Press, 1993.

Ashbee, C. R., *Craftsmanship in Competitive Industry: Being a Record of the Workshops of the Guild of Handicraft, and Some Deductions from their Twenty-One Years' Experience*, London: Essex House Press, 1908.

Bachelard, Gaston, *The Poetics of Space*, trans. Maria Jolas, Berkeley: Beacon Press, 1994.

Barker, Stephen (ed.), *Excavations and their Objects: Freud's Collection of Antiquity*, Albany: State University of New York Press, 1996.

Baudelaire, Charles, *The Painter of Modern Life and Other Essays*, trans. Jonathan Mayne, London: Phaidon, 1964.

——, *The Poems in Prose, with La Fanfarlo*, trans. Francis Scarfe, London: Anvil Press, 1989.

Baudrillard, Jean, *The System of Objects*, trans. James Benedict, New York and London: Verso, 1996.

Beecher, Catharine, *A Treatise on Domestic Economy*, Boston: Marsh, Capen, Lyon & Webb, 1841.

Benjamin, Andrew, *Architectural Philosophy*, London: Athlone, 2000.

—— (ed.), *Walter Benjamin and Art*, London: Continuum, 2005.

—— (ed.), *Walter Benjamin and History*, London: Continuum, 2005.

Benjamin, David N. (ed.), *The Home: Words, Interpretations, Meanings, and Environments*, Aldershot: Avebury, 1995.

Benjamin, Walter, *Selected Writings*, trans. Edmund Jephcott *et al.*, 4 vols, Cambridge, MA: The Belknap Press of Harvard University Press, 1996–2003.

——, *The Arcades Project*, trans. Howard Eiland and Kevin McLaughlin, Cambridge, MA: The Belknap Press of Harvard University Press, 1999.

Benton, Tim, *The Villas of Le Corbusier*, New Haven: Yale University Press, 1987.

Birdwell-Pheasant, Donna and Denise Lawrence-Zuniga (eds), *House Life: Space, Place and Family in Europe*, Oxford: Berg, 1999.

Blau, Eve and Edward Kaufman (eds), *Architecture and its Image: Four Centuries of Architectural Representation: Works from the Canadian Centre for Architecture*, Montreal: Canadian Centre for Architecture, 1989.

Bloch, Ernst, *The Utopian Function of Art and Literature: Selected Essays*, trans. Jack Zipes and Frank Mecklenburg, Cambridge, MA: MIT Press, 1988.

Blonsky, Marshall (ed.), *On Signs*, Baltimore: Johns Hopkins University Press, 1985.

Bolter, Jay David and Richard Grusin, *Remediation: Understanding New Media*, Cambridge, MA: MIT Press, 1999.

Bowlby, Rachel, *Shopping with Freud*, London: Routledge, 1993.

Braham, William, *Modern Color / Modern Architecture: Amédée Ozenfant and the Genealogy of Color in Modern Architecture*, Aldershot: Ashgate, 2002.

Bronner, Simon J. (ed.), *Consuming Visions: Accumulation and Display of Goods in America, 1880–1920*, New York: W. W. Norton, 1989.

Bruno, Giuliana, *Atlas of Emotion: Journeys in Art, Architecture, and Film*, New York: Verso, 2002.

Bryden, Inga and Janet Floyd (eds), *Domestic Space: Reading the Nineteenth-Century Interior*, Manchester: Manchester University Press, 1999.

Buck-Morss, Susan, *The Dialectics of Seeing: Walter Benjamin and the Arcades Project*, Cambridge, MA: MIT Press, 1989.

Burckhardt, Lucius (ed.), *The Werkbund: Studies in the History and Ideology of the Deutscher Werkbund, 1907–1933*, London: Design Council, 1980.

Burgin, Victor, *In/Different Spaces: Place and Memory in Visual Culture*, Berkeley: University of California Press, 1996.

Burgin, Victor, James Donald and Cora Kaplan (eds), *Formations of Fantasy*, London: Routledge, 1986.

Burnett, Ron, *How Images Think*, Cambridge, MA: MIT Press, 2004.

Buruma, Ian, *Anglomania: A European Love Affair*, New York: Random House, 1998.

Cacciari, Massimo, *Architecture and Nihilism: On the Philosophy of Modern Architecture*, trans. Stephen Sartarelli, New Haven: Yale University Press, 1993.

Campbell, Joan, *The German Werkbund: The Politics of Reform in the Applied Arts*, Princeton: Princeton University Press, 1978.

Carter, Michael, *Putting a Face on Things: Studies in Imaginary Materials*, Sydney: Power Publications, 1997.

Charney, Leo and Vanessa R. Schwartz (eds), *Cinema and the Invention of Modern Life*, Berkeley: University of California Press, 1995.

Cieraad, Irene (ed.), *At Home: An Anthropology of Domestic Space*, Syracuse: Syracuse University Press, 1999.

Colomina, Beatriz (ed.), *Sexuality and Space*, New York: Princeton Architectural Press, 1992.

——, *Privacy and Publicity: Modern Architecture as Mass Media*, Cambridge, MA: MIT Press, 1994.

——, 'The Media House', *Assemblage*, no. 27, 1995, pp. 55–66.

——, 'Enclosed by Images: The Eameses' Multimedia Architecture', *Grey Room*, no. 2, 2001, pp. 6–29.

Colomina, Beatriz, Annmarie Brennan and Jeannie Kim (eds), *Cold War Hothouses: Inventing Postwar Culture from Cockpit to Playboy*, New York: Princeton Architectural Press, 2004.

Conboy, Kate, Nadia Medina and Sarah Stanbury (eds), *Writing on the Body: Female Embodiment and Feminist Theory*, New York: Columbia University Press, 1997.

Conrads, Ulrich (ed.), *Programs and Manifestoes on 20th-Century Architecture*, Cambridge, MA: MIT Press, 1997.

Cooper, Nicholas, *The Opulent Eye: Late Victorian and Edwardian Taste in Interior Design*, London: Architectural Press, 1976.

Couldry, Nick and Anna McCarthy (eds), *Mediaspace: Place, Scale and Culture in a Media Age*, London: Routledge, 2004.

Crary, Jonathan, *Techniques of the Observer: On Vision and Modernity in the Nineteenth Century*, Cambridge, MA: MIT Press, 1992.

Crowley, John, 'The Sensibility of Comfort', *American Historical Review*, vol. 104, no. 3, 1999, pp. 749–82.

——, *The Invention of Comfort: Sensibilities and Design in Early Modern Britain and Early America*, Baltimore: Johns Hopkins University Press, 2001.

Csikszentmihalyi, Mihaly and Eugene Rochberg-Halton, *The Meaning of Things: Domestic Symbols and the Self*, Cambridge: Cambridge University Press, 1981.

Dal Co, Francesco, *Figures of Architecture and Thought: German Architecture Culture, 1880–1920*, New York: Rizolli, 1990.

Dannat, Trevor (ed.), *Architects' Yearbook 10*, London: Elek Books, 1962.

Davey, Peter, *Arts and Crafts Architecture: The Search for Earthly Paradise*, London: Architectural Press, 1980.

de Bastide, Jean-François, *The Little House: An Architectural Seduction*, trans. Rodolphe el-Khoury, New York: Princeton Architectural Press, 1996.

de Maistre, Xavier, *A Journey around my Room*, trans. Andrew Brown, London: Hesperus, 2004.

Decker, Hannah, *Freud, Dora, and Vienna 1900*, New York: Free Press, 1992.

Deleuze, Gilles and Félix Guattari, *What Is Philosophy?*, trans. Hugh Tomlinson and Graham Burchell, New York: Columbia University Press, 1994.

Dickerson, Vanessa (ed.), *Keeping the Victorian House: A Collection of Essays*, New York: Garland, 1995.

Donzelot, Jacques, *The Policing of Families*, trans. Robert Hurley, Baltimore: Johns Hopkins University Press, 1979.

Eastlake, Charles, *Hints on Household Taste in Furniture, Upholstery and Other Details*, 3rd revised edn, London: Longmans, 1872.

Eiland, Howard, 'Reception in Distraction', *boundary 2*, vol. 30, no. 1, 2003, pp. 51–66.

el-Dahdah, Farès, 'The Josephine Baker House: For Loos's Pleasure', *Assemblage*, no. 26, 1995, pp. 73–87.

Eley, Geoff and Ronald Grigor Suny (eds), *Becoming National*, Oxford: Oxford University Press, 1996.

Elias, Norbert, *The Civilizing Process: The History of Manners*, trans. Edmund Jephcott, Oxford: Basil Blackwell, 1978.

Emmons, Paul, 'Intimate Circulations: Representing Flow in House and City', *AA Files*, no. 51, 2005, pp. 48–57.

Engelman, Edmund, *Sigmund Freud: Berggasse 19, Vienna*, Vienna: Universe, 1998.

Evans, Robin, *Translations from Drawing to Building and Other Essays*, London: Architectural Association, 1997.

Farmer, Ben and Hentie Louw (eds), *Companion to Contemporary Architectural Thought*, London: Routledge, 1993.

Forty, Adrian, *Words and Buildings: A Vocabulary of Modern Architecture*, London: Thames & Hudson, 2000.

Foucault, Michel, *The History of Sexuality*, Volume 1: *An Introduction*, trans. Robert Hurley, London: Allen Lane, 1978.

——, *The Order of Things: An Archaeology of the Human Sciences*, London: Routledge, 2002.

Franklin, Jill, *The Gentleman's Country House and its Plan, 1834–1914*, London: Routledge & Kegan Paul, 1981.

Freud, Sigmund, *The Standard Edition of the Complete Psychological Works of Sigmund Freud*, trans. James Strachey, 24 vols, London: The Hogarth Press, 1953–74.

Frisby, David, *Cityscapes of Modernity*, Cambridge: Polity, 2001.

Fry, Tony, 'A Geography of Power: Design History and Marginality', *Design Issues*, vol. 6, no. 1, 1989, pp. 15–30.

Furján, Helene, 'The Specular Spectacle of the House of the Collector', *Assemblage*, no. 34, 1997, pp. 57–91.

Fuss, Diana, *Identification Papers*, London: Routledge, 1995.

——, *The Sense of an Interior: Four Writers and the Rooms that Shaped Them*, London: Routledge, 2004.

Gamwell, Lynn and Richard Wells (eds), *Sigmund Freud and Art: His Personal Collection of Antiquities*, Binghamton, NY, and London: State University of New York and The Freud Museum, 1989.

Garber, Marjorie, *Sex and Real Estate: Why We Love Houses*, New York: Pantheon, 2000.

Gay, Peter, *The Bourgeois Experience: Victoria to Freud*, 5 vols, Oxford: Oxford University Press, 1984–99.

Gere, Charlotte, *Nineteenth-Century Decoration: The Art of the Interior*, New York: Harry N. Abrams, 1989.

——, *Nineteenth-Century Interiors: An Album of Watercolours*, London: Thames & Hudson, 1992.

Giedion, Sigfried, *Mechanization Takes Command: A Contribution to Anonymous History*, New York: W. W. Norton, 1969.

Gilloch, Graeme, *Myth and Metropolis: Walter Benjamin and the City*, Cambridge: Polity, 1996.

Ginzburg, Carlo, *Myths, Emblems, Clues*, trans. John and Anne C. Tedeschi, London: Hutchinson Radius, 1986.

Girouard, Mark, *Life in the English Country House: A Social and Architectural History*, New Haven: Yale University Press, 1978.

——, *The Victorian Country House*, New Haven: Yale University Press, 1979.

Gloag, John, *Victorian Comfort: A Social History of Design from 1830–1900*, Newton Abbot: David & Charles, 1973.

Goodwin, Kenneth, 'Morris & Co.'s Adelaide Patron', *Art and Australia*, no. 8, 1971, pp. 342–5.

Gosse, Fayette (ed.), *Joanna and Robert: The Barr Smiths' Life in Letters, 1853–1919*, Adelaide: Barr Smith Press, 1996.

Grant, Charlotte, 'Reading the House of Fiction: From Object to Interior, 1720–1920', *Home Cultures*, vol. 2, no. 3, 2005, pp. 233–49.

Grosz, Elizabeth, *Space, Time, and Perversion: Essays on the Politics of Bodies*, London: Routledge, 1995.

Guallart, Vincente (ed.), *Media House Project: The House Is the Computer, the Structure Is the Network*, Barcelona: IaaC, 2004.

Gunning, Tom, 'The Exterior as *Intérieur*: Benjamin's Optical Detective', *boundary 2*, vol. 30, no. 1, 2003, pp. 105–29.

Gusheh, Maryam (ed.), *Double Frames: Proceedings of the First International Symposium of the Centre for Asian Environments*, Sydney: Faculty of the Built Environment, The University of New South Wales, 2000.

Hansen, Mark B. N., *New Philosophy for New Media*, Cambridge, MA: MIT Press, 2004.

Haraway, Donna, *Simians, Cyborgs and Women: The Reinvention of Nature*, London: Free Association Books, 1991.

Harvey, David, *Paris, Capital of Modernity*, London: Routledge, 2003.

Hays, K. Michael, *Modernism and the Posthumanist Subject: The Architecture of Hannes Meyer and Ludwig Hilberseimer*, Cambridge, MA: MIT Press, 1992.

—— (ed.), *Oppositions Reader*, New York: Princeton Architectural Press, 1998.

Heidegger, Martin, *Poetry, Language, Thought*, trans. Albert Hofstadter, New York: Harper & Row, 1975.

Hermann Muthesius, 1861–1927, London: Architectural Association, 1979.

Heynen, Hilde, *Architecture and Modernity: A Critique*, Cambridge, MA: MIT Press, 1999.

Heynen, Hilde and Gülsüm Baydar (eds), *Negotiating Domesticity: Spatial Constructions of Gender in Modern Architecture*, London: Routledge, 2005.

Hight, Christopher, 'Inertia and Interiority: *24* as a Case Study of the Televisual Metropolis', *Journal of Architecture*, vol. 9, no. 3, 2004, pp. 369–83.

Hirsch, Julia, *Family Photographs: Content, Meaning, and Effect*, Oxford: Oxford University Press, 1981.

Hobsbawm, Eric and Terence Ranger (eds), *The Invention of Tradition*, Cambridge: Cambridge University Press, 1983.

Hollander, Martha, *An Entrance for the Eyes: Space and Meaning in Seventeenth-Century Dutch Art*, Berkeley: University of California Press, 2002.

Holm, Lorens, 'Reading through the Mirror: Brunelleschi, Lacan, Le Corbusier. The Invention of Perspective and the Post-Freudian Eye/I', *Assemblage*, no. 18, 1992, pp. 21–39.

——, 'What Lacan Said Re: Architecture', *Critical Quarterly*, vol. 42, no. 2, 2000, pp. 29–64.

Homes in a Box: Modern Homes from Sears Roebuck, Altgen, PA: Schiffer, 1998.

Hope, Thomas, *Household Furniture and Interior Decoration Executed from Designs by Thomas Hope*, London: Longman, Hurst, Rees & Orme, 1807.

Irving, Robert (ed.), *The History and Design of the Australian House*, Melbourne: Oxford University Press, 1985.

Jacobus, Laura, 'On "Whether a Man Could See Before Him and Behind Him Both at Once": The Role of Drawing in the Design of Interior Space in England, *c.* 1600–1800', *Architectural History*, no. 31, 1988, pp. 148–65.

Jay, Martin, *Cultural Semantics: Keywords of our Time*, London: Athlone, 1998.

Jennings, Michael W., *Dialectical Images: Walter Benjamin's Theory of Literary Criticism*, Ithaca: Cornell University Press, 1987.

Kamper, Dietmar and Christoph Wulf (eds), *Looking Back on the End of the World*, New York: Semiotext(e), 1989.

Kerr, Robert, *The Gentleman's House, or How to Plan English Residences from the Parsonage to the Palace; with Tables of Accommodation and Cost, and a Series of Selected Plans*, 3rd revised edn, London: John Murray, 1871.

King, Peter, *Private Dwelling: Contemplating the Use of Housing*, London: Routledge, 2004.

Kofman, Sarah, *The Childhood of Art: An Interpretation of Freud's Aesthetics*, trans. Winifred Woodhull, New York: Columbia University Press, 1988.

Krauss, Rosalind, 'Léger, Le Corbusier, and Purism', *Artforum*, vol. 10, no. 8, 1972, pp. 50–3.

Kulka, Heinrich (ed.), *Adolf Loos: Das Werk des Architekten*, Vienna: Löcker, 1930.

Lacan, Jacques, *Écrits: A Selection*, trans. Alan Sheridan, New York: W. W. Norton, 1977.

Ladurie, Emmanuel Le Roy, *The Territory of the Historian*, trans. Ben and Sian Reynolds, Hassocks: Harvester Press, 1979.

Lakoff, Robin Tolmach and James C. Coyne, *Father Knows Best: The Use and Abuse of Power in Freud's Case of Dora*, New York: Teachers College Press, 1993.

Lavin, Sylvia, *Form Follows Libido: Architecture and Richard Neutra in a Psychoanalytic Culture*, Cambridge, MA: MIT Press, 2004.

Le Corbusier, *Oeuvre Complète*, 6 vols, Zurich: Les Editions Girsberger, 1957–64.

——, *The Modulor: A Harmonious Measure to the Human Scale Universally Applicable to Architecture and Mechanics*, trans. Peter de Francia and Anna Bostock, London: Faber & Faber, 1961.

Lewis, Arnold, James Turner and Steven McQuillin, *The Opulent Interiors of the Gilded Age: All 203 Photographs from 'Artistic Houses'*, New York: Dover, 1987.

Lilley, Ed, 'The Name of the Boudoir', *Journal of the Society of Architectural Historians*, no. 53, 1994, pp. 193–8.

Loos, Adolf, *Spoken into the Void: Collected Essays, 1897–1900*, trans. Jane O. Newman and John H. Smith, Cambridge, MA: MIT Press, 1982.

——, *Ornament and Crime: Selected Essays*, trans. Michael Mitchell, Riverside, CA: Ariadne Press, 1998.

——, *On Architecture*, trans. Michael Mitchell, Riverside, CA: Ariadne Press, 2002.

Loudon, J. C., *An Encyclopaedia of Cottage, Farm and Villa Architecture*, London: Longman, 1833.

Lubbock, Jules, 'Adolf Loos and the English Dandy', *Architectural Review*, no. 1038, 1983, pp. 43–9.

——, *The Tyranny of Taste: The Politics of Architecture and Design in Britain, 1550–1960*, New Haven: Yale University Press, 1995.

Lukacs, John, 'The Bourgeois Interior', *American Scholar*, vol. 39, no. 4, 1970, pp. 616–30.

Macarthur, John (ed.), *Imaginary Materials: A Seminar with Michael Carter*, Brisbane: IMA Publishing, 2000.

——, 'The Image as an Architectural Material', *South Atlantic Quarterly*, vol. 101, no. 3, 2002, pp. 673–93.

MacCarthy, Fiona, *William Morris*, London: Faber, 1994.

Mallgrave, Harry Francis (ed.), *Otto Wagner: Reflections on the Raiment of Modernity*, Santa Monica: Getty Center for the History of Art and the Humanities, 1993.

Mallgrave, Harry Francis and Eleftherios Ikonomou (eds), *Empathy, Form and Space: Problems in German Aesthetics, 1873–1893*, Santa Monica: Getty Center for the History of Art and the Humanities, 1994.

Marcus, Clare Cooper, *House as a Mirror of Self: Exploring the Deeper Meaning of Home*, Berkeley: Conari Press, 1995.

Marcus, Sharon, *Apartment Stories: City and Home in Nineteenth-Century Paris and London*, Berkeley: University of California Press, 1999.

Margolin, Victor and Richard Buchannan (eds), *The Idea of Design*, Cambridge, MA: MIT Press, 1995.

Menz, Christopher, *Morris & Company, Pre-Raphaelites and the Arts & Crafts Movement in South Australia*, Adelaide: Art Gallery Board of South Australia, 1994.

——, *Morris & Co.*, Adelaide: Art Gallery of South Australia, 2002.

Mertins, Detlef, 'The Enticing and Threatening Face of Prehistory: Walter Benjamin and the Utopia of Glass', *Assemblage*, no. 29, 1996, pp. 7–23.

Miele, Chris (ed.), *William Morris on Architecture*, Sheffield: Sheffield Academic Press, 1996.

Miller, Daniel (ed.), *Home Possessions: Material Culture Behind Closed Doors*, Oxford: Berg, 2001.

Mills, Frederick, *The Art and Practice of Interior Photography*, London: Simpkin, Marshall, Hamilton, Kent & Co., 1890.

——, *Exterior and Interior Photography*, London: Dawborn & Ward, 1895.

Missac, Pierre, *Walter Benjamin's Passages*, trans. Shierry Weber Nicholson, Cambridge, MA: MIT Press, 1995.

Mitchell, Edward, 'Lust for Lifestyle', *Assemblage*, no. 40, 1999, pp. 80–8.

Mitchell, W. J. T., *Picture Theory*, Chicago: University of Chicago Press, 1994.

Morley, David, *Home Territories: Media, Mobility, and Identity*, London: Routledge, 2000.

Morse, Margaret, *Virtualities: Television, Media Art and Cyberculture*, Indianapolis: Indiana University Press, 1998.

Muthesius, Hermann, *The English House*, trans. Janet Seligman, London: Crosby Lockwood Staples, 1979.

——, *Style-architecture and Building-art: Transformations of Architecture in the Nineteenth Century and its Present Condition*, trans. Stanford Anderson, Santa Monica: Getty Center for the History of Art and the Humanities, 1994.

Nash, Suzanne (ed.), *Home and its Dislocations in Nineteenth-Century France*, Albany: State University of New York Press, 1993.

Nesbit, Margaret (ed.), *Eugène Atget: Intérieurs parisiens*, Paris: Musée Carnavalet, 1987.

Olsen, Donald, *The City as a Work of Art: London, Paris, Vienna*, New Haven: Yale University Press, 1986.

Percier, Charles and Pierre Fontaine, *Recueil de décorations intérieures comprenant tout ce qui a rapport à l'ameublement comme vases, trépieds, candélabres, cassolettes, lustres, girandoles, lampes, chandeliers, cheminées, feux, poèles, pendules, tables, secrétaires, lits, canapés, fauteuils, chaises, tabourets, miroirs, écrans, etc. etc. etc.*, Venice: Joseph Antonelli, 1845 [1801].

Pevsner, Nikolaus, *The Englishness of English Art*, Harmondsworth: Penguin, 1976.

——, *Pioneers of Modern Design from William Morris to Walter Gropius*, Harmondsworth: Penguin, 1991 [1936].

Poe, Edgar Allan, *The Works of Edgar Allan Poe*, Chicago: Stone & Kimball, 1894.

Posener, Julius, *From Schinkel to the Bauhaus: Five Lectures on the Growth of Modern German Architecture*, London: Lund Humphries for the Architectural Association, 1972.

Praz, Mario, *An Illustrated History of Interior Decoration from Pompeii to Art Nouveau*, trans. William Weaver, London: Thames & Hudson, 1964.

Preiss, Ken and Pamela Oborn, *The Torrens Park Estate: A Social and Architectural History*, Adelaide: K. Preiss & P. Oborn, 1991.

Proust, Marcel, *In Search of Lost Time*, trans. C. K. Scott Moncrieff and Terence Kilmartin, 6 vols, London: Vintage, 1996.

Rabinow, Paul (ed.), *The Foucault Reader*, Harmondsworth: Penguin, 1984.

+RAMTV, *Negotiate My Boundary! Mass Customization and Responsive Environments*, London: Architectural Association, 2002.

Reed, Christopher (ed.), *Not at Home: The Suppression of Domesticity in Modern Art and Architecture*, London: Thames & Hudson, 1996.

——, *Bloomsbury Rooms: Modernism, Subculture and Domesticity*, New Haven: Yale University Press, 2004.

Rice, Charles, 'Evidence, Experience and Conjecture: Reading the Interior through Benjamin and Bloch', *Home Cultures*, vol. 2, no. 3, 2005, pp. 285–97.

Riley, Terence, *The Un-Private House*, New York: Museum of Modern Art, 1999.

Risselada, Max (ed.), *Raumplan versus Plan Libre*, New York: Rizolli, 1989.

Robinson, Henry Peach, *Art Photography in Short Chapters*, London: Hazell, Watson & Viney, 1890.

Rose, Nikolas, *The Psychological Complex: Psychology, Politics and Society in England, 1869–1939*, London: Routledge & Kegan Paul, 1985.

——, *Inventing Our Selves: Psychology, Power and Personhood*, Cambridge: Cambridge University Press, 1996.

——, *Governing the Soul: The Shaping of the Private Self*, 2nd edn, London: Free Association Books, 1999.

Rosner, Victoria, *Modernism and the Architecture of Private Life*, New York: Columbia University Press, 2005.

Rowe, Colin, *The Mathematics of the Ideal Villa and Other Essays*, Cambridge, MA: MIT Press, 1976.

Royle, Nicholas, *The Uncanny*, Manchester: Manchester University Press, 2003.

Rugg, Linda Haverty, *Picturing Ourselves: Photography and Autobiography*, Chicago: University of Chicago Press, 1997.

Rybczynski, Witold, *Home: A Short History of an Idea*, Harmondsworth: Penguin, 1987.

Saunders, David, 'So I Decided to Go Overseas', *Architecture Australia*, vol. 66, no. 1, 1977, pp. 21–7.

Sbriglio, Jacques, *Le Corbusier: The Villas La Roche-Jeanneret*, Basle: Birkhauser, 1997.

Scarry, Elaine, *Dreaming by the Book*, Princeton: Princeton University Press, 1999.

Schivelbusch, Wolfgang, *The Railway Journey: The Industrialization of Time and Space in the 19th Century*, Leamington Spa: Berg, 1986.

Schorske, Carl, *Fin-de-Siècle Vienna: Politics and Culture*, New York: Vintage Books, 1981.

Schumacher, Thomas, 'Deep Space', *Architectural Review*, no. 1079, 1987, pp. 37–42.

Schwartz, Frederic J., *The Werkbund: Design Theory and Mass Culture before the First World War*, New Haven: Yale University Press, 1996.

——, 'Ornament and Spirit, Ornament and Class', *Harvard Design Magazine*, no. 11, 2000, pp. 76–84.

Schwarzer, Mitchell, *German Architectural Theory and the Search for Modern Identity*, Cambridge: Cambridge University Press, 1995.

Seale, William, *The Tasteful Interlude: American Interiors through the Camera's Eye, 1860–1917*, 2nd revised edn, Nashville: American Association for State and Local History, 1981.

Semper, Gottfried, *The Four Elements of Architecture and Other Writings*, trans. Harry Francis Mallgrave and Wolfgang Hermann, Cambridge: Cambridge University Press, 1989.

Shamir Zion, Adi, 'New Modern: Architecture in the Age of Digital Technology', *Assemblage*, no. 35, 1998: pp. 63–79.

Sidlauskas, Susan, *Body, Place, and Self in Nineteenth-Century Painting*, Cambridge: Cambridge University Press, 2000.

Silverman, Kaja, *World Spectators*, Stanford: Stanford University Press, 2000.

Silverstone, Roger and Eric Hirsch (eds), *Consuming Technologies: Media and Information in Domestic Spaces*, London: Routledge, 1992.

Simmel, Georg, *The Philosophy of Money*, trans. Tom Bottomore and David Frisby, 2nd enlarged edn, London: Routledge, 1990.

Slingsby, Robert, *A Treatise on Magnesium Flash-Light Photography for Various Subjects with Methods for its Application Practically Considered*, London: Marion & Co., 1890.

Smith, George, *A Collection of Designs for Household Furniture and Interior Decoration*, London, 1808.

Stallybrass, Peter and Allon White, *The Politics and Poetics of Transgression*, London: Methuen, 1986.

Steedman, Carolyn, *Strange Dislocations: Childhood and the Idea of Human Interiority, 1780–1930*, Cambridge, MA: Harvard University Press, 1995.

Stevenson, J. J., *House Architecture*, 2 vols, London: Macmillan, 1880.

Stevenson, Katherine Cole and H. Ward Jandl, *Houses by Mail: A Guide to Houses from Sears, Roebuck and Company*, Washington, DC: The Preservation Press, 1986.

Stewart, Janet, *Fashioning Vienna: Adolf Loos's Cultural Criticism*, London: Routledge, 2000.

Stewart, Susan, *On Longing: Narratives of the Miniature, the Gigantic, the Souvenir, the Collection*, Baltimore: Johns Hopkins University Press, 1984.

Stoichita, Victor, *The Self-Aware Image: An Insight into Early Modern Meta-Painting*, trans. Anne-Marie Glasheen, Cambridge: Cambridge University Press, 1997.

Tafuri, Manfredo, *Architecture and Utopia: Design and Capitalist Development*, trans. Barbara Luigia La Penta, Cambridge, MA: MIT Press, 1976.

Tafuri, Manfredo and Francesco Dal Co, *Modern Architecture*, trans. Robert Erich Wolf, New York: Harry N. Abrams, 1979.

Taylor, Peter, *Modernities: A Geohistorical Approach*, Cambridge: Polity Press, 1999.

Taylor, William, 'Characterizing the Inhabitant in Robert Kerr's *The Gentleman's House*, 1864', *Design Issues*, vol. 18, no. 3, 2002, pp. 27–42.

——, *The Vital Landscape: Nature and the Built Environment in Nineteenth-Century Britain*, Aldershot: Ashgate, 2004.

Teyssot, Georges, '"Water and Gas on All Floors:" Notes on the Extraneousness of the Home', *Lotus*, no. 44, 1984, pp. 83–93.

——, 'The Disease of the Domicile', *Assemblage*, no. 6, 1988, pp. 73–97.

——, 'Boredom and Bedroom: The Suppression of the Habitual', *Assemblage*, no. 30, 1996, pp. 44–61.

——, 'A Topology of Thresholds', *Home Cultures*, vol. 2, no. 1, 2005, pp. 89–116.

Thornton, Peter, *Seventeenth-Century Interior Decoration in England, France and Holland*, New Haven: Yale University Press, 1978.

——, *Authentic Décor: The Domestic Interior, 1620–1920*, New York: Viking, 1984.

Tournikiotis, Panayotis, *The Historiography of Modern Architecture*, Cambridge, MA: MIT Press, 1999.

Tristram, Philippa, *Living Space in Fact and Fiction*, London: Routledge, 1989.

Trotter, David, 'Some Brothels: Nineteenth-Century Philanthropy and the Poetics of Space', *Critical Quarterly*, vol. 44, no. 1, 2002, pp. 25–32.

20 Maresfield Gardens: A Guide to the Freud Museum, London: Serpent's Tail, 1998.

van Duzer, Leslie and Kent Kleinman, *Villa Muller: A Work of Adolf Loos*, New York: Princeton Architectural Press, 1994.

Vernant, Jean-Pierre, *Myth and Thought amongst the Greeks*, London: Routledge & Kegan Paul, 1983.

Vidler, Anthony, *The Architectural Uncanny: Essays in the Modern Unhomely*, Cambridge, MA: MIT Press, 1992.

——, *Warped Space: Art, Architecture, and Anxiety in Modern Culture*, Cambridge, MA: MIT Press, 2000.

von Moos, Stanislaus and Arthur Ruegg (eds), *Le Corbusier before Le Corbusier: Applied Arts, Architecture, Painting, Photography, 1907–1922*, New Haven: Yale University Press, 2002.

Wagner, Otto, *Modern Architecture: A Guidebook for his Students to this Field of Art*, trans. Harry Francis Mallgrave, Santa Monica: Getty Center for the History of Art and the Humanities, 1988.

Watson, Janell, *Literature and Material Culture from Balzac to Proust: The Collection and Consumption of Curiosities*, Cambridge: Cambridge University Press, 1999.

Wigley, Mark, *White Walls, Designer Dresses: The Fashioning of Modern Architecture*, Cambridge, MA: MIT Press, 1995.

Wolff, K. H. (ed.), *The Sociology of Georg Simmel*, New York: Free Press, 1950.

Wood, Denis and Robert J. Beck, *Home Rules*, Baltimore: Johns Hopkins University Press, 1994.

Zimmerman, Claire, 'Photographic Modern Architecture: Inside "the New Deep"', *Journal of Architecture*, vol. 9, no. 3, 2004, pp. 331–54.

Index

Page numbers referring to illustrations are in **bold** type